MANAGING THE MOBILE WORKFORCE

Leading, Building, and Sustaining Virtual Teams

DAVID CLEMONS and MICHAEL KROTH, Ph.D.

New York Chicago San Francisco Lisbon London Madrid Mexico City
Milan New Delhi San Juan Seoul Singapore Sydney Toronto

The **McGraw·Hill** Companies

1 2 3 4 5 6 7 8 9 10 DOC/DOC 1 9 8 7 6 5 4 3 2 1 0

ISBN: 978-0-07-174220-7
MHID: 0-07-174220-4

McGraw-Hill books are available at special quantity discounts to use as premiums and sales promotions or for use in corporate training programs. To contact a representative, please e-mail us at bulksales@mcgraw-hill.com.

This book is printed on acid-free paper.

Library of Congress Cataloging-in-Publication Data
Clemons, David.
   Managing the mobile workforce : leading, building, and sustaining virtual teams / by David Clemons, Michael Kroth.
      p. cm.
   Includes bibliographical references and index.
   ISBN 978-0-07-174220-7 (alk. paper)
      1. Telecommuting—Management. 2. Mobile communication systems—Management. I. Kroth, Michael S. II. Title.

   HD2336.3.C55 2011
   658.3—dc22   2010026308

Praise for *Managing the Mobile Workforce*

"This dynamic group of workers represents the future of work. Understanding how they work, the tools they need to be successful and the dynamic nature of their workflow is essential for today's business leaders. Work is no longer about location; it is about communication."
—Brent Lang, president and C.O.O., Vocera Communications

"Clemons and Kroth make a compelling argument for the speedy adoption of the officeless office. Their thoughts on how people management, as opposed to technology management, will determine success for an organization is truly insightful."
—James D Johnson II, senior director of marketing,
Avery Dennison

"This is a great read for anyone in the field of business, technology, education, human resources, community development, and government."
—Patricia Kempthorne, president/CEO, Twiga Foundation, Inc.

▶ CONTENTS

▶ **Acknowledgments**   v

▶ **Introduction: Why Should You Read This Book?**   vii

**Part One: Thinking Strategically about
the Mobile Workforce**   1

▶ **Chapter One: Moving to Mobility**   3
   Creating Mobile Urgency—Let's Get Started!

▶ **Chapter Two: Discovering a New Workforce Paradigm**   21
   Check Your Assumptions about the Future at the Virtual Door

▶ **Chapter Three: Presence**   51
   Being There Even When You're Not

▶ **Chapter Four: Trust or Bust**   71
   Breaking Trust Is the One Thing That Can Immobilize
   a Mobile Workforce Faster Than a Dropped Call

▶ **Chapter Five: Strategic Leadership in a Virtual World**   93
   Creating Sustainable Competitive Advantage

Part Two: Performance Management and the Mobile Workforce   **117**

▶ **Chapter Six: Autonomy or Not Autonomy?**   **119**
That Is the Question

▶ **Chapter Seven: The Mobile Performance Management Process**   **137**
Reducing the Distance between Manager and Worker

▶ **Chapter Eight: Hiring and Preparing Great Mobile Talent**   **157**
Getting the Right People on the Virtual Bus

▶ **Chapter Nine: The Eight Principles Model**   **183**
Motivational Tools for Mobile Leaders

Part Three: Technology, Tools, and Teams   **205**

▶ **Chapter Ten: Keeping Up with the Phoneses**   **207**
Using Metaskills to Keep Pace with the Increasing Evolution of Hardware and Software

▶ **Chapter Eleven: Developing Your Virtual Team**   **221**
Reconfiguring the Process

▶ **Notes**   **245**
▶ **Index**   **257**

▶ ACKNOWLEDGMENTS

This book is a direct result of many passionate people who shared their ideas and experience with successful working models regarding the global mobile workforce. As a result of our interviews with thought leaders and global enterprise executives and managers, we have captured solid advice to offer anyone wanting to deploy a mobile workforce.

We want to thank the creative team at Achieve Labs who gave their time and advice regarding content and design, including, Dave Jansik, Taylor Clemons, Heather Jones, Lehi Wayman, Megan Sutton, and Jon Marecki. Also, we owe much to Janet Caldow, Camille Venezia, and those who provided advice and coaching during the initial stages of writing chapter formats and styles. It's amazing what we learned along this process, it was a complete turning point.

The University of Idaho has been generous in giving Michael time to write this book, and his colleagues have been both encouraging and helpful. Jerry McMurtry and Charlie Gagel were not only supportive but also instrumental in making it possible for Michael to participate in the writing of this book.

There are many people who shared ideas and helped us to connect with people to interview. We want to especially thank Patricia

Kempthorne, who took a personal interest in our book and introduced us to several people we interviewed who we could never have connected with otherwise.

Our new friends at McGraw-Hill have been wonderful. Mary Glenn and Emily Carleton were the first people there who believed in this book and moved it forward, and we have been so lucky to work with Mary Therese Church, Ron Martirano, and Daina Penikas, who are true professionals and highly skilled in their work. They are easy to work with and have added so much value to the book.

Finally, thanks to our families and friends, who are our bedrock. Our wives, Violet Clemons and Lana Kroth, have seen us through all the late nights and weeks and months of writing, patiently supporting us and motivating us to complete our project. Thank you for your love and great support. Now we can get on with our family plans!

From David:

Michael Kroth, my mentor and friend, has been the anchor needed for this book project and without him this book would not have been completed on time or at the level of professionalism accomplished. My gratitude for his patience and inspiration to all of us, as well as his positive cheerful attitude for steering the project to completion, is immeasurable.

From Michael:

When I began this project I felt like I was a fairly good author. David Clemons opened my eyes to writing possibilities I had never imagined. He has been an inspiration to me, helped me to dream about what this book could be and do far more than I would have otherwise. David has also been fun and easy to work with, and has deep integrity, which is very important to me. His enthusiasm is absolutely energizing. Most of all, he has deep experience in the world of mobility, and I have learned so much from him, not only about this book, but about life and leadership, every time we meet. It has been an honor and a pleasure to write this book with my friend, David Clemons.

B uilding a mobile workforce can be a competitive advantage for your company. It can also be a powerful threat in the hands of your competitors. In a global market for talent, the best employees can work anywhere. Do you have job alternatives that will appeal to workers of the twenty-first century? Does your corporate strategy envision a mobile workforce? Are you prepared to lead one? Do you have the capability to find, get, keep, and support mobile workers? Is your organization technologically savvy—do you have the meta-capabilities to keep up with the constant technological innovation that will require new hardware and software regularly?

If you want to get a leg up on the competition, you should read this book. If you want to provide the most flexibility for your workforce and options for yourself as a leader, you should read this book.

It has been estimated that the number of worldwide mobile workers will reach one billion by 2011, which includes nearly 75 percent of the U.S. workforce.[1] These new, technology-enabled workers will have unlimited, global job opportunities and easy access to companies that will value them. The question you need to answer right now is, do you have a mobile workforce strategy that is compelling enough to attract the best talent to your company, and then to keep them?

▶ THE BAGEL FACTOR

Like many successful collaborations, ours started while breaking bread together. We (the authors, David Clemons and Michael Kroth) had just coasted in from a beautiful mountain bike ride to Blue Sky Bagels on the corner of Fourth and Main in Boise, Idaho. David ordered his classic asiago bagel with no butter, and Michael his blueberry bagel with way too much butter. Then, what we have come to call "the bagel factor" came into play.

"The bagel factor" occurs when otherwise mobile workers meet face to face, often over dinner or during some social function but also during professional meetings, and the magic of relationship occurs. As we'll find later in this book, most mobile workforce leaders still believe that regular face-to-face meetings are essential for building a strong connection with their virtual workforce. In our case, the idea of writing a book together emerged after about half a bagel apiece.

David has provided leadership in digital content and digital learning since 1990. He is recognized within the CD-ROM and online learning industries as being a successful entrepreneur and innovator for many years. He is the president of LearnKey, Inc., and the founder of Achieve Labs Inc., (LearnCast.com and Push Mobile Media) which are focused on mobile workforce strategy and educational delivery platforms.

At the beginning, Michael knew almost nothing about mobile technology. (One of his early questions was, "What's an SMS text?") He had been an organizational consultant for many years and an author of three books. As a professor in the field of human resource development he had both practical and scholarly experience. He was interested in how leaders would be able to create healthy, highly motivating work environments for this newly emerging mobile workforce.

The possibility for synergy, combining our two sets of complementary experiences and knowledge, and writing a book together about managing the mobile workforce, was born over a bike ride and two bagels.

▶ THIS BOOK IS VERY DIFFERENT THAN WHAT WE IMAGINED IT TO BE!

Interestingly, many times book introductions are written last as authors finalize their book. The reason for that makes sense: the authors have learned much along the way. That has been our case as well.

We originally thought that we would be spending a lot of time talking about technology, but as we looked more deeply into what successful mobile workforce managers must do, we realized that the technology, while important, was just the ante to get in the mobile workforce game. The successful leaders who consistently distinguish themselves, we found, are those who take the principles of leadership and apply them to the specific challenge of mobile workforce management. As Hewlett-Packard's Bill Avey told us, you need to have good technology to be successful, but then what determines success is whether or not, from a leadership perspective, you can bridge the distance gap and create essential personal relationships.

Within a span of just over three months we interviewed 39 leaders about managing a mobile workforce. We didn't interview them just to obtain quotes to validate our views; we interviewed them to learn. Their experiences and views changed what we thought this book should cover.

The online devices your employees are using right now—mobile phone, netbook, whatever—are the *least* important factor for your organizational and competitive mobile workforce success. Sooner or later anyone can get the same devices you have. *More* valuable will be the applications you are using. *Most* critical will be whether or not you have created a work environment that attracts, motivates, trains, enables, and retains the talent you need to stay ahead of the competition and meet your goals. There are many sources for finding out how to make the technological choices managers need to make—this book has a single-minded concentration on what is required to develop and lead the mobile workforce that is rapidly emerging today.

▶ WHAT IS A MOBILE WORKFORCE?

The first question we faced was to ask ourselves what exactly a mobile workforce is. That definition has evolved in our minds since we started. This description has been a good starting point:

> *Mobile workers are those who work at least 10 hours per week away from home and from their main place of work, on business trips, in the field traveling or on customer premises and use online computer connections when doing so.*[2]

This 10-year-old definition still seems basically accurate. For now, we suggest defining the mobile workforce as follows:

> *Mobile workers are available and accountable anywhere and anytime. The mobile workforce may be located at home or on the road, or it may simply be moving within your own corporate settings. Mobile workers perform critical jobs for an organization, using secure Internet connections, collaborating from near to as far as anywhere on the globe you can imagine, using the most appropriate hardware and software needed to get the work done. The most effective mobile workforces have the support and leadership of management, who provide both the technological and organizational tools to assure success.*

Actually, of course, the mobile workforce extends beyond Earth. Consider astronauts, perhaps the iconic mobile workforce, operating out of space shuttles and space stations to be a part of this virtual community of people who are no longer constrained by a physical location or even the bonds of gravity.

We will reconsider the definition of a mobile workforce as we proceed through the book. Is it location that defines mobility? Is it electronic communication? Is it a strategy, a way of thinking, or how people act?

Managing the Mobile Workforce provides executives, managers, and members of the mobile workforce with a holistic approach to hiring, motivating, training, leading, supporting, and retaining this exploding mobile population. It is intended to help enterprise executives make strategic decisions about leading a global workforce that will beat the competition, improve profits, and attract and retain an engaged, flexible, motivated, and healthy workforce.

We share the stories, experiences, and wisdom of people ranging from first-line supervisors to leaders of global enterprises. Managers will find useful advice from industry leaders about leading and the tools needed to support the unique team of remote workers.

▶ **WHAT WILL YOU GET OUT OF THIS BOOK?**

The advice we share is crafted from the experiences of many organizations, ranging from small, entrepreneurial companies to the U.S. federal government and its two million workers. The leaders you will read about offer inspiring and straightforward advice about the dos and don'ts of mobile workforce leadership. The timing and the opportunity of this topic is so engaging and appealing that it has been relatively easy to schedule interviews with otherwise hard-to-access leaders. They have shared their stories with us because they know this is the cutting edge of workforce strategy. Each chapter features one or more leaders who have found real-world solutions to real-world problems. Each has used forward thinking and strategic planning to first build his or her mobile workforce and then to keep it engaged in contributing to the company's bottom line.

As coauthors, we bring a unique combination of experience to this book. One or both of us have been entrepreneurs, developers and marketers of distance education and training products, organizational consultants, and researchers. We will share equally diverse experiences from leaders of successful companies such as Deloitte, LEGO, Samsung, Citrix, KPMG, and Hewlett-Packard; these people tell interesting stories about creating highly successful mobile workforces. These leaders have workers who might never see a corporate building or meet their managers face to face. We will share stories from global leaders who have taken the risk to unleash their workers from the chains of daily commutes, nine-to-five business hours, and the same old cubicles they've sat in day after day after day. After day. Millions of workers have been tied to these kinds of constraints for months, years, and sometimes decades and now are being given much more flexibility.

Thought leaders such as Stephen M. R. Covey and Joel Barker apply principles of leadership thinking to the emerging mobile workforce in this book; leaders from organizations like Citrix (which offers the popular GoToMeeting) and Wifi.com, which provide the tools for enabling effective workforce management, talk about the new world of telework. We provide research, examples, and tools managers and employees can use immediately to develop genuine, highly motivating work and work environments.

This book is the first we know of to do all this:

▶ Talk about the dichotomous choices leaders have to make about mobile worker autonomy
▶ Explore the convergence of e-presence, social presence, and leadership presence
▶ Extend the idea of a "platform" beyond technology to include strategic leadership and workforce practice
▶ Devote an entire chapter to the relationship between trust and mobile leadership
▶ Rethink the sequence of team development for mobile workers
▶ Provide meta-strategies for efficiently keeping up with the changing world of technology

▶ ONE MORE REASON TO READ THIS BOOK

Throughout the book you will find links to mobile exercises and other information that you can use on your mobile device immediately.

Each will be an example of how you can apply what is in this book to your own mobile workforce. *We call these* "freemiums"—*they are an added value to you for reading this book. We think you will find them—by themselves—worth far more than the purchase price of the book.*

Use these freemiums to collaborate, talk about your experience, offer suggestions, and share with your colleagues. They are an added value of this book, which we feel can help jump-start the development of your mobile workforce.

▶ OUR TEAM

The social media and mobile workforce tools available today gave us the opportunity to write this book with the support of an online team of experts who care about this book, each operating virtually from a different location. Not for us the life of the solitary author bent over a candle in front of the fireplace! Just like the powerful potential of a mobile workforce working together while spread across vast geographical areas, we drew from the expertise, imagination, and experiences of successful artists, business and community leaders, thought leaders, and entrepreneurs from around the world. Some we interviewed, some we asked to help us with the content, and some—such as our families and friends—we just asked to encourage and to support us. We think the result of asking all these people to be a part of our virtual team is far more robust than if this book had come from just the two of us.

▶ WHAT MAKES THIS BOOK DIFFERENT

Many books about the mobile workforce focus on how to deploy mobile technology. But the hardware and software required will change exponentially more quickly than any enterprise leader can hope to keep up with. (You get the idea: when you've tried to keep up with technology in your own life, just about the time you get the latest netbook the next one has made it extinct.) The leaders in companies we've interviewed have told us that the key is not providing the latest gadget to their employees but instead is providing a trusted, supportive work environment for employees, where people are so emotionally committed that they will go above and beyond the call of duty to assist the organization in its efforts to succeed, help each other overcome obstacles, and constantly learn how to produce the highest-quality product and/or service even in an ever-changing, competitive world.

The more we work with organizations around the world, the more we realize that there is much more to managing a mobile workforce than simply sending one's sales and support staff into the field with a smartphone. That's why we think *Managing the Mobile Workforce* will make a huge difference in your ability to approach this incredible opportunity—and threat—to your company in a way that ensures long-term success.

▶ INTERVIEWS FOR THIS BOOK

We interviewed 39 executives and thought leaders for this book. Nearly all of these interviews were conducted by both of us, and we found the interviewees an extraordinarily rich source of information. Not only did these busy people share their valuable time with us, they also shared their acumen and their passion for executing mobile work strategies effectively. They did much more than just share quotable quotes we could use to back up themes that we wanted to share with readers; they also shaped our thinking in significant ways. This book is much different, and talks about much different topics, than we had originally anticipated because of the wisdom of the people with whom we were able to meet.

We developed both a broader and a deeper understanding of managing the mobile workforce because the people we interviewed were so diverse. We interviewed senior executives—with titles such as chairman, EVP, VP, CEO, general manager, or director—of national or global enterprises, as well as thought leaders, senior consultants, non-profit CEOs, on-the-ground managers working in the field, and entrepreneurs. We talked with people from a wide range of sectors, including technology, transportation, government, health care, education, consulting, insurance, finance, manufacturing, and services. Our interest was to gather information from highly successful leaders who have established highly effective mobile workforces.

Almost no one we asked to interview turned us down. People were eager to share their stories and insights, and clearly they were bullish about the prospects for mobile work, both immediately and during the next few years. Their enthusiasm reaffirmed for us that this book is both timely and needed. It has been a heady process!

These interviews led to wide-ranging discussions that we share throughout this book. We gleaned abundant insights into management processes and issues affecting the mobile worker. We heard stories about how companies developed their mobile workforces. We learned what worked and what didn't. We recorded amazing success stories and case studies from which any manager responsible for mobile workers can benefit. Our interviewees pulled no punches. While all of the advice and data we collected is valuable, none was more compelling than what we heard from the executives who believe their companies could not survive today without a mobile workforce.

We developed an interview guide and used it from start with the intent of providing some structure to the interviews, giving the interviewees the ability to prepare ahead of time, and to assure that we were getting the information we needed. However, that guide evolved as we learned more, and we customized it to target the particular knowledge and experience of the person we were interviewing. We shared an interview guide ahead of time with most people, but there were times when we just used it ourselves to remind us of key questions we wanted to cover.

Most, but not all, of our interviews were recorded—with the permission of those we interviewed—and then were transcribed. We gave each of our interviewees a chance to review what we'd written about them so they could make corrections or add comments if they wished.

Meeting and learning from the people we interviewed was one of the most meaningful benefits we have received from writing this book, and we think you will feel the same way.

We will be sharing throughout the book the knowledge, experience, and advice we collected from these leaders. Some of you will find this information persuasive enough to embark upon a mobile workforce strategy; others will say it's not enough to convince you to take the plunge.

Here is some of what we heard:

▶ "It requires more effort to communicate and more frequent communications."
▶ "Few managers who deploy a mobile workforce have any specific training."
▶ "I've seen a whole bunch of failed experiments where companies put the wrong technology in the hands of the people."
▶ "Companies get hell-bent on pushing technology before people are ready for it."
▶ "It is so easy for text or e-mail be misconstrued or misunderstood. . . . On the other hand, it's so easy to spend too much time typing and logging e-mails, answering questions, and having unproductive dialog."
▶ "It is easy to lose trust when you are not making connections."
▶ "Team conflict in a remote setting is harder to resolve, and it impacts production and performance."

This was not a scholarly study. Ours was not a systematic investigation, and we did not collect, test, evaluate, or analyze any data systematically. Rather, we interviewed people who we thought would have informative experiences, perspectives and stories.

Throughout the book we share stories and insights we heard from these leaders, as well as information from scholarly studies and the popular press.

▶ A MANUAL FOR DEVELOPING AND SUSTAINING A MOBILE WORKFORCE

We've organized this book to provide tools you can use to support the practices needed to lead a virtual organization. In every chapter we will share leadership stories, ideas, and tools that you can apply to your organization.

Part 1, *Thinking Strategically about the Mobile Workforce*, will cause you to think differently about the future work landscape than you have ever done before. Chapter 1, *Moving to Mobility*, describes the need for leaders and workers to be prepared for a world in which nearly every person will be working "mobilely." Chapter 2, *Discovering a New Workforce Paradigm*, starts with paradigm busters. We talk about organizations such as Vocera Communications and Deloitte LLP, in ways that will challenge you to think about the opportunities technology provides your organization. Chapter 3, *Presence*, proposes a new "presence" paradigm, which takes into consideration technology (telepresence, for example), social (virtual relationships, for example), and leadership (charisma at a distance?) presence. Chapter 4, *Trust or Bust*, is completely devoted to the need for and qualities of trust in virtual situations. Stephen M. R. Covey lends his considerable expertise to showing how principles of trust can be applied to mobile workforces. Chapter 5, *Strategic Leadership in a Virtual World*, draws upon the leadership of people such as John Berry, the Director of the U.S. Office of Personnel Management, to explain the strategic thinking, leadership, and execution that is required to move to a mobile workforce. Here we talk about the importance of a "strategic platform" for moving to mobility.

Part 2, *Performance Management and the Mobile Workforce*, lays out the process of managing the performance of mobile workers. In Chapter 6, *Autonomy or Not Autonomy? That Is the Question*, we show two different approaches to mobile performance management. Both can be very effective. In Chapter 7, *The Mobile Performance Management Process*, we start with Con-way, a $3.7 billion trucking, logistics, and intermodal services company, and demonstrate how it approaches performance management in today's trucking industry. Chapter 8, *Hiring and Preparing Great Mobile Talent*, talks about getting the right virtual team on board; and Chapter 9, *The Eight Principles Model*, talks about what great companies, such as Melaleuca, Inc., do to motivate a globally dispersed workforce.

Part 3, *Technology, Tools, and Teams*, is the ultimate how-to manual. Here, in Chapter 10, *Keeping Up with the Phoneses*, we share how to how to stay up to date as the swirl of mobile devices and software changes almost daily. Finally, Chapter 11, *Developing Your Virtual Team*, shares what leaders in international organizations such as LEGO and Hewlett-Packard do to create highly motivated, creative teams across the globe.

▶ PUTTING HEART INTO MANAGING THE MOBILE WORKFORCE

Sometimes matters of the heart are concrete. As examples, David had heart surgery about four months before we began working on this book and Michael had heart surgery about a month before it was due to the publishers. Our commitment to this book has moved far beyond anything physical, however—we have developed a passionate desire to help leaders move to the more diverse, flexible, strategically powerful, and healthy work environment that is the promise of mobile workplaces everywhere. Our hearts are devoted to this future. Won't you join that journey with us? We hope you find some answers inside the pages of this book and the mobile experience we will provide you along the way.

► PART ONE

**Thinking Strategically about
the Mobile Workforce**

CHAPTER ONE

Moving to Mobility

Creating Mobile Urgency—Let's Get Started!

This is not just being on the phone anymore. This is now about an extension of my life. This is an extension of my personality. If you look at the decline of traditional land lines from the carriers, the trends are compelling. People are using this as their primary device. It is functional that way.
—PETER DENAGY, SAMSUNG TELECOMMUNICATIONS AMERICA, SENIOR DIRECTOR AND GENERAL MANAGER, U.S. ENTERPRISE MOBILITY ENABLEMENT[1]

The world is in the midst of a mobile feeding frenzy. The explosion of wireless broadband networks, mobile devices, social networking, cloud computing, and a global economy is changing communications and computing at an unprecedented pace. Organizations of all kinds will find the prospects of lower costs, more localized service, and ultra-motivated mobile workers to be exhilarating. For businesses, the stage is set to take advantage of the incredible opportunity to apply new forms of work and technologies that will lead to competitive advantage in their markets. It's not about getting your hands on the latest toy; instead, it's about getting your head wrapped around a corporate mobile strategy that works for your organization. How can you exploit mobile technologies to leverage your business? How do you transition your workforce into a mobile environment in ways that competitors cannot easily replicate?

Take out your mobile phone. Yes, it's okay to do so right now. Text the word "MOBIFORCE " to 878787 to register in our Mobile Workforce Registry. When you register, you will instantly receive a text message with content from us regarding building your mobile workforce. Open the text message, and click on the link that's provided within the SMS message. Within seconds, you will be connected to a mobile world of content.

You will find what we call "freemiums" like this in each chapter of the book. Just look for icons similar to what you see here and then experience what mobile workers throughout the world now have access to—globally available, useful knowledge that can be accessed and applied immediately.

▶ THERE'S AN APP FOR THAT—THIS BOOK!

C level executives (CEOs, CFOs, COOs, and other top corporate officers) need to rethink their businesses from the perspective of a mobile workforce environment. How can products or services be differentiated with mobile technologies? Are there cost advantages? Can business cycle times be reduced? Customer service improved? How can your workforce be transitioned so workers excel in a mobile environment? How will you sustain that new paradigm? A robust mobile technology infrastructure is foundational, but, ultimately, achieving competitive advantage will depend upon your people, not your technology.

Let's begin by exploring the current mobile ecosystem and why it's so important to rethink what you are doing and how you might push forward with a new mobile strategy.

▶ UNPLUGGED: BUSINESS STRATEGY AND THE MOBILE TECHNOLOGY ENVIRONMENT

It is almost impossible to overstate the mobile revolution. The ability to communicate quickly, to receive and send information at a moment's notice, and to collaborate on urgent company issues easily from anywhere in the world is essential in today's business environment. The Internet surrounds us like the oxygen we breathe, saturating our personal and professional space. Having the capacity to connect 24 hours a day, 7 days a week (24/7) is now an expectation, just as is turning on a radio and assuming music will emerge, or flipping through channels on your digital TV with your remote. It's always on. You are within reach of a mobile network from a mobile carrier or local Wi-Fi hot spot just about anywhere you go. The Internet has become a lifeline for all of us. Moving at *the speed of life*, we expect technology to keep up with us, with the consequence that we too are "always on." When we finally sit down with a tasty cup of java or at our favorite deli, we know we can connect with our company, our employees, our partners, and our personal network of contacts.

Always-on broadband connections set us free, but they also create a new set of business rules and business expectations. In the last five minutes, how many times has your mobile device alerted you of incoming e-mails, a personal text message, a Twitter message, or a news alert? We now expect information to be, literally, at our fingertips at all times. Instant information is pushed at us from everywhere on a global scale. Some people consider this to be an intrusion, a total interruption of their focus. Others recognize the unlimited opportunities inherent in mobile technology, mobile applications, and mobile management strategies that can be leveraged to achieve sustainable competitive advantage.

Connections alone don't solve the total puzzle. It takes an ocean of technology and supporting hardware to connect the dots. Technology needs to be managed, monitored, updated, and easily used. The better the solution, the less training and information technology (IT) support users need. Technology today can be implemented at every organizational level and for almost every business process needed.

Technology controls the Internet and the massive amounts of communication flowing from city to city, country to country, and even from globe to globe. And it just keeps getting better. How? Well, for one, technology seems to have taken on human characteristics. It's friendlier than ever before. It's smart enough to work in the ways we think and behave. It anticipates our desires. It's proactive enough to stay just a bit in front of our needs by delivering information almost immediately, with more relevance, with content more targeted to what we need— sometimes even before we know we need it. And it does all this anywhere and anytime through the mobile devices we hold in our hands.

Urgency
If you don't have a mobile strategy for your organization today, you are already behind. If you haven't even thought about it, you may never catch up.

You can't help but observe the growth of Twitter racing over the planet with a billion "tweets" per month, or the hundreds of millions of LinkedIn members sharing professional career information, or the millions of digital books being downloaded through Amazon or Barnes & Noble, or the billions of downloads of the Apple iPhone applications that entertain us and provide very useful applications to make our lives easier.

Who would have thought that Apple Inc. could have driven a mobile market vast enough to inspire three billion mobile app downloads by January of 2010? This power brand is unlike any other, and its innovation and ability to deliver the best user experience has been a fascinating success story that is exciting to watch. It has us "iTuned" for new announcements. By launching the iPad in 2010, Apple primed the pump for all its other products and services. Apple reconfigured the business it is in, but, more powerfully and pervasively, it destroyed assumptions about what constrains the way all organizations and sectors might communicate and interact with one another and the world. There is now a riot of creative, innovative activity capitalizing on the opportunity that has become newly visible—just like it always does when there is a major paradigm shift in the way people view the world.[2]

The fact is that mobile connectivity is rapidly becoming the standard rather than the exception. Remember the dinosaurs? That's your product or service if you aren't carefully considering how you might apply connectivity to it. New products with broadband connection to the Internet that are now showing up at consumer stores such as Target, Best Buy, and Staples are replacing those products that don't have it. Manufacturers who know how to produce technology products that integrate wireless may survive; those that don't, surely won't. Consumers of the past uploaded and moved information in raisin-sized Internet bytes compared to consumers today, who can move truckloads of data, video media, and urgent communications over VoIP (Voice Over Internet Protocol) in fast, easy-to-use services.

Mobility lives on the Internet. It breathes on terabytes of information and serves billions of people at the same time. We seemingly can't live without our Internet connections and the fanfare we receive on our favorite social media sites, such as Facebook, MySpace, Twitter; video portals, such as YouTube; or our personal blogging sites. Like it or not, most of us have become dependent on the Internet to help us keep up with our friends and family, not to mention our work.

There is no question that, whether we like it or not, the Internet connects us to urgent, important information; provides us a lifestyle filled with individualized products and services that entertain, educate, and inform us *on demand;* and introduces us to new ideas, ways of thinking, and people.

The mobile phone industry, and others, have powered up the perfect solutions for all of us if what we want is to stay connected to work and play. Technology devices give us the freedom and power to live and work where we want. Mobility is not just for the rich or for executives or for powerful people anymore. Everyone wants to connect, to call, to text, to search, to navigate, to listen, to translate, to coach, to train, to collaborate, to upload, to share (and do just about anything else you can think of)—*and they can!*

▶ **WHAT IS MOBILITY?**

Someone with mobility has the ability to move from room to room, building to building, city to city, or country to country without losing the ability to function successfully. Even when we are moving outside the wired-in service territory, the disconnect is only temporary. Even when service is weak or spotty, we can quickly connect with our family or our boss. Even when we are sharing confidential information a continent away, we know it is secure.

Already there are large pools of Wi-Fi installations and Wi-Fi towers that allow people to move seamlessly among mobile carriers. It won't be too long before most or all of the planet will have seamless connectivity. Then how will you hide from your boss? (Or from your employees . . .)

Most people couldn't care less about the technology that undergirds their mobile devices. They just want them to work. It won't matter much to your employees that you spent thousands of hours and millions of dollars to get them just the right device, software, and knowledge management system. All they want to know is whether all that stuff will help them to get the job done or whether it will be an obstacle.

Technology is complex, but your customers and employees expect it to be intuitive. They want technology that is simple, works the way they think, and supports the way they act. *Technology—for the average worker—has to understand us a lot more than we need to understand it. It needs to follow our behaviors and interests, not to dictate them.* This is a very complex request, but the winners of the technology race will be those that get this right. They will study deeply the connection between the human interface with technology. The more effortless that interaction, the better.

Compelling Research, Polling, and Opinion about the Mobile Workforce

Current research and industry trends support the urgent need to take action in forming a mobile business strategy. At the very least, companies must reflect upon whether a distributed, mobile business strategy will help them to become competitive or stay competitive, and whether the lack of one will knock them off the playing field. A mobile business strategy has the potential to help companies to achieve *sustainable* competitive advantage.

The adoption rate of global mobile technology, tied to a workforce that understands how to use this technology, is a recent paradigm shift of grand scale. The Yankee Group reports that in the year 2009 the enterprise customers who purchased mobile technology for their employees had reached 550 million mobile subscriptions globally, with a projected 12.7 percent cumulative growth rate through 2013. That's reaching levels of more than 668 million small, medium, and large enterprises. IDC research reveals that more than 1.6 billion people used the public Internet in 2009, and it predicts a total Internet population of more than 2.2 billion people by 2013.

According to the IDC Worldwide Mobile Worker Population Forecast, the U.S. mobile workforce will reach a 75 percent adoption rate of mobility by 2011. The study projects the existing adoption rate of mobile Internet subscribers to double by the end of 2013. China is reported to use the public Internet more than any other country, with 359 million users in 2009, compared to the United States, with 261 million Internet users in 2009. India is projected to have the fastest Internet growth before 2013, doubling its total user count.

The largest growth in mobile computing is expected to be in online mobile business applications, corporate e-mail, and mobile blogs. Unsurprisingly, more than one researcher believes that paying attention to the "mobile workforce trend" will be a smart decision for you and your company.

Research shows that consumers are readily using mobile phones, with subscriptions at 3.9 billion in 2008 and predicted to reach 5.6 billion by 2013. IDC predicts that by 2013 the worldwide shipments of *smartphones* will exceed 390 million units shipped. Growing at a compound annual rate of 20.9 percent. Moreover, while 27 million phones had Wi-Fi capabilities in 2007, the number will reach 400 million by 2012. [3]

▶ A WORKFORCE THAT CAN EXECUTE A MOBILE BUSINESS STRATEGY

How can you differentiate your workforce from competitors who are chasing the same competitive advantage? It won't be accomplished simply by scooping up the latest technology. Sure, knowing what technology investments to buy and how to use the latest software and hardware are fundamental competencies just to stay in the game. *But that will not give you long-term competitive advantage.*

Let's assume you have developed a business strategy to exploit the enormous potential of mobile technologies. Let's assume you've identified ways to leverage this strategy to achieve competitive advantage. While the strategy and the technologies are essential, technology is nothing more than competitive parity. Your competitors have or soon will have access to the same mobile technologies you have. So how do you turn parity into competitive advantage? It comes only by leveraging the use of technology to advance core business strategies. And, that depends on your *people*. Without a companion mobile *workforce* strategy, the best mobile business strategy will falter.

▶ WHAT TO CALL IT?

Deciding the terminology to describe your mobile workforce is important so that your company understands whom you are talking about. The terms "mobile workforce," "tele-workforce," "distributed workforce," and "virtual workforce" are used interchangeably on a global basis. In this book, we refer to individuals who are not physically located within a centralized physical building and those who move between work locations within a centralized location, and who are able to access company resources through private networks, the Internet, and mobile networks as "mobile workers." More than one mobile worker (such as a manager with several mobile workers) would be considered a "mobile workforce." The mobile workforce can include both employees and contractors who provide valuable services to either not-for-profit or for-profit entities.

Mobility Makes Sense for Both Workers and Managers
For an individual, learning how to join the mobile workforce can be a smart move. Mobility provides a flexible lifestyle that is highly valued by most mobile workers. If you want to work from a small village in Italy, you can. If you want to walk into any cafe in Toronto and connect to colleagues and clients, you can. If you want to wear your pajamas to work every day, you can. You can even moonlight simultaneously if you want to work part time with companies headquartered in Bonn, London, Santa Fe, or just about anywhere else on the planet.

For a manager, mobility means having access to a global talent pool. If you want the best engineers in the world to work for you, it doesn't matter if they live in India, Cleveland, or Buenos Aires. Need to have a talented graphic artist? No problem. How about someone living in Paris? Or Lithuania? Or Hamburg? Does your business strategy call for a flexible, distributed sales force situated throughout Europe, South America, or Asia—or all of the above? The solution lies in the palm of your hand.

▶ DEVELOPING A MOBILE WORKFORCE STRATEGY

Developing a high-level mobile workforce strategy can be broken down into four specific steps.

Step One: Evaluate for Strategic Fit
Some organizations are going to be more likely candidates to move to a mobile work environment than others. Some *parts* of an organization may be better candidates than others. Here are some factors to take into account when considering a move to mobility:

▶ *What are your competitors doing?* If everyone in your industry is moving to mobility and you aren't, that's a red flag.

▶ *How might moving to mobility change the competitive playing field in your industry?* If all your foes are making customers come into a central location, could you provide on-location service if you had a mobile workforce? Could you become the low-cost provider if you didn't have to pay for office space?

▶ *In what ways could workforce mobility further your competitive strategy?* If you want to expand to additional markets, would having a mobile workforce make it easier? If you are developing core competence in a particular area, would access to mobile talent worldwide make a difference?

Step Two: Assess the Costs and Benefits

There are many potential benefits to having a mobile workforce; here are a few:

▶ It opens a window to competitive advantage over competitors.
▶ It improves customer relationships.
▶ It reduces costs of salespeople, travel, and facilities.
▶ It increases employee productivity. (Employees are less distracted and more motivated, and they use time more efficiently.)
▶ It locates employees geographically near customers.
▶ It improves work–life balance and employee flexibility, including reduced commute time.

There are potential costs involved as well; here are a few:

▶ It requires an investment in technology, both hardware and software. (What will this cost you? An estimate of the hard numbers is necessary.)
▶ Time for managing is increased. For example, more communication is needed. Many executives we interviewed told us there is an appreciable amount of "extra work" associated

with day-to-day communication for a mobile workforce. So the question becomes: how much time is needed to "replace" face-to-face meetings and other interactions that occur naturally in a colocated environment?

▶ There are additional nontechnology costs. As the mobile workforce develops, the enterprise leadership and management teams needs to accept the added costs to hire, train, and support a mobile workforce. If sufficient resources are not dedicated to these initiatives, the company risks high employee turnover, decreased loyalty, and lost productivity—*the opposite of what should occur!*

▶ There might be employee and managerial resistance. If you don't handle this transition well, you might hurt the organizational structure and create a dysfunctional workforce.

Step Three: Plan and Align the Organization

Aligning people with new initiatives can be a daunting task even for the most seasoned executive. Transitioning to a mobile workforce requires significant changes you'll have to plan for in human resource management policies and procedures, information systems, legal issues, and training capacity. And that's not all. You'll need buy-in from each of the affected business units. Each department stakeholder needs to play an important role in the identification of objectives, opportunities, and the risks inherent in a mobile workforce. Each brings a unique perspective in transitioning from a traditional workforce to a mobile workforce. You are going to want advocates who understand the business strategy, objectives, alignments, and requirements of the company. Your managers may be the most important constituency you need to consider, because managing a mobile workforce takes a lot of time and dedication. You'll have to motivate and train your managers to lead this newly organized workforce.

Stakeholder collaboration optimizes the efficiency and effectiveness of the transition to a mobile workforce. Here are some alignment issues you'll need to consider:

▶ *Written policies.* These policies are updated based on the needs and objectives of the business unit. The value of written policies is that they easily can be distributed for compliance requirements and signed by the employees, to confirm receipt of the policies.

▶ *Management.* Sales and IS/IT must work together regarding the cross-management needs of hardware, software, and support.

▶ *Software and hardware applications.* Selection and purchase of software should be considered a cross-business unit concern. Training and support are cost centers to the enterprise that get heavy hit with support needs if the applications selected are hard to learn and/or the hardware fails.

You will want to plan this transition carefully, perhaps piloting the proposed changes and thereby developing early adopter advocates.

Step Four: Execute and Improve
After all the assessing, planning, and aligning, it's time to step off the edge and give it a try. That's the only way you'll learn what works and what needs improvement. Again, pilot projects can mitigate your risk and add advocates for the change.

> **Seven Strategies to Consider When Building a Mobile Workforce in Your Organization (People, Process, and Technology)**
> 1. *Center of Excellence.* Build a team that is responsible for the definition and details of creating a mobile workforce. Buy-in of executive members is critical, based on cost, risk, and return on investment (ROI). Appoint team members who will create policy and a companywide vision for

the adoption and implementation, support services, and budget of your mobile workforce. This leadership group should provide quality advice to the executive team, and it should be trusted to execute the right plan based on cost, risk, and ROI. The team will help determine expectations and accountability.

2. *Integrate mobile practices and technology into existing systems.* Every company has people, processes, and systems that can be leveraged. For the largest ROI, utilize existing people you have and their knowledge base, and existing IT personnel and technology in which the company has already invested. Often, integration should not require complete upgrades or replacement. Look for suppliers who take interest in your company requests and suggest modifications that further your business focus.

3. *Keep policies straightforward and technology simple to use.* Create policies that empower mobile workers to be more efficient, that define more efficient procedures, and encourage the selection of technology solutions that are interchangeable within your platform. Make policies that employees can understand. Policies set the stage for both success and failure. Analyze what has already impacted the company regarding people, processes, and efficiencies. Security continues to be a top concern for companies. However, by defining the security policies and the hardware and software platform, and by assigning roles and rights-based access to company information, the enterprise can lower the overall risk of information.

4. *Define roles and expectations.* One of the most important factors in hiring and managing is having absolute role clarity within the job description. Managers need to set expectations, actually manage these roles, and become coaches.

5. *Collaborate.* The success or failure of any technology is based on user experience and user feedback. Consider suggestions and feedback to be high-priority communications. Create a pilot group. Allow it time to use the technology and to provide feedback regarding the usefulness of the software, the process, and benefits of improved efficiency, communications, and productivity.

6. *Train, learn, and improve.* Train everyone, but be sure to train managers to be mobile leaders. All managers should learn the current evolving "best practices" associated with managing mobile workers. They also need to understand the key motivators of the employees—the behavior models of every worker. Determine as a leadership group what inspires the workforce to make their deadlines, to report the numbers and the impact areas, and to communicate more effectively. Determine the expected frequency and channels of communications and accountability. Provide access to a secure, comprehensive company knowledge base and make it available to all mobile workers.

7. *Support mobile workers as if they were customers.* Executives say that they recognize the value of mobile workers. That means supporting the needs of those employees and contractors and providing reliable solutions to their problems. Mobile workers need the relationship to be built on trust. They also need to have confidence that the company is paying attention to their efforts and production. Keep your eye, and budget, on meeting the needs of these people.

▶ MOBILE PLATFORMS NEED TO BE INTEGRATED INTO THE CORE OF EXISTING BUSINESS SYSTEMS

Your IT leadership will have to take the lead on providing the technology solutions your mobile workforce will require but you should have a working knowledge and familiarity with the various systems which may be needed, depending on your organization's size and purpose.

There are a number of ways to integrate new technology into the existing framework of business systems. The paragraphs that follow describe five predominant ones. These enterprise tools are the primary components of a comprehensive mobile workforce integration solution.

Enterprise Resource Planning

Generally associated with an enterprise, the Enterprise Resource Planning (ERP) system is responsible for providing secure data to serve all departments within the enterprise. It manages that data and ensures that there is access to it. The ERP system interfaces within the enterprise back-end software services, such as order entry, accounts receivables, general ledger, purchasing, warehousing, and human resources. This is not a complete list; however, it defines the primary functional responsibilities of the ERP.

Customer Relationship Management

In addition to the ERP, many enterprises use a customer relationship management (CRM) system to plan, schedule, and control the sales efforts and activities of the organization's sales teams. Many successful companies utilize CRM to increase their profitability. They do so by engaging the entire enterprise, on a daily basis, in efforts to collect information about their customers and report on their activities. This intranet and extranet solution allows instant access to secure customer data about prospecting, presales activity, and postsales activity. Customers who are entered into the system can be tracked to show communication behaviors and buying trends that help create a "sales pipeline" report for sales management. The primary departments that use this software are the sales team, including the call center, marketing, field services, and technical support. The goal of the CRM is to provide accurate customer information, which allows management to plan its ROI.

Content Management System

Within the enterprise, the need to find and access digital files using a secure Internet connection both within the physical enterprise location and outside of the brick and mortar is met by using a content management system (CMS). This system allows its members to authenticate their personal identification and gain access to digital files, such as customer records, documents, spreadsheets, presentations, and audio and video files from practically anywhere. Within a collaborative space, the enterprise uses the CMS so people can work together when accessing, uploading, editing, storing, and managing documents. There is a single point of search and distribution of these files. Industries may also call this their EDM (electronic document management), DMS (digital management system), or EMS (electronic management system).

Learning Management System

Enterprise global training groups and regional training teams often use a network-based aggregation system that manages learning content, member activity reports, and member information. Within the internal network space and/or the Internet online space, content flows to its members based on assignments, job functions, roles, and requirements. The content may or may not have assessments to track the performance of the users. This learning management system (LMS) can be a highly developed collaborative workspace within departments and the entire ecosystem of the enterprise or something much simpler. An LMS can also provide performance management that includes employee reviews and appraisals, competency management, skill gap evaluations, and succession.

Content Delivery Network/Content Distribution Network

The content delivery network (CDN), also known as the content distribution network, is an optimized network infrastructure. It includes both storage hardware and transmission hardware that distributes requested content. Generally, enterprise customers secure third-party services to provide an "outside of the firewall" distribution plan of media and access points. Customer-facing data, which demands a faster user experience, requires these access points, which are placed on the CDN. The biggest users of the CDN today are those who require large repositories of video and audio media.

▶ SUMMARY

In this chapter we provided a general introduction to strategies for moving to mobility. You found your first "freemium" and access to additional online content related to the concepts we cover in the book. We shared why we think the time is now, not later, for you to consider developing a mobile workforce, and some initial thoughts about what a strategy for doing that might look like. Finally, we provided descriptions of five often-used business systems that are useful for integrating your mobile workforce solutions. In the next chapter we'll ask you to think about rethinking your paradigms about the workforce.

▶ CHAPTER TWO

Discovering a New
Workforce Paradigm

Check Your Assumptions about
the Future at the Virtual Door

A paradigm is a set of rules and regulations (written or unwritten) that does two things:
it establishes or defines boundaries; and
it tells you how to behave inside the boundaries in order to be successful.
—JOEL BARKER, *Paradigms: The Business of Discovering the Future*, P. 32

The work itself should determine the best method, time, and place for its accomplishment. You wouldn't ask a farmer to come in to the office from eight to five to get his or her work done. Cattle need to be fed and crops need to be harvested where they are and in their own time. Our beliefs about these matters are based upon an industrial model that is out of date. It's time to go forward by thinking back—perhaps to the world of the craftsperson, who works where she chooses to work, with the tools she picks to shape her creation, and at a pace that she chooses, confident and skilled in the knowledge of what it takes to build an end product about which she can be proud, and which her customer will purchase.

▶ **MOVING TO MOBILITY IS NOT A CHOICE YOU HAVE TO MAKE**

Have we convinced you yet that moving to mobility is inevitable for your organization? If not, that's what we'll try to do in this chapter. Here we'll talk about why it is imperative to think about your organization in new ways if you want to survive and thrive. We'll share why moving to a mobile workforce is practically unavoidable. It doesn't matter if your organization has 300,000 employees or 15. It is not a choice you have to make. *It's happening!* Your decision will be *when* to move to mobility, not *if,* and even that choice may also be made for you, as your employees acquire devices and software that give them many work options. Isn't it nice to have one fewer decision you have to stew over? In this chapter we'll share not what to do but how to think about it. The world is transforming before your eyes—are your *paradigms* keeping you in a box?

Just so you know, the work paradigm has already changed. If you move to mobility now you are not on the cutting edge—you are already following. *The horse has already left the barn!* Here we will share how the new paradigm solves problems the old one couldn't, and what the new rules are. We'll ask you to define the mobile workforce more broadly than you may have ever done before. We'll share what we've learned from talking to leaders of global companies—how they have "re-visioned" their workforces and are changing industry workforce practices—and the industry itself.

Many companies believe they could not exist today without their mobile teams. The business model has changed. Soon you almost certainly will be, if you aren't already, dependent on work being completed by people you don't see simply by walking down the hallway. Your workers—able to choose from employers all over the world—are already a lot less dependent on you than you may think. Working virtually is a win-win relationship—it's a new way to play the game and win as an organization, and it can contribute to a much appreciated work–life balance for you and your workforce.

Paradigm Buster Number 1: Mobile Technology Is Changing Not Just *Where* We Think People Should Work, but *How* the Work Gets Done

Brent Lang is president and COO of Vocera Communications, a provider of wearable instant voice communication technology for mobile workers in hospitals, retail stores, and hospitality locations.[1] Now, that doesn't sound all that earthshaking until you start thinking about what the applications might be in, say, a hospital setting. It turns out that this technology actually redefines business processes and changes the way work gets done. "You can think of it as a work flow tool," Brent told us.

In a hospital, employees are often on their feet, moving. They use their hands a lot—interacting with patients or using special equipment—so they need them to be free. If urgent needs come up, they may have to move to a different part of the building very quickly. "We call these guys and gals 'corridor warriors,'" Brent says, "because that is where they spend their time—in the tiled halls of the corridors of a hospital or the carpeted hallways of a hotel or in a library." Their work style is very different than that of the classic office worker who sits all day at his or her command center (most often a desk with a phone, computer, book shelves, and—if lucky—a window to the outside world).

Contrast that with a nurse wearing scrubs with no pockets who walks four to six miles a day. If a patient or doctor needs to get in contact with a clinician the matter is usually important and urgent. Brent's product is a wearable badge that enables instant communication between workers no matter where someone is within a building. All the worker has to do is say the name of the person she wants to contact, the role that that person plays, or the group in which that person is a member by using voice commands through her badge. No hands. Instantaneous communication with any key worker. Maximum mobility. Problem solved.

But it turns out the business opportunities that come with this easy-to-use mobility-enabling device are far greater than you might imagine.

For example, Brent's badges have been used to improve patient flow. The throughput of an operating room can be increased by using them to reduce the time it takes to clean the room and coordinate the next patient coming into the room. That can shrink the backlog of people waiting, which is also good news for patients and their families. Hospital revenues increase too.

Just as important, these wearable devices also increase patient safety by improving response time so life-threatening events can be dealt with more quickly. The patient experience in general also improves, because not only is response time faster but the noise level is lower. There's no need for loudspeakers to call people. A soft voice command into a badge fits the ticket. (When will airports figure out a way to apply this, eh?) Patients can sleep without interruption.

These badges can also improve efficiency by reducing, for example, the distance a nurse may have to walk. Brent says this kind of communication tool can even affect how buildings are designed. Instead of needing the classic hospital hub-and-spoke system, where people shout down hallways to find people, they can be instantly located no matter where they are. The building can be designed accordingly.

That is just touching the surface. The badges can also contact members of a stroke alert team who are scattered throughout the hospital with just one voice command. And even that's not all, according to Brent:

> Many times, emergency departments get overcrowded. When they get overcrowded to a certain, severe degree they actually start turning ambulances away. They call it "diversion." They can literally force an ambulance to go to another hospital. One of the things that we've been able to do with some of our hospital customers is eliminate that problem through the improvement of the work flow process of how they are handling their emergency department.
>
> The way it works is when the emergency department gets to a certain level of occupancy, they actually send out a broadcast alert message to their Census Alert Team. The Census Alert Team knows that, based on a newly defined process, if you are in housekeeping, you start cleaning rooms. If you are a transport tech, you start moving patients out of the emergency department. If you are a discharge clerk, you start discharging patients as appropriate. It is amazing how much inefficiency is left in the system and as a result you can get more people out of the hospital and more beds emptied in the hospital to get people moved from the emergency department into the actual hospital thereby essentially creating more space in the emergency department for new patients coming in.
>
> We had a hospital here locally that had been on diversion for over 60 hours for three consecutive months and were on the verge of being fined by the State of California because they had basically surpassed the limit that was allowed in their environment. They implemented this new process with basically different colors representing different levels of urgency. It is just like our national security, with green, yellow, orange, and red. Based on creating this gate system using these colors and pre-defined workflow processes, they were able to eliminate diversion from their emergency department completely. That is an example where, yes, communication played a role in it but it was a question of us coming in and enabling them to create a whole new process for how they manage people inside of that environment.

Corridor warriors may be retail workers, manufacturing workers, security teams—anyone who is mobile throughout the day. They don't get into cars or planes to move around. They aren't sitting at a desk. They are, Brent says, "the forgotten worker," because most mobile technologies are focused on traditional road warriors.

What if, someday, everyone had a device like this and could be contacted immediately anywhere in the world? What if it weren't a badge anymore but something implanted inside the body? Is it possible? We think so.

Imagine the possibilities for your organization.

Paradigm Buster Number 2: Working Away from the Office Won't *Hurt* Your Career, It Will *Help* It

To be competitive globally your company has to attract and retain the top talent in the world. If you are an enterprise leader, what do you do? Pay exorbitantly? Lessen the amount of work? Lower expectations? Stop asking people to travel? For Sharon Allen, chairman of Deloitte, none of those solutions were good enough. [2] Instead, Deloitte created and instituted "mass career customization."

Jodi LaBrie is a senior manager at Deloitte, and she told us how mass career customization (MCC) works for her. [3] Jodi manages nine employees. The day we talked with her, four of those people were in the office, one was home with a sick child, and the rest were in clients' offices or elsewhere. Jodi uses e-mail and Deloitte Online—which tracks and gives the team access to each project—to help keep up with everyone. The work is accomplished at a high level of quality and on time, and everyone is happy with the work arrangement. Especially Jodi.

Jodi has chosen to work on a reduced, 60 percent workload level. Right now that fits her life. In the past, she told us, that wouldn't have been possible, because in public accounting there are very clear levels: staff, senior, manager, senior manager, and partner, and if you didn't move right up the chain, that was it—you went up or you were out. The next step for Jodi should be partner, but that's not what she wants—now. "There are definitely sacrifices you have to make to make partner," she says. "That is just the reality of it. Given where I am in my life, I don't want to be partner right now." But she doesn't want to close that door either, which is what would have happened in the past. MCC gives her another option. It allows flexible work, including mobile work, that fits the needs of professionals like Jodi.

MCC, according to Cathleen Benko and Anne Weisberg in their book, *Mass Career Customization*, "does for careers what mass product customization (MPC) has done for the consumer products industry: replace a one-size-fits-all approach with a bevy of customized product offerings." Similarly, MCC, they say, "delivers distinct competitive advantage through increased employee job satisfaction and loyalty; greater potential for the kinds of continuous, long-term relationships with higher-performing employees that improves productivity; and lower costs related to less employee churn."[4] In short, you get to hang on to high-value employees like Jodi.

"You can choose when and where you are doing the work," Jodi told us. "That is the thing about Deloitte. They [local partners or the larger organization] say they aren't so concerned about you sitting at your desk at specific hours as [they] are about knowing that your clients are being handled and the work is being done. How and where you work—as long as your clients are okay with it and you are getting a good work product—whatever you do is great."

In a MCC environment, not only can you choose your workload, you can also have choices about where and when that work gets done, how quickly you want to move to increasing levels of authority and responsibility, and what role (e.g., individual contributor or manager) you wish to play. Those choices interact to make up your current job, and allow you to customize your desired career as you go along. As Benko and Weisberg say, this gives the company lots of flexibility to optimize employee potential, effort, and loyalty. As our friend Jodi says, it not only attracts people to the company but "it [also] keeps people here too. I've had various other opportunities over the years. My schedule would be eight to five, and I'd be expected to be sitting at my desk. It is hard to imagine doing that. I have people I report to, but it feels like I'm my own boss. I'm managing my time. I do what I do. I don't feel like I have someone over my shoulder all the time, and that is a really huge selling point."

At an organization like Deloitte, with around 165,000 employees in 140 countries, "mass" seems like an appropriate term, "customization" individualizes it, and "career" is the medium through which people get the work done over time. So let's go back to Sharon Allen, the company's chairman, to consider what that means—and how that affects the paradigm of virtual work—for enterprise leaders. Deloitte has the highest percentage of regular telecommuters—93 percent—of all companies on *Fortune* magazine's 100 Best Companies to Work For list in 2010.[5] Like all effective leaders, Sharon started with a simple example when we asked her how telework touches her own job.

> *The very best example of how telework is supporting my own career is today's example. That is because as the chairman, while I live in Southern California, my office is in New York, and I benefit from the team that is spread throughout the country. The technology that supports us is really what makes that all work. For instance, when I moved from Portland to Los Angeles, I was fortunate enough to have my assistant, Cindy Hoppe, and her family actually move along with me. She supported me here when I was the regional managing partner. When I took on the chairman's role about seven years ago, after a period of time she recognized I was traveling a lot—the majority of the time, in fact—[and] she basically came to me and said, 'Why is it I commute an hour and a half each way to work into Los Angeles if you're never here?' Good question, right? She moved back to Portland, and works out of her home office and supports me every day as my executive assistant. She picks up my Los Angeles phone from her desk in Portland. She even supports one of the regional managers in L.A. as well. She backs up his assistant because they are able to stay connected so well through technology with the instant messenger communication. Even though she is remote, she can stay connected to his office. My speechwriter happens to live in North Carolina. Bob, [Sharon's chief of staff] works from his office in New York but occasionally from his home in New Jersey. Dana, [in our public relations group] is in New York. My team is basically spread all over the country.*

I'm able to take advantage of the very best resources from wherever they might live. The whole technology that really supports our being mobile and my personally being mobile is what makes my life a whole lot easier.

An Interview with Sharon Allen, Chairman of the Board, Deloitte LLP

We sat down (virtually) with Sharon Allen to discuss the mobile workforce. With the highest percentage of regular telecommuters on *Fortune* magazine's 100 Best Places to Work, we were aware that Deloitte knew something many much smaller companies don't—that flexible work environments are both good business and good for the people who work there. What we didn't know was whether the "good for the people who work there" was just lip service or a serious matter for Deloitte. After just a few minutes it was clear that Sharon was passionate about the people part, too.

"The whole notion of focusing on individuals and individuals' competencies and how individuals can succeed is core to our culture," she told us. "It is all about people." The mobile workforce "is a competitive advantage. . . . It has improved the work satisfaction, productivity, and our workforce's feeling about their ability to have more engagement with what they are doing and more control over what they are doing."

But it is not, she emphasized, about working less hard. "Sometimes people get the perception that if you're working on any kind of a flexible arrangement or even telecommuting that you are really not working as hard. It is important to be clear that that is not the case. You may be working *less* by choice—a flexible work arrangement that actually has [fewer] hours—but it doesn't mean you are working less hard. I think it is very important we always keep that in mind in relation to people's expectations when they come into or-ganizations and how they play that out in the context of their day-to-day work."

The mass career customization program evolved from initiatives to improve retention of women at the firm, she told us. Their research helped them understand the impor-tance of workplace flexibility. Today the results benefit all of the organization's employees. "I absolutely believe that tele-work helps facilitate work–life fit as we call it for individuals within our organization." Does telework give the company and its employees more opportunities for customization? "With telework, it ties in very appropriately with the whole notion around flexible work options and how and where people work," says Sharon. "The telework concept is what, in so many ways, facilitates our process around enabling mass career customization."

Virtual work environments are opening up the floodgates for con-sidering organizational structures that wouldn't have been dreamed of before. One of the primary worries of employees who are considering telework is that "out of sight, out of mind" will hurt when it comes to career progression. Leaders who are considering telework worry that key employees who aren't tethered to an office will fly to other organi-zations that promise rapid career progression. Sharon Allen and De-loitte have capitalized on the opportunities that telework provide to do the opposite—keep great employees who have very high employee satisfaction.

Have you thought about how your mobile workforce paradigm could be limiting your business potential?

Ten to fifteen years ago the world seemed much rounder; in busi-ness it seemed to revolve around and around with standard telephone calls, handwritten messages, some voice mail, and of course snail mail. Face to face was the most important business communication component when structuring deals and winning new business. Today, the world has simply flattened, as Thomas Friedman has so famously described.[6] Now people can work on international teams with colleagues in many cities and many countries, depending on where the talent resides.

Paradigm Buster Number 3: Mobility Isn't Just Letting Your Employees Work Away from the Office—It Incorporates Every Form of Mass Communication That Has Come Before

A great way to get perspective on how the cell phone has busted previous paradigms about the mass media is to think about what Tomi Ahonen proposes as the *7th of the Mass Media*.[7] According to Ahonen, mobile technology has outpaced all forms of mass communication media. There are twice as many cell phones as TV sets, four times the number of cell phones as personal computers (PCs), five times as many cell phones as cars, and three times as many cell phone subscriptions as Internet users. Mobiles (as Ahonen calls them) can do everything other forms of media can do and can additionally initiate, respond to, and dialogue with others. (You really need to read what Ahonen has to say—he has fascinating statistics, such as 60 percent of the people take their cell phone to bed every night—*what other communication medium can boast that?* Over 50 percent of e-mail users expect a response with 24 hours, but *84 percent* of Short Message Service [SMS] users expect a response *within five minutes*. Think of the implications of that—and we haven't even started talking about the apps that are available for cell phones.)

Ahonen describes each of the mass media that have emerged throughout history, and how each one transitioned to the next. They are: (1) print, (2) recordings, (3) cinema, (4) radio, (5) TV, (6) Internet, and (7) mobile, which materialized in the 2000s. The cell phone, Ahonen says, will become more and more the "predominate" media channel, by "cannibalizing" elements from all the previous ones. The cell phone can do everything all the first six media can do—and more. He lists seven unique benefits that mobile possesses:

1. The cell phone is the first truly personal mass media channel.
2. The cell phone is permanently carried.
3. The cell phone is the first "always-on" media.
4. Only the cell phone provides a built-in payment channel. All you have to do is "click to buy."
5. The cell phone is available at the point of creative impulse, enabling user-generated content. The camera phone sits in your hand (video and podcast recorder as well as picture taker), ready to use at a moment's notice.
6. The cell phone is the first media with near-perfect audience data.
7. Only the cell phone captures the social context of media consumption.

What's on the mobile channel?

The mobile channel includes mobile hardware, such as laptops, wireless modems, and handheld personal digital assistants (PDAs); mobile collaborative software; mobile productivity software and mobile carriers; Wi-Fi connections; and mobile Internet connections.

Mobile is the mass media channel, your on-the-go station. The static images are small, but the value of the information accessed while being mobile is more valuable because it can be accessed anywhere. If the small screen is the only option we have, we learn to use its "value proposition" very quickly and adapt to the mobile screen limitations. The younger "Y" generation—those Game Boy enthusiasts who grew up on hours of microscreen focus—are really the same customers today of mobile devices and their powerful access to all mass communication channels at once. People in other countries that have not already experienced the early innovation of mobile gadgets and mobile phones are learning

to use mobile purely from necessity—in some extreme remote areas it's the only form of communication and media
portal.

Today's workforce is changing into an army of well-
equipped professionals who are not afraid to spend most of
their day accessing a mobile computer device.

Think about the qualities that Ahonen describes in terms of your workforce. Mobile is the first "always present," "always on," and always within-arm's-distance communications channel. You now have the ability to skip all the previous media. You can communicate via written word, voice, or video. You can search for information, and receive it, in those three modes as well. You have instant access to anybody on your team and can meet anytime. You can communicate immediately with your direct reports, the whole company, or the world. If you need to let people know something urgent—or if there is something pressing going on that you want to know about—you can do it or get it in real time. Right now. You can make information more secure than your locked four-drawer file or than your bank lockbox. You can teach, meet, share information, study prototypes, and even conduct complex, sensitive medical operations virtually.

Your organization is probably mobile already. Do you get messages from people not in the office now, perhaps sitting in a subway or taxi or in a hotel room? Do people send you the latest presentation or document on your phone while you're sitting at home eating dinner? They are working mobilely, and so are you.

Paradigm Buster Number 4: Work and the Worker Do Not Have to Be in the Same Location

Former Principal Investigator of the Afghanistan Water Agriculture and Technology (AWATT) project, Bob Grassberger, seems like the typical "road warrior" we conjure up when thinking about mobile work: harried, tired, and—though still thrilled with the work—ultimately burned out from traveling. When asked about his travels, Grassberger remarked, "I spend a ton of time in cities that I never see. I arrive, usually get on a shuttle or catch a cab to a hotel, hold meetings at the hotel, catch a cab to the airport, and fly home."[8] We'll learn in Chapter 3 that many of these workers will be able to reduce their travel time as telepresence technology, such as Hewlett-Packard's Halo system, becomes more available, or by using more traditional methods, such as cell phones, VoIP, or virtual offices. And in this chapter we've already learned that some mobile workers—"corridor warriors"—can take their work with them as they roam through hallways, buildings, or stores.

But what would happen if *the work itself* could be executed separately from the worker? Sharon Kay, in a piece called "Remote Surgery," describes one possibility:

> *A patient is prepped for surgery. The anesthesiologist asks him to count backward from 10—he fades out at 5. Everyone in the operating room is wearing scrubs and a mask, but one critical person is missing—the surgeon. Not only is the surgeon absent from the operating theater; he's not even in the same hospital, or on the same continent! He's actually performing surgery from thousands of miles away in a room with dimmed lights, multiple television monitors, a surgical console, and a computer that connects him via a high-speed fiber-optic link to robotic arms in the operating room. It's called telesurgery—a technology with far-reaching implications.[9]*

The first transatlantic surgery occurred on September 7, 2001, when a 68-year-old woman in Strasbourg, France, had a gall bladder operation led by a surgeon in New York. Dr. Richard Satava, Professor of Surgery at the University of Washington Medical Center and Senior Science Advisor at the U.S. Army Medical Research and Materiel Command, believes that surgery will be completely automated 40 to 50 years from now. Telemedicine, according to the American Telemedicine Association, is "the use of medical information exchanged from one site to another via electronic communications to improve patients' health status."[9] The potential—as technology and our ability to use it improves—for this kind of mobile work is unfathomable.

Is There a Hologram in the House?
One of our grand challenges at TATRC [Telemedicine and Advanced Technology Research Center] is to develop the roadmaps for a "holographic doctor" when a human attendant is not available, and for just-in-time training and guidance to a human when a physician is not available.
—2009 Annual Report, TATRC

As an example, suppose that Jake has been seriously injured on the battlefield and desperately needs expert diagnosis; then, quite possibly, complicated and immediate surgery is necessary. Yet he is two continents away from the surgeon who can conduct the operation. That is one of the challenges the Telemedicine and Advanced Technology Research Center (TATRC) is dedicated to solving.

TATRC is part of the U.S. Army Medical Research and Materiel Command. Its initiatives are wide ranging, and include the "Hospital of the Future," creating a virtual human advisor, medical robotics (such as a neck and spinal injury assessment device), simulation and training technology (such as a simulation-based open surgery training system), and a project to use cell phones for electronic disease surveillance. Another of the many examples of TATRC's cutting-edge work is the teleconsultation program the U.S. Army started for deployed forces in 2004. Since then, using Internet access and personal digital cameras, they have completed 5,700 consultations, giving timely assistance to thousands of deployed personnel. Another example—a complete robotic combat casualty extraction and evacuation system—has been developed to reduce the risk of injury for combat medics and other rescue personnel. Still another example is a smart device being developed for telesurgery and telerobotics. It will be able to adapt quickly to abrupt changes (e.g., available network bandwidth). This will make surgery for wounded soldiers more effective, allowing experts to assist or perform surgery at a distance.

Your ability to be in one place and to have the fruit of your work simultaneously occur in another will burgeon as these kinds of products come of age. One of TATRC's portfolios is health information technologies, and one project it is overseeing is being led by Healthwise, Inc. Dave Foster, the director of product management at Healthwise, told us, "The same technology that is allowing a radiologist to see information about a patient hundreds of miles away is also going to allow a doctor to see information about a patient and provide a virtual information prescription to them."[10]

Brian Dolan is the cofounder and editor of MobiHealthNews, an online daily trade journal covering the emerging wireless health space. Part of his job is to think about the future of health care. He goes even further than Dave. Among his predictions is that in just a few years wireless health sensors will be prescribed by physicians to assess heart conditions, which "will allow physicians to remotely monitor patients and get new, more comprehensive information unlike any information they've had before." [11]

Don't you think that, if doctors can conduct surgery half a world away, your workers might, someday, be able to do their work at a distance too, and not simply by communicating with members of your team or clients? Can you picture the truck driver who operates his truck in Cincinnati while he's sitting in his living room? Or the mechanic who fixes specialty cars two states away? Or the professor who teaches students all over the world? (Wait—that's already happening!) How about having virtual police officers? Can you visualize holograms that give out virtual tickets or stop cars while the officer sits safely in her car or back at the department several miles away?

Impossible? Rethink those assumptions. They are limiting the way you think about mobile work. Maybe you'll be the first in your industry to construct homes at a distance. Maybe you'll be the first chef cooking at restaurants on three continents during the same night. Maybe your company will be the first to provide a virtual plumber. Maybe . . . .

Paradigm Buster 5: You Are Not Alone—Everyone Is Doing It

Thus far, we've given you four great paradigm busters. We'll try one more for now, and if that doesn't cause you to think about the mobile workforce differently, please go hop in your Ford Pinto, stick an eight-track tape in your stereo, bop over to the local eatery, and play some Pong. The world of work is changing—either get on the train or we'll teleport you outta here.

Here's the deal: the train really is leaving, and you don't want to be stuck at the station. We'll now share just a few of the vast amounts of data—available in industry reports but also, if you don't trust us and want to do a little research on your own, is just a few simple clicks of your browser away. That will, hopefully, convince you that the work world as we know it is changing irrevocably.

To appreciate the unstoppable emergence of the mobile technologies and the interest of employees to not be tethered to an office desk, let's look at a few important statistics and industry trends. According to the latest industry research conducted by Comstat, IDC, In-Stat, and the Yankee Group, the consensus seems to be that many companies must move to a distributed workforce model either to get competitive or to stay competitive. Today, the enterprise is faced with higher costs in all areas of business operation, physical offices, global competition, issues regarding global talent pools, use of Internet technology and team collaboration challenges, as well as the cost to update the outdated technology used within most companies.

Facts and Figures

The Bureau of Labor Statistics reports that the proportion of U.S. workers taking advantage of flexible work schedules has more than doubled since 1985, and now represents 25 million workers, or 27.6 percent of the full-time workforce. Further, the increase in flexibility is widespread across demographic groups, with little difference in the numbers of men and women taking advantage of flexible schedules.

A 2004 study for the International Telework Association and Council (ITAC) by Dieringer Research Group reports that the number of employed Americans who worked from home, from as little as one day a year to full time, grew from 41.3 million in 2003 to 44.4 million in 2004, a 7.5 percent growth rate.

A study by iGillottResearch Inc., an Austin-based strategy consulting firm, estimates the U.S. mobile workforce stood at 56.6 million in 2004, but that figure will rise to more than 61 million by 2009. The firm defines a mobile employee as anyone who is out of his or her office—including other parts of their building—more than 20 percent of the workweek.

A 2004 IDC study estimates a 650 million global mobile work population. The United States reported a 20 percent growth in mobile workforce population from 2005 and 2006.

In 2006, Business in Motion, an enterprise news and information portal, released its findings from a global study of 375 global executives in 36 countries reporting a 20 percent gain in personal productivity of employees using mobile technology within their daily job functions.

A 2007 study by Cisco, "Understanding and Managing the Mobile Workforce," reported that within two years of the study over 870 million mobile workers would connect to their corporate headquarters by electronic means of laptops and mobile devices.

A study by market research firm IDC predicted that 164.7 million smartphones would be shipped worldwide in 2009—a figure expected to reach 363.2 million in 2012. Moreover, while 2007 saw 27 million phones with Wi-Fi capabilities, the service will reach 400 million by 2012.

Studies confirm that the traditional office hours of nine to five in many cases are being replaced by greater flexibility and choice of when and where employees begin and end their workday. This results in strategic and bottom-line improvements to those companies.

There is mounting evidence that policies that support flexible and mobile work strategies within the corporation boost worker productivity, aid employee attraction and retention, and reduce employee health-care costs.[12]

In 2009 it was estimated there were around 4.6 billion mobile cellular subscriptions worldwide. Compare that figure to the estimated 1.7 billion who were using the Internet at that time. The International Telecommunications Union reports that there remains a "digital divide" and developing countries are still far behind developed countries. Internet penetration, for example, in developing countries was only 18 percent at the end of 2009, while it had reached 64 percent in developed countries.[13]

Advantages to Going Global

Teams that communicate over time zones and geographical distance can get their company's products and services to the marketplace cheaper, faster, and on time, and they can get better customer service ratings.

Okay, so everyone is doing it and it's making a big improvement. Now, what makes it work? Lots of people have been studying that too. We'll talk at length about that throughout the book. For the moment, take a look at what one research study shows.

Knoll, Inc., looked at several Global 100 companies representing five different industries, and it found four "best practices" for increasing organizational effectiveness and performance:

1. Flexible policies attract and retain top talent through development and deployment, deliver measurable results that benefit the business and the employee, including annual savings on corporate health-care costs and absenteeism and turnover.
2. Mobile and flexible work arrangements are not simply "perks"; they increase organizational effectiveness, financial performance, and market valuation.
3. Knowledge-based work relies upon "time" as the resource that drives productivity. "Time" is shared between employees and the organization, replacing the traditional measurement of "time spent behind a desk."
4. Mobile work strategies support knowledge-based work, enhancing productivity while reducing real estate costs, increasing worker productivity, and requiring less real estate and fewer physical systems to facilitate the workforce.[14]

▶ JOEL BARKER: OUR PERSONAL PARADIGM CONSULTANT

Now we turn to the expert on paradigms, Joel Barker, because the best way to facilitate transformational thinking is by reconsidering your paradigms. *We think Joel Barker is the Soul of Schema, the Master of Mental Models, and the Pater of Paradigms!* The term *schema*, which refers to mental representations people have, is mostly associated with psychology. Peter Senge popularized the idea of mental models, or the maps we carry inside our heads. And Thomas Kuhn, of course, famously used paradigms to explain the structure of scientific revolutions.[15] But it was mostly Joel Barker who applied the idea of paradigms, and how they can both constrain and facilitate change in the world, to business. Joel is a futurist; though he is perhaps best known around the world as the "Paradigm Man." As the author of *Paradigms: The Business of Discovering the Future*[16] Joel is credited with making popular the concept of paradigms and paradigm shifts.

Joel had obviously given a good deal of thought to our interview ahead of time. Instead of us asking all the questions, Joel, like a good consultant (or scientist) would, asked us questions and made us think. He asked us to think more deeply and to question the definition of mobile workers we were using; he suggested we list all the problems that can now be solved with mobility that could not have been solved before, and to consider the problems that mobility can't solve. We talked about what happens when paradigms shift (the rules and boundaries change) and which of those are now occurring in the workforce. This list helped us think about our "paradigm busters," mentioned previously, where the rules are clearly changing. Take a look at Table 2.1, The Changing Rules of Today's Workforce. What would you add?

Table 2.1 The Changing Rules of Today's Workforce

Old Rules (Assumptions)	New Rules
Work is a physical place (as in, "I'm going to work.")	Work is something you do (as in, "I have work that needs to be accomplished.")
Work takes place between 8 A.M. and 5 P.M.	Work takes place between when is it assigned and when it is due.
Employees have to be controlled	Employees are responsible for results.
Work has to be completed at the same place where the worker is located.	Work (e.g., surgeries) can occur far from where the employee is located.

Old Rules (Assumptions)	New Rules
Relationships are limited to whom I can meet personally.	You can interact with almost anyone you want online and develop deep relationships with people you've never met face to face.
Work I initiate occurs when I initiate it.	This one is a little tricky. With technology (e.g., an online class), you can set up the work—the communication, the work process—which can occur asynchronously (i.e., at a different time).
What would you add?	

Now, let's examine the old rules (assumptions) and new rules we identified in the table a little more deeply. This will start your thinking, but there are many more assumptions that may be holding back your thinking that you can identify on your own.

Old Rule (Assumption): Work is a physical place (as in, "I'm going to work").
New Rule: Work is something you do (as in, "I have work that needs to be accomplished").

Work is no longer *the* place where people gather to get things done. It's not *the* location with technology, and resources, and human connection that enables employees to be productive. It is *a* place where these things occur—not the *only* place. In fact, in the future most people may never step foot into the type of central location that, for the last century, has been called "work." Work *can* occur *anywhere*, and *should* occur where it can be completed the most effectively and efficiently. Why in the world spend society's money to keep building roads and infrastructure and buildings when we don't have to? Why clutter the ozone with unneeded pollution? Sure, sometimes the best place to work is at a particular location, but it might not be a 20-story building where every employee has an office; instead, it might be at a coffee shop down the street from the person with whom you are collaborating.

So, test the assumption with every one of your employees: do they have to "come to work"? Or can they "do the work" someplace else? (This one exercise can save you a lot of money.)

Even better, if your employees don't have to "come to work," doesn't that mean you can hire the best person for the job, no matter where in the world she or he is?

What's Coming Down the Pike?

Based on the availability of technology, business is morphing into *its own freeway* of global connections, enabling employees to work outside the corporate box, connecting into the secure corporate intranets, extranets, and global Internet from just about any environment, anywhere.

No longer does an employee have to drive an hour to work through a maze of highways and frustrating traffic jams to get to a colossal enterprise, walk past a security guard desk to access a 6-by-8 cubicle with a computer having a secure connection, or to be on a conference call in the corporate conference room. That's the old paradigm, an outmoded assumption about where I have to sit—or drive to—in order to be productive.

Old Rule (Assumption): Work takes place between 8 A.M. and 5 P.M.
New Rule: Work takes place between when it is assigned and when it is due.

Why in the world does everyone have to come in to work at the same time and leave at the same time? It's crazy! Not only does that lead to a massive waste of facilities and equipment (everything is empty and turned off from 5 P.M. to 8 A.M.) but it is misguided from the start. Work should occur when and where it is best accomplished.

> Drive Time + Clocked-in at the Cubicle vs. Answering E-mails in Morning Slippers with Coffee. Hmmmm . . . .

The risk of allowing employees to manage their own time and location, deciding when and where they work, is a small one if the expectations are clearly set up-front. When the employee is managed by performance objectives, based on delivered output, then the pressure to perform is a constant motivator for the mobile worker, 24/7.

There is a "happiness factor" and productivity scale regarding those employees who really like working from home, or on the road, but specifically not in an office, 8 A.M. to 5 P.M. With a mobile workforce "micromanagement" just doesn't work. It's not accepted or needed. The mobile worker who is an independent thinker and is able to evaluate objectively and solve problems commands respect and provides a measurable ROA based on performance measurements rather than on the number of hours worked. Working mobilely can create a life–work balance that scores high on the "happiness factor," and managers in this new environment understand its value.

Old Rule (Assumption): Employees have to be controlled.
New Rule: Employees are responsible for results!

We'll talk in Chapter 6 about ROWE, a Results-Only Work Environment, but for now ask yourself why employees like Jodi LaBrie love to work at companies like Deloitte. It's because they are responsible for results! People *hate* to be micromanaged. Let desired results and a great work environment take the place of control. Let workers dictate their own hours, where they work, and with whom they interact. In that climate you are a coach, a booster, a resource provider, and a blocking tackle—clearing the way so that people can succeed.

Most of us have had more than enough bosses in our lives who posed as parents and treated us as little kids.

Old Rule: Work has to be completed at the same place where the worker is located.
New Rule: Work (like surgeries) can occur far from where the employee is located.

We've seen how technology gives, and will increasingly provide, more opportunities to separate ourselves physically from the work we do. Sure, we'll always be working to produce results, but the actual materialization of our efforts may occur elsewhere.

Old Rule: Relationships are limited to whom I can meet personally.
New Rule: You can interact with almost anyone you want online and develop deep relationships with people you've never met face to face.

This is an obvious one, with unobvious implications. Just as corridor warriors can connect with anyone on the team by speaking into a badge, your workforce has *zero* degrees of separation from anyone. Employees can send a note to the newspaper reporter who has been hounding you for information, or one to the Securities and Exchange Commission, attaching just about anything they want. They can—like we did for this book—meet virtually with some of the most powerful executives and thought leaders in the world. They can "tweet up" with a group of concerned people in a nanosecond. Now, more than ever, the way you lead this connected workforce will either strengthen your organization beyond what you could have hoped or smash it on the shoals of distrust and dishonor.

Yes, the mobile workforce is changing the rules!

▶ WHAT PROBLEMS CAN THE NEW MOBILE WORKFORCE PARADIGM SOLVE THAT THE OLD ONE COULDN'T?

We should have thought right off the bat to list the problems the new paradigm solves, but it took Joel, reminding us of Rule Two, to actually do it. They seemed so obvious, but Joel had thought of some that we'd missed.

One substantial benefit, he said, was that *you can bring talent together in a way that you couldn't before.* "The worker will go where the work is, so you get this ability to cluster and focus talent that was much more difficult [to get] before." Another, he said, is that *people can work from their own homes and still keep their jobs.* Workers have more options when there is, for example, reorganization—they don't have to sell their houses. He asked us what some other benefits were, and we came up with the following items:

1. Organizations can be *less asset dependent* (e.g., have fewer buildings), solving the need to cut unnecessary costs.
2. *Knowledge is universal.* It's available to anyone, anytime, no matter where they are, helping to solve the problems that having less-than-perfect knowledge causes. It's especially troubling, isn't it, when you know that the information you need exists in some file cabinet somewhere already, but you just don't know where. That's not so much a problem with readily available electronic knowledge.
3. *Access to people is instant and always available.* This solves the problem of finding people when you need to get things done.

These initial thoughts led to further dialogue about something else:

4. In general, *connectivity untethers people* from offices ("I don't need one") and file cabinets ("I have them with me wherever I go").

All those old "rules" we assumed were "truths" just aren't longer.

~~Location, location, location~~
Connectivity, connectivity, connectivity
With virtual mobility, location becomes increasingly irrelevant. Connectivity anytime, anywhere is everything.

Joel continued—as our virtual thought-leader consultant—to prod us. What do you *lose*, he asked rhetorically, with the new rules? "Loss of personal touch," he started, "in particular loss of physical cues, are going to make a huge difference." The nonverbal cues, such as how people unconsciously read the size of the pupils in another's eyes, will be gone.

Another loss will be fewer opportunities for folks to connect face to face and create "verges," as he calls them. Verges occur when people "bump against stuff you would never bump against otherwise." Verges—these unlikely intersections—create conversations, ideas, partnerships, new processes, and innovations.

The list grew some more. No paradigm shifts are without losses. Will working mobilely increase or decrease anxiety as people contemplate their job security? What will it do to our personal privacy? Will it reduce those great opportunities to go to barbecues together and build otherwise unthinkable relationships with unlikely people? All of these are potential losses with the new paradigm.

When we were done talking with Joel we were mentally exhausted. Thinking about paradigms stretches your brain cells! Ever the gentleman, he encouraged us to continue contemplating the rules, the problems, and the problems that will be solved by the mobile workforce paradigm.[17]

▶ THE MOBILE WORKFORCE—A WORKING DEFINITION

So now when we think of mobile work we can consider several dimensions. First, the mobile worker may be physically separated from his or her boss, coworkers, or other key constituencies, such as clients. Second, the mobile worker may or may not be physically separated from a work location, such as an office, retail establishment, or warehouse. Third, the mobile worker may or may not be initiating the work in the same place as it is being executed, thereby being physically separated from the work that's occurring elsewhere. Fourth, the worker doesn't even have to be awake when the work is being completed. Last, there is no one—no one—in the world of the mobile worker who can't be reached within seconds. The possibilities for building (or destroying) relationships are unlimited.

One thing to know about paradigms is that they are provisional. They are works in progress. You can hold them for a minute, a month, or a lifetime—but the rules and boundaries can change at any time. As we learn more about this rapidly changing mobile workforce phenomenon our definition of it will change, and yours may be different than ours.

The quality that is common to all mobile work is *connectivity,* which is why technology is the *sine qua non* of all modern mobile workforces. Even at its most rudimentary—using phone booths, signal flags, or the telegraph—mobile workforces have to be connected at some level. At its most sophisticated, technology makes the mobile workforce appear to be present, even when people are far away.

The Mobile Workforce

What is the quality that is common to all mobile work? It's *connectivity.* A mobile workforce is joined together, virtually, through technology, to get work done for an organization, a cause, or a goal, anywhere and anytime.

▶ THE MOBILE WORKFORCE SUCCESS SUMMARY

In this chapter we've looked at five paradigm busters, each with compelling stories behind them. We've examined the changing rules of today's workforce and problems the new paradigm doesn't solve, and may even cause. Finally, we've proposed a working definition of the mobile workforce for your consideration. In Chapter 3 we'll talk about Presence—how people separated by thousands of miles can feel like they are in the same room together.

Meet Jerrod

This bio describes an existing mobile worker. His story is real and so is his perspective. Here he discusses the positive life–work balance achieved with his employer by working mobilely.

Hi, my name is Jerrod. I am here to tell you about my job. For the past seven years I have been a mobile worker.

I am 35 years old and married. I am working as a professional in the medical equipment industry in a very large company. I have held a variety of sales roles leading cross-functional teams and consulting with customers. At present, I'm engaged in sales training and development.

I have been with the company about four years now. I must admit, I enjoy working from home. This is the most economical arrangement for both me and my employer—not to mention that I am much more productive. I spend about 50 percent of my time outside my home office working with sales professionals. The other time is divided between preparation, designing training, and updating our programs to better leverage technology available.

Despite our remote geography, we manage to work quite well as a team. We spend upwards of 15 days per quarter working together onsite. When we are working remotely, we use a host of supporting tools, such as Web and teleconferencing, Skype, or just plain phone and e-mail, to keep in touch.

In all, I have a very attractive work–life balance. I don't have to spend time in traffic. I do, however, tend to spend a considerable amount of time flying. I work more than 50 hour weeks, but it doesn't seem like work, just something I need to accomplish.

A drawback of working remotely is a tendency to sneak into the office to complete just one small task. That task can turn into hours if you don't have clear boundaries.

Overall, the remote work arrangement is beneficial to me, my family, and my company. I get to spend more time at home, have flexible hours, and schedule around important events outside of work. The company saves the cost of providing an office [and] benefits from more hours worked and enhanced productivity. Overall, I feel this is a healthy arrangement, both for me and my company.

▶ CHAPTER THREE

Presence

Being There Even When You're Not

When you can have two people sitting in the room on opposite sides of the planet and not feel like they're having a remote meeting, I think you've achieved telepresence. When you feel like the technology is getting in the way of the discussion, as it does during video conferencing, then you don't have telepresence.

—BILL AVEY, DIRECTOR, WW STRATEGY AND MARKETING,

HP LASERJET AND ENTERPRISE SOLUTIONS, HEWLETT-PACKARD[1]

We couldn't wait to experience the latest in "telepresence," the term the electronics industry is calling the newest generation of teleconferencing systems. Telepresence products have seen enormous growth recently, and companies like Hewlett-Packard (HP) and Cisco now offer high-definition, high-tech products designed to make you feel like you are right in the room with others who might be a half a world away. Now we were about to take a look at HP's telepresence product.

Presence
▶ Being There
▶ The impression or sense that something or someone is
  close by

We walked into HP's Halo Collaboration Meeting Room, which, after all the high expectations, seemed just like a small meeting room with six comfortable chairs lined up on one side of a curved wood table. The difference, however, stared us in the face. On the other side of the table three large screens lined the wall. Sitting above these was a collaboration screen that, we would learn later, projects an image so clear that engineers, designers, managers, and others, located anyplace on the globe, in real time, can use it to see and work from detailed, complex figures. Sitting life-sized in those screens, looking us right in the eyes, was Bill Avey, WW Strategy and Marketing, HP LaserJet and Enterprise Solutions, Hewlett-Packard.

As Bill explained Halo we noticed several things. When we walked across the room the cameras followed us, just like our eyes would follow a person in a normal meeting setting. Also, Bill told us, unlike the opening to the old *Brady Bunch* TV show, where you see nine videos of people who are unconnected in real time, with Halo technology you get the feeling that the people in the virtual meeting are right across the table. Just as in a traditional meeting, when a person is speaking in a Halo Meeting Room all eyes appear to be right on him. When the baton is tossed to another person, everyone seems to face her as if she were right across the table—even though she might be in Singapore. Halo Meeting Rooms even have the exact same furniture and design in all of their locations, which reinforces all participants' feelings of being in the same room. Also, unlike the audio delay you hear when news reporters are being interviewed from far-flung areas of the world, Halo has no "latency," or delay. Imagine talking back and forth with people all over the world just as if you were having a normal conversation over a cup of coffee. More importantly, Bill told us that he had recently negotiated multimillion-dollar deals with various clients around the world using Halo Collaboration Meeting Rooms. In the past, he would have had to travel to a face-to-face meeting for something that important. What's going on here?

HP is not the only company developing and selling telepresence products. Cisco, for example, has a product it calls "Cisco Telepresence," Polycom has something it calls "Immersive Telepresence," and Tandberg's Telepresence T3 has "astonishment as standard." "The fidelity," Tandberg says, "with which Telepresence T3 captures every sound, every gesture, and every facial expression supports the kind of natural interaction that enables you to get on with the business at hand."[2] And that's just the start; other companies are also in the game and the race is on. The business goals are clear. Each of these companies is battling to create the best new telepresence products and to develop market share in this field. By the time this book gets into your hands, we are likely to see products we can't imagine now from new

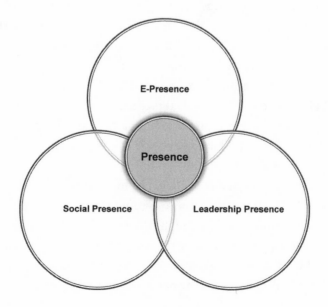

or merged companies. The business goal for customers is also clear: to create the experience of "presence," no matter where employees, clients, or consumers are located.

Unfortunately, that won't happen.

At least it won't happen in the near future. Nothing, according to Avey, will ever replace the need to meet employees or clients face to face from time to time. You can't go to dinner with a high-definition screen, he says. We agree. You can't give a hurting employee a hug or shake the hand of a new customer with telepresence. You can't smell the sweat of an anxious project manager or watch your boss pace in his office, awaiting the board meeting. Yet that day, we believe, is coming.

▶ PRESENCE AND DISTANCE

What does "presence" have to do with managing virtual workers? Let's dig a little deeper.

Peter Senge and his colleagues in their book, *Presence*, speak of presence in terms of being totally in the present moment, fully aware, deeply listening, with a sense of being connected. Presence, they say, "starts with understanding the nature of wholes, and how parts and wholes are interrelated." [3] Imagine being totally present and mindful and open to experience, to learning, to others, to nature, and to the interconnected ecology of the world. As we will see later, presence can be thought of as e-presence, social presence, and leadership presence. The surprising idea about presence is that it doesn't depend upon being in the same physical location—and in fact may have nothing to do with location at all.

Let's consider the notion of distance for a minute. Karen Lojeski and Richard Reilly, in their book *Uniting the Virtual Workforce*, ask us to redefine distance. [4] Geographic distance is what we commonly think of, and Lojeski and Reilly remind us that companies like Hudson's Bay Company, the premier fur-trading business in the 1700s and 1800s, had managers distributed far and wide, communicating asynchronously, and rarely meeting face to face. The Roman Empire, they point out, is another example of a global organization that managed different cultures and economic groups for centuries. Managing a geographically dispersed workforce is nothing new.

But distance, the authors say, is more than geography. It can also mean emotional separation or time separation. Their term, "virtual distance," refers to the psychological distance that occurs when people interact primarily through electronic media. This virtual, emotional distance is affected by physical (geographical, temporal, organizational) factors; operational (day-to-day communications interactions, multitasking, technical support problems, uneven dispersion of people throughout the organization), and affinity (cultural, social, relationship, and interdependence) distance.

But that's just part of the story. What if you considered distance to be connected to interpersonal interaction?

Virtual distance is related to what Michael Moore has called "transactional distance," [5] which he applied to distance education. Transactional distance, he said, is not simply geographical distance for teachers and learners but also the psychological and communications space between them that must be crossed. He believes that dialogue, structure, and learner autonomy can reduce this distance between learners and teachers. Dialogue occurs with respectful and active listeners; positive, purposeful, constructive, and valued interactions; and with the intent of improving student understanding. Structure is the rigidity or flexibility of program objectives, teaching strategies, and evaluation methods. It really reflects how far the program can be responsive to each learner's needs. Learner autonomy represents the extent to which the learner, rather than the teacher, determines the goals, learning experiences, and evaluation decisions. These considerations, when taking the needs of individual learners into account, can help course designers develop learning experiences that respond to both learners and the context for learning. Interestingly, transactional distance is something virtual leaders deal with every day.

For managers of the mobile workforce, the implications are clear. Until such time as science can make the physical distance seem like nothing, attention must be paid to reducing the psychological distance between workers and managers. We will share specific "how-to's" in later chapters, but for now it's important just to know that technology is a way, but not the only one, to reduce that distance.

Reducing the Distance Between Leader and Worker

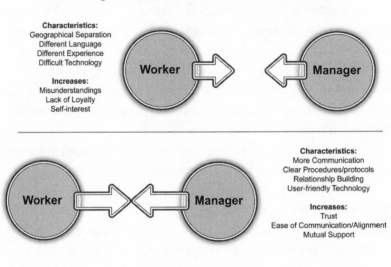

▶ PRESENCE—THE FUTURE

Picture your workforce 30 years from now. How will you be communicating with them? iPads will be long gone. No one will be carrying around an Android or a BlackBerry. HP's Halo Meeting Room will have lost its wings by then. What will they be carrying, or will they be carrying anything at all?

Technology has progressed so rapidly over the last few years that a person has to believe that anything that can be imagined can also be developed. Past experience is instructive. What one generation perceives as magic (e.g., regeneration of body parts, radio waves, miraculous cures) the next generation of scientists invents. We believe that the ability for people dispersed throughout the world to perceive themselves as totally "present" with their work teams will become closer and closer to reality. That is, science will discover the means for people to perceive they are almost, but not perfectly, actually in the same room with others located anywhere in the world and, theoretically, anywhere in the universe.

But wait—is that as far as it might go? Just almost? Will we ever actually totally experience ourselves as copresent with others even if they are a thousand miles away? We think the answer is yes. If holograms (remember Princess Leia from Star Wars: "Help me, Obi-Wan Kenobi; you're my only hope"?) have now been experimented with by CNN news, as they were during the 2008 election, why can't we imagine a meeting room full of holograms? Science is becoming increasingly hard for thinking people to underestimate, and leaders in every endeavor—military, business, politics, education—do so at their own risk.

Just as technology—video, voice, print, instant messaging—will converge, so will social and physical sciences. Psychology, sociology, and learning will team up with physics, chemistry, and biology to draw people located at a distance so close together that they will believe they are actually shaking those hands, passing that bottle of wine, and hugging the employee who just lost a relative. One day this will be true, and at that point, instead of calling it "telepresence" we may as well just call it "presence" because we will, indeed, be there.

▶ PRESENCE—THE PRESENT

We know that scientific advancements will bring geographically distant workers ever closer perceptually, make communications ever easier, and make technology ever more invisible. With the manager-employee relationship, geographical distance will become less and less of a barrier. As we have seen above, managers will, however, always need to attend to psychological, communication, social, trust, and other leadership issues with their mobile workforce.

Presence: Being there, the impression or sense that something or someone is close by.

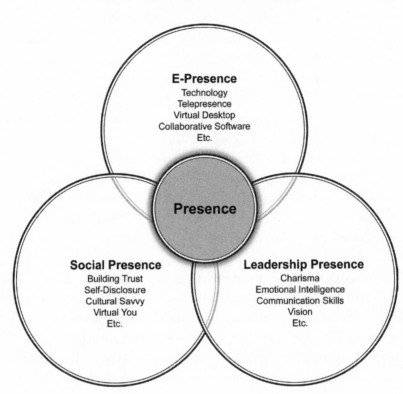

E-presence and the Mobile Workforce

The ability of technology to close the distance between manager and workers gets continuously better. We have moved from the telegraph to the telephone to telepresence. When Bill Avey started working at HP, it was hard to have a phone conference but was easy to send voice mail. There was a time he would check his voice mail in the morning and have 19 messages. Today it's moved to e-mail. E-mail is being displaced by instant messaging. Video conferencing can cost nothing. Holograms you can touch and feel are already in the making.[6] This is the e-present, and keeping up with it is an ever-moving target.

The Virtual API: Greg Kaiser, President and Chief Business Development Officer, ISB Global

Greg Kaiser is one of those people who seem like a walking electromagnetic force field. We interviewed him in a coffee shop, but the place didn't seem big enough to hold all the ideas he threw at us over the course of a late afternoon. He's had a busy career already, and one supposes that he is really just getting started. A key person in quadrupling the Blanchard organization, he has since gone on to work with many of the world's thought leaders. An entrepreneur and successful professional speaker in his own right, he currently works around the globe as president of ISB Global, which is the parent organization of the International Speakers Bureau.

We were intrigued when he used the term API (application protocol interface), to talk about what mobile workforce managers can do to put structures and processes into place to connect people. An API, in layperson's terminology, basically allows two things to talk to each other. In computerese, it's the interface between two software programs that allows them to interact with each other. So the "human API" is the person who connects it all together for the mobile workforce. He explained it to us:

If we envision this archetype of the mobile worker and what [he or she needs], and that the manager's responsibility is to anticipate that, and to put into place structures that support the direction that we want this independent agent, this mobile worker, then we want to structure their direction and structure [around] what they do but do it in a way that is encouraging to them rather than enforcing to them. We need to anticipate the experience [he or she is] going to have as a mobile worker and marry that to our strategic agenda.[7]

An API, then, is a metaphor to describe how a manager can assess, plan for, and then design ways for managers and members of their workforce to interact. "We acknowledge," Greg told us, "that people thrive on networks, they thrive on support, and they thrive on interaction. I think we need to channel and create that interaction to bring people along." That means anticipating what workers might need to do their work—information resources, preloaded software and work tools, networks both electronic and social, or any other kind of structure or process that will facilitate that interface between the worker and other workers, the worker and the manager, and the worker and external environment.

What a human API does, then, is to bring a sense of presence to mobile workers. Presence in this sense bridges technology and people, connecting the worker with what is needed to do the job. To Greg it can be even more esoteric, yet pragmatic. "How do we encourage people," he asks, "to use their own energy but then create natural pathways for that energy to follow such that they are motivated [more easily], helped to find information, plugged into the network that they need with the least amount of investigation and energy required, and . . . get the most return on their investment of time and energy?"

The human API—the next frontier in socio-technoengineering! What kind of interface will you be?

Social Presence and the Mobile Workforce

Charlotte (Lani) Gunawardena wanted to know what causes people to be perceived as "real" in an online learning relationship.[8] Gunawardena, born in the tropical island of Sri Lanka, and an award-winning faculty member at the University of New Mexico, is an acknowledged distance education expert around the world. The problem, she knew, was that people learning at a distance can feel isolated. The solution, building relationships between students and teachers, improves both communications and learning.

Improved "social presence," or that degree of being perceived as a real person, has been found to improve trust, conflict resolution, interpersonal relationships, and perceived learning—all key issues for the mobile workforce—in online classes. Learners view teachers with high social presence as more effective and positive than those who can't manage it. Further, this holds true in cultures as diverse as Morocco, Sri Lanka, and China. Simple strategies, such as coaching and encouraging online participation, asking for self-introductions, and encouraging private messages between students, increases social presence.

Lani told us that understanding the cultural context is very important because some strategies that would be effective in one cultural setting would be counterproductive in another. "One technique for building social presence is to share photographs and let people see each other," she said. "[But] people in Asian countries and also in Morocco, when I did my study there, are little bit hesitant to share their photograph with people they don't know." So she didn't ask them to share pictures until after the academic activity was over. When she was doing training in Sri Lanka, she asked people to choose an icon or image that represented them rather than posting a picture. "They loved the idea, because it gives them the freedom to express themselves. . . . What happens is when you post a photograph the stereotypical notions of the person get in the way of you being able to communicate."

She teaches students all over the world, many of whom she never meets, and they can develop into very close learning communities. The trick is to get to know each other, and she uses online icebreakers, introductory surveys, Web sites that feature pictures from different countries, and other tools to reduce the distance—cultural, geographical, hierarchical, structural, experiential, educational—between people.

Making different kinds of media available for people to communicate, she says, helps. E-mail, group conferencing, both asynchronous and synchronous tools, audio and video and text, instant messaging, and whatever can be made available gives people the opportunity to use what they prefer and to move—if they choose—to the more personal communications that build relationships, trust, and shared support. "What I was realizing," she said, about working with a Sri Lankan organization, "was that few of them would ever say face to face what they were saying online. The online medium actually broke the barriers for them to be able to communicate with each other across hierarchies—across power distance—as a learning participant. You have to understand the culture in order to be able to facilitate that."

Lani was curious to know if social presence also affects learner satisfaction, so she, along with colleague Frank Zittle in one of her earlier studies, asked students participating in an interuniversity virtual conference how factors, such as social interaction, having a sense of an online community, being comfortable conversing, having the ability to form individual impressions of other participants, the personableness of the online discussions, and the moderation style, were related to their satisfaction with the experience. It turns out that social presence is a very strong predictor of learner satisfaction.

She went on to explore the role social presence has in other venues. She found, for example, that self-disclosure, expressing one's identity, building trust, dealing with conflict, knowing how to deal with silence, and innovatively using language to adapt communication were keys to developing social presence in different cultural contexts. Since her initial work, social presence research has expanded to look at how social presence affects such things as online product sales, online trust, and the creation of successful e-learning environments.

But, come on, social presence may be important when teaching students, but it can't make any difference when managing a mobile workforce. Can it?

It's only important if you want to build loyalty, identity, and support for your organization. It's important to leaders who are working globally, Lani says, "if they want workers who are scattered all over the world to feel that they are part of an organization." Do you want your workers to feel like they belong to your organization? To relate to the organization? To be woven into the organizational culture? Then it's important to build social presence and a sense of community. If people are self-contained, or if it doesn't matter whom they work for, then building social presence isn't very important. But for most organizations that want to build and maintain high-performing teams, it is crucial.

Social presence is a key for creating trust, motivation, and loyalty for organizations with mobile workers. One of the biggest challenges for leaders of a mobile workforce is to reduce the sense of isolation that people working away from the office, in coffee shops or home offices, feel day to day. Managers who really get it, who know that leading workers at a distance is more than zipping out the latest company update, will thrive because they will know how to create the loyal, trusting, passionate, online communities that bring out the best in workers of every age and profession.

How important is social presence for leaders trying to create a passionate mobile workforce? It's indispensable. The *sine qua non*. Pick your generation or perspective—without understanding social presence your work environment is only as good as the next software upgrade, and your workers will only be as loyal as the next paycheck. Developing social presence is just one of the secrets we share in this book for developing a passionate mobile workforce.[9]

Personal Presence—The Virtual You

The ability to communicate quickly, to receive and send information at a moment's notice and to collaborate easily from anywhere in the world, is essential in today's business environment. Connecting 24/7 has become the norm and an expectation, like turning on a radio or TV and expecting the programs you normally enjoy to magically appear. Our lives are surrounded with technological systems that are expected to work all the time. The reboot is fast when there is a problem, taking just a few seconds or a few minutes and, generally speaking, all systems are back up working, including the Internet and the mobile networks. No matter where you are or what you are doing, you are almost always within reach of a mobile network from a mobile carrier or local Wi-Fi hot spot. The Internet has become a traveling connection for all of us. Moving at *the speed of life*, we expect technology to keep up with us so we can remain "always on." And when we sit down for that focused moment with a tasty cup of java or at our favorite corner deli, we know we can connect virtually into our companies, our clients, and into our personal lives.

Always-on broadband connections give us freedom. This powerful new Internet is creating a new set of business rules and business expectations. For the mobile workforce today, the issue is not about *where you work* (geographically speaking) but is more specifically weighted on *how you work in the virtual space* using technology, and how you present your style and the real "virtual you." Everyone who connects to us, chats with us on MSN/Skype, text messages us, reads our e-mails, or sees and hears us online through collaboration tools, draws conclusions about who we are, many times without ever meeting us face to face. They measure our character, trustworthiness, personality, sense of humor, likeability, communication style, and competence from our ability to communicate online. Most importantly, they develop a perception of our *personal virtual brand.*

The Virtual Mobile Worker (YOU): How Are *You* Viewed in a Connected, Virtual World?

A few months back I attended a local conference with an interesting group of presenters, experts within the social media space, Justin Foster and his partners within Tricycle. Their message to our group was about personal branding. He helped us understand how our own personal brands are made, how people remember them, and how "sticky" they can be—both good or bad. Our group, the attendees who were practically strangers, worked up a few on-the-fly reviews of the perceptions we had of each other after only a few seconds of conversation.

Everyone sizes you up within seconds of visual or audible contact and remembers the small details about you, those small things that build your personal persona and personal brand. It all happens automatically. Once your personal mobile brand is established, it's difficult to change it.

People remember your personal brand based on a visual and auditory pattern, and they remember the perception of you from the way they feel about you. What they remember quickly gets set in concrete. Why is this important for members of the mobile workforce?

When you connect a mobile workforce through technology, everyone has a personal virtual brand, a personality that comes through the mobile lines, over the Internet, through the SMS and Webcasts. Your "virtual-you" follows you, and your reputation is built. How people perceive you influences their behavior and whether they will trust you, think you are competent, laugh at you behind your back, or deem you a good—or a bad—vendor, client, or partner. Their perception will determine whether they buy your product. Their perception will determine whether they follow your leadership.

After just a few hours of this "personal branding" seminar, I learned something that was a personal awakening that rocked my personal "safe mode." As a mobile worker I have learned to move fast to cover a lot of ground. Meeting people in person and online has always been my road warrior role. Communication skills have become the value proposition I bring to the enterprise every day—that is, when my virtual self is effective. When it's not, business suffers.

There it was, staring me right in the face—my online virtual me. I realized the advice others would give me—to listen more. Actually that's a bit too nice—"shut up" might be more accurate!

For me it was an awakening, a shock to my self-perception. It was a slap in my virtual face, which shook the belief system I held about myself, the way I interact with others, and how others viewed my online persona.

If you don't like your personal brand, you should continue to improve your communication skills. That's what I've done. Work on it, and listen to the responses others receive and share with you when you are together in a group setting. Record your online and face-to-face sessions, and listen to how you present your ideas and your style. It's not a simple thing to listen to yourself. It can be disturbing—even frightening. Many people do not like to listen to their own voice or to see video of themselves and yet that is exactly how you will be judged as a mobile worker. What you say and write online—and how you do it—creates your mobile identity, and it's an indelible record.

This one simple seminar about the personal virtual you should be a prerequisite for all mobile workers, and espe-

cially for managers and executives. It had delivered the truth I needed to hear. To this day, the name badge I wore at the seminar is still placed on the dashboard of my SUV— in plain view for everyone, and especially me, to see. It says, "It's your brand—own it." Since that seminar I have thought often and deeply about how others perceive me in a virtual online world, and especially as a remote mobile worker who connects with clients, executives, managers, and team workers using technology and through my personal, virtual brand "me."

–DAVID CLEMONS

Leadership Presence and the Mobile Workforce

Stage presence is that quality some actors have in person or on the screen to draw people to them. Some think it is inborn magnetism, and some believe it can be learned. Some people just seem to have "it," and we laugh at them even before they tell the joke, cry with them as if our own best friend died right up there on stage, and consider ourselves part of their family. When some actors walk on stage, even in something as large as a stadium, they own us, we are connected to them, and we feel like they are performing just for us.

Belle Linda Halpern and Kathy Lubar, coauthors of the book *Leadership Presence*,[10] make the link between stage presence and leadership presence. Leadership presence to them is "the ability to connect authentically with the thoughts and feelings of others in order to motivate and inspire them to achieve a desired outcome." They propose four steps to cultivate it, using the acronym PRES: P means Being *P*resent, which is being fully focused on what is going on. R stands for *R*eaching Out by listening to others and building authentic relationships. E represents *E*xpressiveness, using words, the tone and rate of speech, and body language to express messages clearly and to take advantage of the power of communication. Self-knowing is represented by *S*. That means being self-aware, guided by priorities and core values, and acting based upon those things rather than blowing with the wind.

Transformational and charismatic leaders have been studied extensively.[11] Transformational leaders have a compelling vision, are involved in advancing or improving society or the organization, and have charisma. Leaders who are simply charismatic may or may not transformationally advance society—think Hitler or Jim Jones—and may or may not simply be self-serving. Transformational, charismatic leaders, however, have vision and are focused on the future. They are great communicators. They build trust in their leadership through the strength of their conviction and self-confidence and by being committed to their followers' needs and not simply their own self-interest. They develop personal, strong bonds with their followers, in part by being emotionally sensitive to their followers' needs and by being emotionally expressive. They are, in short, *present* in their work and in the lives of their followers. Great leaders don't have to have charisma, as Jim Collins reminded us in *Good to Great*, but they do establish *leadership presence* by building relationships.[12]

We started this chapter with Bill Avey, who demonstrated cutting-edge telepresence technology for us. We end with Bill, who reminded us that great leaders transcend technology. He doesn't see the leadership role itself changing with the advent of more sophisticated electronic tools, just that leaders will be thinking about different things. A virtual leader, for example, will always have to work hard to establish and communicate the vision but will do it using the tactics that are available, even if that means putting a vision statement in his or her virtual room—as Bill does—so that it pops up every time a team meeting begins. "The good leaders I've seen end up figuring out a way to be good leaders. I just don't see the technology as making the good leaders good. It's that the good leaders figure out how to use the technology."

Until the day comes that technology becomes sophisticated to the point that we can suspend belief enough to perceive that we are actually in the presence of another person halfway around the world there will be a need for physical meetings. In the meantime, savvy leaders will do what leaders have always done: use the tools at hand to get the job completed. It's figuring out the best ways to be "present," as Senge thinks of it, with workers who are half a world away, whether that's through regular face-to-face meetings, telepresence technology, or e-mail. If you're Bill Avey, you establish that presence in many ways, but it always includes developing a personal relationship. "You can't always talk about work," he says. On Monday he'll ask people how their weekend went, and on Friday afternoon he'll ask them what they're doing over the weekend. He shares that kind of information about himself too. "Somehow you have got to inject the watercooler on to the telephone."

Bill, for whom telepresence through Halo is a way of life, believes that nothing totally takes the place of actual presence.

"If you never go to dinner, you don't know about people's personal lives," he says, "and if you never know about their personal lives, you never make those connections."

When working cross-culturally, this is even more important. "People take pride," Bill says. "You know, every time I go to Guadalajara they're going to take me to La Distillere. And they're so proud of it and it's part of the experience." When you are working around the world, he believes, the rules aren't exactly the same. "I've got to believe that people that are closer and develop relationships are always going to be at an advantage over those that aren't."

"Going to dinner" seems symbolic of the idea of developing personal relationships in whatever way possible. For Bill Avey, and for so many others we've interviewed, those relationships form the backbone necessary for effectively leading a mobile workforce.

▶ SUMMARY

If you are a successful manager of a geographically dispersed workforce, we don't have to tell you that leading it is far more than mastering the available technology. It is also very much about reducing the distance—the communication, emotional, psychological, and social distance—between you and your workers. It is about developing a presence wherein people feel connected to each other, to you, and to your organization no matter how many miles separate them. It is about establishing your virtual you—that identity that helps people come to know you more deeply. In future chapters we'll talk about specific skills and techniques that will help you to choose the right people for mobile work, and how to motivate and train them, build virtual teams, manage performance, and to keep up with ever-changing collaborative soft- and hardware. The underlying principle of all these objectives will always be to reduce distance and to develop presence.

CHAPTER FOUR

Trust or Bust

Breaking Trust Is the One Thing That Can Immobilize a Mobile Workforce Faster Than a Dropped Call

At the end of the day it is all about trust.
—PETER L. DENAGY, SAMSUNG TELECOMMUNICATIONS AMERICA,
SENIOR DIRECTOR AND GENERAL MANAGER, U.S. ENTERPRISE
MOBILITY ENABLEMENT[1]

Bob Grassberger is an entrepreneur. He has owned several of his own companies and has been the COO of a successful start-up, high-tech knowledge management company. He has a doctorate in organizational learning and instructional technologies. He is smart as a whip. He understands business. He knows all about economics. Yet managing a multimillion-dollar international project in multiple countries challenged all his considerable skills.[2]

Until recently, he led a $20 million project focused on building capacity in Afghanistan. The objective was to enhance farm household incomes, create rural jobs, and improve rural livelihoods by teaching new skills and transferring new technologies. "My team was truly global," he says. "It was comprised of people from five countries, working in multiple time zones and in several organizations."

His ability to manage this mobile team has been tested in various ways. First, he had people on his team from a number of countries. "People come with varying perspectives, and communications, especially at the start, which have to be consistently monitored," he says.

Second, he had inter-institutional cultural issues. His project involved organizations from multiple government organizations and educational institutions. "There was jealousy across organizations about how much budget each is given as well as the amount of recognition each is given for contributions to the project." Finally, he didn't have the opportunity to pick his own team. Therefore, he didn't have established relationships with members from the start. "I had some folks whose egos were well ahead of the organizational good," he says. "When you see hoarding of information, it is a pretty good indicator that the people are putting themselves ahead of the team good."

Bob believes that developing and maintaining trust was one of his most important jobs. "When the trust bonds fail or are weak," he says, "immense energies get directed at politics and building allegiances rather than working as a team." His previous experience had taught him the importance of building social capital—the value created through the relationships people in the organization have—for helping to assure the highest level of productivity. He believes that the most important part of building high social capital is the need to establish that elusive thing called "trust."

We won't pretend it's going to be easy—establishing trust mobilely is one of the most difficult things you'll have to accomplish as a leader, and yet it is the key to long-term success for your project and for your organization.

▶ WHY TRUST IS IMPORTANT

The people we interviewed told us that trust is essential for managing a mobile workforce. You can't listen to a management guru or pick up a book on leadership that doesn't extol the virtues of trust for building teams, organizations, and relationships between leaders and followers. For virtual teams, trust is even more crucial. Our friend Kit Brown-Hoekstra, writing with Brenda Huettner and Char James-Tanny, says trust is even more important virtually because the supervisor can't manage by "walking around." When employees work away from the office "the supervisor must have a high degree of trust in the employee, as well as being comfortable with a certain lack of control, for this situation to work."[3]

Trust also makes a big difference in the quality of your team's decision making. Author Jana Kemp believes that trust affects not only decision making itself but also what happens *after* decisions are made: "When there is no trust, no confident decision-making for positive action can occur. When there is trust, decision-making can occur with the hope for positive implementation to follow."[4] Without that trust, good luck. Moving from a consensus style of decision making to a command-and-control type of decision making, she says, can "break the trust" of a team. Command and control at a distance is nearly impossible; you are going to have to trust the members of your team to solve problems, think creatively, and take the initiative when opportunities come up. If they wait for you to give them instructions every time a decision has to be made, you are in big trouble.

In fact, your ability to do something special with your organization will rest on the ability to establish trust. James Kouzes and Barry Posner, best-selling authors of *The Leadership Challenge*, when talking about the practice of Enabling Others to Act, include an entire section about creating a climate of trust. They start by saying, "At the heart of collaboration is trust. It's the central issue in human relationships within and outside organizations. Without trust, you cannot lead. Without trust, you cannot get extraordinary things done."[5]

So if you want to get things done you'd better spend as much time establishing trust as you do picking your team's mobile device. Without it, your best employees will flit to other opportunities, you'll reap subpar performance, and your job of leading the organization will be like trying to worry that cord you pulled out of your sweatpants back through the belt loop, or like pushing a string up a hill. It will be much harder than it needs to be.

▶ THE SPEED OF TRUST APPLIED TO MANAGING THE MOBILE WORKFORCE: AN INTERVIEW WITH STEPHEN M. R. COVEY

We caught up with Stephen M. R. Covey in Dallas early one morning just before he was headed to the airport. Clearly a road warrior himself, he was enthusiastic about discussing how the principles in his best-selling book, *The Speed of Trust: The One Thing That Changes Everything,* pertain to leading a mobile workforce.[6]

Covey, the son of *The Seven Habits of Highly Effective People* author, Dr. Stephen R. Covey, has a success record founded on his own ability to build trust as the CEO of a high-performance business. When Stephen was entrusted with leading the Covey Leadership Center he was able to double sales and to increase profit by over 1,200 percent. Not only that, during his leadership the company branched into 40 countries and increased shareholder value from $2.4 million to $160 million. How did he do it? According to Dr. Covey, one word—trust. He was trusted and he also offered trust to others which, Dr. Covey says, increased performance to a level the company had never experienced before.

The Speed of Trust shares principles of trust and behaviors that build trust with self, in relationships, and with stakeholders. Also included in this book, which is jam-packed with tools, examples, and techniques, is wisdom about how to inspire trust.

Trust isn't just something nice to do. There is an economics of trust, Stephen says. The penalty for lack of trust is less speed and higher cost. He calls it "the trust tax." The reward for a high-trust culture, alternatively, is "the trust dividend." As in his own executive leadership experience, high trust leads to quantifiable results. It is a "performance multiplier, elevating and improving every dimension of your organization and your life." It improves, he says, your energy, passion, enjoyment, collaboration, execution, engagement, partnering, innovation, and relationships with all stakeholders, including your family, friends, and community.

We wanted to know if Stephen thought trust was important when leading a mobile workforce. It didn't take us long to find out. "In a mobile environment," he told us, "there is an even greater premium put upon modeling the behaviors that build trust. In the *Speed of Trust* book I highlight these 13 behaviors that are common to high-trust people (high-trust leaders, high-trust companies). Those same behaviors will be important for mobile managers and a mobile workforce. [They] may be of even greater importance, because you may not be together."

As we'll learn throughout this book, the principles of leading are the same when managing either a colocated workforce or a mobile one, but the strategies and techniques may be different or have a different emphasis. Building trust is no different, Stephen told us. The principles are the same—talking straight, transparency, clarifying expectations, delivering results, and keeping commitments. "The practices may change a little bit in terms of the mediums and frequency of communication and the focus," he said. "I would differentiate more between the practices than I would the principles."

Stephen told us that two behaviors are particularly important in a mobile setting—clarifying expectations and practicing accountability:

> *You need to get your mobile employee to really focus on those two, because the whole premise of the mobile workforce is really based heavily on trust. It is saying that we can get our work done without all necessarily having to be present in the same place to do it. The idea that everyone has to be present in the same place might have some merit in certain circumstances where there is a synergy taking place. With all the platforms and medi-*

ums available today to communicate and collaborate, it is not required
anymore. What is required is that there is an element of trust and that
there is confidence that people are clear on the expectations, and doing the
right thing, following through.

The more clearly you make those expectations in a mobile work
environment, the higher the level of trust you can build. Without
clear expectations people will be wondering what they are supposed to
be doing. And in a mobile setting, accountability initially may need to
be more frequently reported in order to reinforce those expectations.

Trust is built on credibility—your competence and your character.
And it is the result of your behavior. A virtual environment puts a
great premium on establishing credibility and your behavior, Stephen
said, because it is harder to see it than when in face-to-face situations.
That is why it is so important for leaders in virtual situations to clarify up front the expectations of themselves and the team. Extending
trust, Stephen told us, is also crucial.

"Extending trust is the best way to make trust," he told us, and
shared an example.

> *I talked with one virtual worker who said that early on as she started*
> *to work virtually the key was to earn the trust of their manager. They*
> *had to do some things early on that they might not have had to do in a*
> *proximate, on-site location. Once they established they could be trusted,*
> *they found they were extended even more trust because they'd earned*
> *it—they'd proven it. More was granted. I asked what they had to do*
> *early on. What they highlighted was they had to communicate more. They*
> *had to make it clear early on what they were working on and what they*
> *were doing. They did that. They maybe over communicated, but what*
> *happened was it gave people some sense of certainty. It gave them some*
> *clarity of what was happening.*

The trust had been earned. Once it had been earned, the fact that
it was virtual didn't matter enormously, and the relationship was able
to go further, faster. As Stephen relates:

Let people know what you are doing and why and that the trust you are extending is not a blind trust that is indiscriminate, but it is also not a distrust because of the fact they aren't present and proximate. Rather, you will extend a very explicit, smart trust based upon these expectations and this kind of accountability. You then model it. You lead out first. This may take, initially, a little more communication. You still are able to communicate even if you aren't present in person. You can communicate by telephone, online, e-mail, and so forth. Sometimes in these settings, especially early on, we may need to communicate more than we will later, as we are trying to show our performance and connect with people. You just want to make sure that early on you feel like you are on the same page.

Smart Trust

Stephen distinguishes between what he calls blind trust, distrust, and smart trust. Someone who trusts blindly will "get burned," he says. "That's being gullible." The person who distrusts everyone is equally poor. Those people view life through a lens of suspicion and only really trust themselves. *It is just too risky to trust other people*, they think. There is a cost to the team, a culture, a company, and relationships from not extending trust. Stephen told us about a retail store whose manager was so worried about shrinkage on his racks that he tied down the sunglasses so no one could steal them. The results, of course, were disastrous, because no one could try them on. There is a risk in trusting, but there is also a risk in not trusting.

The third alternative is what he calls "smart trust," and it is particularly needed in a mobile workforce. Smart trust takes into account the risks involved, the credibility of the people involved, and the situation. It is built by setting clear expectations and accountability for those expectations, being transparent, extending trust, receiving trust, and reciprocating that trust. "It becomes a virtuous upward cycle of trust and confidence creating more trust and confidence," Stephen said.

It's not just giving indiscriminate blind trust to virtual workers. Nor is it distrusting them, being suspicious of their motives and behaviors, and looking over their shoulders every 30 minutes to see if they are really working, which can lead to a vicious downward cycle of distrust and suspicion. Rather, he says, we want to keep that cycle going upward:

> *We want to avoid the extremes of blind trust and distrust and find the third alternative, smart trust that really comes to life and is especially vital in a virtual environment. That smart trust is balancing that high level of trust but equally high analysis so that we use good judgment. That is both directions—the judgment of the mobile managers extending smart trust to their people and the judgment of the mobile workforce coming back and illustrating how they are appropriately running with that trust that's been given.*

It is this kind of smart trust, he says, that really enables a virtual workforce to take off.

Trust is essential for building teams, leading organizations and, especially, working at a distance. Remember that girlfriend you tried to keep when you each went to a different university? That relationship was not very easy, was it? If you've ever had a long-distance personal relationship, you know how hard it is to maintain trust over time and geography. It's no different with your workforce. Trust building takes extra effort, and the consequences, good or bad, are magnified. Trust reduces transaction costs, increases productivity, makes communication easier with less need to over explain situations, reinforces interpersonal relationships, supports employee motivation, and allows work to be delegated with confidence.

Lack of trust, on the other hand, leads to the rumor mill, political manipulation, lack of loyalty; employee beliefs about management "cheating" and taking advantage of them; leader beliefs that employees are loafing, hoarding information (or sharing that information with competitors), and turnover; and people watching out for their own backs instead of watching your back.

▶ **RELATIONSHIPS**

More than anything, trust is about building relationships with people. Over time, as those relationships become strong, trust becomes something of value in your organization. Don Cohen and Laurence Prusak dedicated an entire chapter to the topic of trust in their book, *In Good Company: How Social Capital Makes Organizations Work*, and say that "social capital depends on trust. The relationships, communities, cooperation, and mutual commitment that characterize social capital could not exist without a reasonable level of trust. . . . We see trust as a necessary condition of social capital, and its natural starting point."[7] Leaders today realize more than ever that social capital provides sustainable competitive advantage to organizations that need an edge when everything else seems readily available for purchase. You can't buy trust—you have to earn it.

The strength of those relationships, built on trust, will determine how information will be shared and its quality, the risks people will take for the organization and its people, the loyalty they will demonstrate, and the tightness of purpose they will share to accomplish goals. For teams working at a distance, these relationships are critical for long-term success.

▶ COMMUNICATION

Managers who want to develop trust with mobile employees do everything in their power to communicate regularly and effectively. For Melaleuca, a company that has grown globally by leaps and bounds, trust is critical, according to company president McKay Christensen, and communication essential to build and maintain it.[8] He told us:

> *It is almost everything. It is so easy to lose trust when you're not making connections. We have one employee who is based out of Kentucky, but he manages several employees who live here in Idaho Falls. . . . What you see tends to happen is that the employees here in Idaho Falls—because they are at a distance—they tend to latch on to another manager here or another group here. It is easy to let discord and out-of-presence conversations erode the trust between one person and another. If communication slips at all, you start to guess, you start to assume—those things start to erode trust. It is a very difficult relationship to manage. The most important thing is that there still has to be face-to-face connection and communication. It costs money, and you just have to spend the money to make it happen. It is well worth it at the end of the day.*

Regular, focused communication is essential. Don't assume your employees halfway around the world will call you when a problem is brewing. You have to take the initiative and facilitate the discussion. It is a continuous responsibility that you must not overlook.

▶ TRUST-BUILDING PRINCIPLES

We have found by interviewing leaders of multinational, highly successful, mobile workforces of all sizes that the principles for building and maintaining trust are no different for employees working at a distance than they are for those who work in one location. What is different, however, are the strategies used to build upon those principles and the magnitude of effort required. People are people, no matter where they are located. As Michael Kroth, coauthor of this book, said in *The Manager as Motivator*,[9] everyone is the same, and so you have to study human nature; and everyone is different, so you have to study the human situation—which, in this case, is one of people interacting to complete work and perhaps never meeting each other. Ever.

What, then, does research and experience tell us managers must do to create trust in their organizations?

▶ TRUST IS A PROCESS

Just as in a personal relationship, in a work relationship, or between leaders and workers, trust is developed over time. It can be destroyed with just one miscommunication or violation. Nan Russell, in *Hitting Your Stride*, says, "Like love, trust is cultivated, grown, and nurtured. We make authentic trust. We make it by what we do and how we do it."[10]

Roger Mayer, James Davis, and David Shoorman wrote an influential article in 1995, revisiting it in 2007, proposing a model of organizational trust that throws light on what will build trust with your employees. We share some of the basic elements here.[11] One of the most important things to remember is that trusting involves taking risks.

Taking Risks

Jon Katzenbach and Douglas Smith (*The Wisdom of Teams*) provide one of the best books about teams, how they're formed, and how they move to high performance. They talk about the importance of individuals on the team taking the risks required, of which "the most formidable involve building the trust and interdependence necessary to move from individual accountability to mutual accountability.

People on real teams must trust and depend on one another—not totally or forever—but certainly with respect to the team's purpose, performance goals, and approach. For most of us such trust and interdependence do not come easily; it must be earned and demonstrated repeatedly if it is to change behavior."[12]

Trusting people means allowing yourself to become vulnerable to their actions and the consequences of their actions. Your employees take the risk that you will do what you say and do what they expect leaders with integrity to do—that you'll pay them what you promised, that you'll be fair in distributing rewards for work that is accomplished, that you'll stay on the right side of the law and ethical behavior, and that you'll look out for their best interests. You take the risk with employees that they are doing the work they say they're doing, that they are not selling company secrets to competitors, and that they are fully sharing information not only with you but also with the rest of the members of your team.

So, a good deal of the development of trust depends upon how much risk each of the members is willing to take on—how vulnerable they will allow themselves to become. If the risks are low, people are more willing to take them. If they are high—perhaps when people are dealing with sensitive information—people have to thoroughly assess how trustworthy they believe the other party is before trusting them. When Stephen M. R. Covey talks about extending trust in a virtual environment he is talking about taking risks in a thoughtful way.

Trustworthiness

To build trust, especially with a team of people located anywhere on the planet, you have to be trustworthy. Lisa Haneberg, in *Focus Like a Laser Beam*, says, "If you are not trustworthy, you will have trouble engaging your team, and both focus and results will suffer. . . . When employees feel they cannot trust you, they hold back because they don't want to get burned for caring about the business. Intimacy and trust feed each other. When you trust someone, you share yourself. When you share yourself, you build trust."[13]

Mayer, Davis, and Schoorman summarized the characteristics of trustworthiness they found in the literature and believe the most important are ability, benevolence, and integrity. We'll examine each of these in the paragraphs that follow.

ABILITY

To trust another person, you have to believe that that person *can* come through with what he or she promises. A good part of that belief is determined by your perception of that person's skills, competencies, and influence, which may be high in one area and low in another. One employee may be great at making Web pages but have no skill whatsoever in writing press releases. You find him trustworthy to complete the first task but not the second. Your employees may perceive your ability to come through with promised merit bonuses to be high, based on past performance; or low, if you were not able to produce them last year as you'd guaranteed. The degree to how trustworthy they find your assurances this year will vary accordingly.

Do your employees believe you have the ability to run a complex mobile operation? Do they think you have the competence to train, lead, and motivate workers all over the world? Would they stake their careers on your capability to acquire the right hardware and software and then to bring everybody throughout the organization up to speed, including yourself? Do they believe you have the influence within the organization to make good on your promises for compensation, promotion, or the other support your organization needs for success? The degree to how trustworthy they find your leadership abilities will vary accordingly.

BENEVOLENCE

Benevolence is the degree to which your employees have faith that you care about them for reasons beyond their usefulness in getting things done. For workers, then, to think you are trustworthy they must not only think you *can* come through for them but that you also, beyond that, *want* to do good for them. From your viewpoint, you will find employees trustworthy when they not only have the skills, knowledge, and abilities to complete deliverables but when they additionally want the best to happen for you. In either case, a person is believed to be trustworthy when he or she not only *can* do something but *wants* to do it.

INTEGRITY

Finally, a person is believed to be trustworthy if she or he shares and follows a set of principles the other person also thinks is important. Both the principle sharing and the principle following are important. These are issues of character, consistency, and shared values.

If you promised to promote the most qualified candidate to a job, had the power to promote whomever you wanted, also had a genuine desire to promote a particular employee, but instead promoted the vice president of marketing's son as a favor to her, how trustworthy would your employee perceive you to be? If your contract employee made a commitment to follow you to the next project, you then offered him the work, you both had developed a close off-the-job personal relationship, but at the last minute he was lured away by a more lucrative offer, how trustworthy would you believe him to be the next time he promised to follow you to the next project?

Greg Lowitz is the Executive Vice President of Sales and Business Development at RipCode, pioneers in mobile video transcoding and mobile video delivery systems.[14] He told us:

> *Trust comes from honesty, integrity, and having frank conversations around issues—not hiding your agendas. Trust comes from leadership. If you demonstrate leadership and reinforce core values of integrity, your team will see that, see that is what you value, and tend to reflect that back to you.*

It takes all three—the ability to do what you commit to do, the desire to help the other succeed, and a set of valued principles that both parties follow—to build long-term trust in your organization.

Propensity

A person's inclination to trust another person or organization is affected by his or her past experiences. If you have been burned in a relationship or two before, you are less likely to trust again. If you have had a series of highly satisfying relationships in the past, you are more likely to take the risk of trusting the next person. Don't be surprised if employees who have been led down the Primrose Path only to be fired, furloughed, or faked out don't leap into your arms when you swear to take them to the Promised Land. If you or your organization has a reputation for making hollow guarantees, don't expect workers to fall down on their swords for you when you make your newest pronouncement. That's why breaking your word for short-term gain has long-term consequences.

Different people also have differing tolerances for risk taking. Some people are more secure than others psychologically, socially, and/or financially. Each person comes with a different personality and personal situation.

Context

The willingness to trust also depends on the situation. If the overall company is in freefall, employees are less likely to trust that it will be able to fulfill its promises. If the culture of the organization is one of manipulation and raw power plays, it doesn't matter how trustworthy a particular manager is, employees are less likely to place their trust in the hands of others who have power over them. If the peril is very high, the willingness to trust is affected. If the organization has a very controlling environment, then there is little need to develop trust—each person's actions are instead prescribed by the rules or regulations of the organization.

Outcomes

Finally, a person's willingness to trust a leader or organization will depend on what happened the last time he or she trusted that same leader or organization. A leader's willingness to trust his or her employees develops based upon whether that person does what she promises. Lori Coruccini, the Founder/CEO, of Predix Inc., a national company that specializes in leveraging behavior to develop productive, high-performance teams, says, "Typically there is a behavioral reason that somebody will not trust somebody. We see it all the time. That's an example of the owner not letting go or even the management not letting go in the field because of not trusting what's going to be done."[15]

This isn't the same as having a propensity to trust, which occurs because of some past personal or professional relationship or of a personality trait; instead, it is the direct result of the specific relationship between employee and manager or employee and organization. If the last interaction has been one of perceived betrayal, then gaining that trust again is less likely to happen. If there have been a series of outcomes that have resulted in perceptions of betrayal or just unfulfilled promises, then trust building is even less likely to occur. The opposite is true. When someone comes through, when the organization does what it has promised, when an employee delivers on time, then trust builds. That is why trust can take a while to grow. Long-term, deep trust depends on a series of outcomes occurring over days, months, and years.

Loss of Trust

Whenever trust has been extended but then lost, it is very difficult to recover, because the other party has been burned. All the promises you may make to compensate for the fact that you didn't come through with the compensation or pay you'd vowed for good performance will not take the place of behaving with integrity and doing what you say you will. "You can't talk yourself out of a problem that you've behaved yourself into," Stephen Covey told us. "We've got to behave our way out of the problem we've behaved ourselves into. In fact that is the only way out. The words may help, but it ultimately comes down to behavior."

▶ MOBILE TRUST-BUILDING STRATEGIES

Building trust is a process that occurs over time. It is dependent upon human nature, so the principles are same for everyone. And it is dependent on the human situation—in this case, a workforce that is working mobilely. Because the principles are the same but the workforce is at a distance, in some cases the leader simply has to do the same things—but more often or more strongly—that a person would do to build trust if the workforce were located in the same place. In some cases, a leader has to adjust for this more complex situation. The following are the most important actions you can perform to increase trust in your mobile organization.

Use Performance and Performance Evaluation as a Tool to Increase Trust

Perhaps the most effective way to increase trust is to establish clear, achievable, and observable objectives with your mobile workforce members and then to evaluate performance based upon those. Use evaluation as an opportunity to give developmental and performance feedback so the worker knows specifically where he or she succeeded, fell short, and has the opportunity to improve. Setting these kinds of objectives and giving this kind of feedback is very important when employees are working mobilely, because leaders won't have the opportunity to drop in and observe people working on a day-to-day basis, and it also assures workers that they will be judged on merit and not preferential treatment.

McKay Christensen, president of Melaleuca, believes the biggest trust-building meetings for virtual workers are scheduled business reviews. It is easy with a mobile workforce to forget to have scheduled business reviews. Approaching a business review that will be conducted at a distance forces a manager to give it much thought.

"A scheduled business review does a lot of things," he says. "It causes you to come prepared, it causes you to think about what communication is going to happen. I find that more trust happens in scheduled distance meetings than in just running them unscheduled, and it is easy to run them unscheduled."[16]

During a virtual business review meeting, McKay says, you can sit at your computer during the conversation; write down decisions made, issues discussed, and follow-up items; and then send something in writing immediately following that discussion to everyone involved. "It increases follow-up, connections, efficiencies, and all of those things," he says.

Performance evaluation should occur often and be used as an opportunity to keep people on track. If you do it regularly it is less ominous and more business as usual. Also you'll know much more quickly when things are going off track. The spirit of evaluation should be one of support and desire to help workers succeed.

The more difficult it is to observe behavior, the more important it is to give objective, high-quality feedback so workers understand the basis for evaluation. To really build trust, consider asking your workforce to evaluate you occasionally too—and give them a chance to do it anonymously. How you react to their feedback—by changing your behavior, if needed, or by acting defensively—will either build or erode your trust with them.

Start Getting to Know Each Other Personally Early

One of the most important ways for people to evaluate whether they want to trust another person is by getting to know him or her socially. People want to know about others' lives—what they're interested in, what their families do, what they care about, and other information about them. Strong, high-performance teams find that their personal relationships often last longer than the team itself.

Start your online meetings with introductions and personal updates, and ask people to share non-work-related information about themselves. Ask them to post their pictures or short movies. The idea is to build interpersonal connections that are not directly work related but that start to bind people together. If you can, find ways to meet occasionally with your workforce face to face, when you can break bread together, and celebrate personal victories or regret losses together.

Be Consistent

Be consistent in every way—rewards, the messages you send, whom you recognize and why, how you treat people, how you make decisions, the values you support. Doing so tells people if you are just blowing in the wind, depending upon the situation involved, or can really be relied upon. Don't react with a meow to one set of bad news and then with a roar to an equivalent set. People won't know what to expect from you. No one likes to walk on eggshells.

Consistency when working mobilely is at least twice as important as it is when people can see you in action every day, because they will use their imagination to fill in the gaps. If you are consistently inconsistent on some matters, they will assume that you can't be trusted in any matters at all.

Don't Overcompensate by Being Overcontrolling

It's natural to feel insecure when beginning to manage a mobile workforce. You can't see, hear, touch, or smell what's going on nearly as concretely as you could before. Your tendency may be to micromanage. Don't. Overly controlled work environments tell your workforce that you don't trust them. They also don't allow trust to develop because every action is prescribed. One of the biggest demotivators in the workplace is micromanagement. You don't want an experienced, highly productive performer sitting around waiting for instructions from you. Clear goals and expectations? Absolutely! Micromanagement? No.

In fact, manager overcontrol is really a symptom of insecurity, according to Camille Venezia, the founder and owner of Venezia Enterprises. "The command-and-control system," she says, "reflects a deep mistrust of employees' competence and commitment. It overemphasizes sanctions as a way of forcing compliance. The question should be more: how do we create a high-trust, low-fear culture? In such an environment, information is widely shared, contentious opinions are freely expressed, and risk taking is encouraged because mistrust demoralizes and fear paralyzes."[17]

Clearly, when working with someone new, you'll have to calibrate how much direction and support he or she will need. We talk in Chapter 11 about the importance of establishing protocols, procedures, and other ways of working together early in the team development process. Beware, however, of carrying these efforts too far, and stifling the team's growth and trust development process. For trust building to flourish, people on your team have to be able to take risks and fail, learn to depend on other people, and develop their ability and reputation for being dependable themselves.

Shoot for Early Small Successes

The way people are perceived early in their relationship will affect all future perceptions. If the very first thing I see you do is steal from me, I'll view every other thing you do in light of the fact that I think you are a thief. If the very first thing I see you do is miss a deadline, then I'm likely to consider you to be the kind of person who misses deadlines, even if you have made every single deadline since then. So, it's important to give your workforce, individually and collectively, opportunities to demonstrate trustworthiness that are likely to be successful from the very start.

Deal with Conflict Immediately

In a mobile environment, it's easy for conflict to escalate rapidly. When trust is low, simple e-mails may be interpreted as being threats. Offline communications may be perceived as giving preferential treatment. Assignments may be viewed as giving power to some and taking power away from others. When those things happen, you have to step in quickly. You can't just take someone out to lunch and talk through the problem. You can't get two people in a room and say they're not leaving until the problem is resolved. You can't wait until the problem is too hard to settle.

Open up discussions about problems that "can't be discussed." Don't let the rumor mill go wild. Address the unspoken biases, jealousies, and historical mistakes that permeate the feelings people have about their work environment. Admit your own weaknesses and mistakes—everyone else is talking about them, why shouldn't you? Get it out on the table, and deal with it.

Provide Regular Forums for Group Discussion

As a mobile manager, you don't have the benefit of people dropping by your office to kick a problem around; therefore, you have to provide the container for the can to be kicked around in. You want to make it safe for people to share thoughts, ideas, and fears they have with one another. Your ability to do that will demonstrate to people whether or not you can be trusted with their vulnerability.

Encourage people to challenge others in supportive ways. Get people into the habit of bringing up outlandish ideas, which everyone can applaud for their creativity. Encourage improvement but not perfectionism. Debrief failures for opportunities to learn, not to blame. Every time you support people for allowing themselves to be vulnerable you provide opportunities for building trust.

▶ SUMMARY

Trust is something that is invisible to the eye but has tangible results. It is based on the relationships people have with one another. Trust is a source of sustainable competitive advantage. A lack of trust can devastate the most talented workforce. The principles of trust are the same regardless of the situation, but leading a mobile workforce requires more emphasis on communication, setting expectations and accountability, extending trust, and acting as a role model. Trust takes time to build, but it can be destroyed faster than a dropped call.

CHAPTER FIVE

Strategic Leadership in a Virtual World

Creating Sustainable Competitive Advantage

How do you keep that competitive advantage? I think that a little bit of that has to do with staying current on the technology itself but more importantly keeping the edge on how you develop and focus on your culture. That is really the primary benefit. Telework, frankly, is a facilitator but focusing on the culture itself is what achieves your objective.

—SHARON ALLEN, CHAIRMAN, DELOITTE LLP[1]

President Barack Obama dubbed it "snowmageddon," and headlines described it as pummeling, walloping, crippling, and paralyzing. "It" was the blizzard that closed down Washington, D.C., for almost a week in February 2010. More than 200,000 federal workers were told to stay home. With a cost of $100 million a day to shut government down, the decision to open government for business or to remain closed was not a trivial one. Ironically, the determination was made by the same person who had made telework—the most strategic long-term solution for this kind of crisis—his first major initiative when

◄ 93

sworn in as director of the Office of Personnel Management (OPM) just nine months earlier.

John Berry was the man on the hot seat (or should we say *"cold seat"*?) that day. Though his telework efforts were just getting started at the time, about a third of the employees at the OPM and the General Services Administration (GSA) logged onto their agencies' computers during the storm, probably from home. The U.S. Patent and Trademark Office, which has emphasized telework for years (more than 80 percent of its eligible staff regularly do some telework), reported production at 85 percent of normal levels during the blizzard—when the government was officially closed. Instead of a total snowpocalypse, the government's work was being done.

Can you imagine how little real impact a blizzard would have if every federal employee were teleworking? Can you imagine how the ability to telework might mitigate the risk of losing critical government operations during crisis situations such as a pandemic, natural disaster, or attack? Continuity of operations for all federal agencies is a strategic imperative for the protection and health of the country. Telework, Berry believes, is one important element that can keep things going. And he's not the highest level person in the federal government who supports it as a workforce strategy. So does the president of the United States, as Berry mentions below.

The Czar of Cool, John Berry, Director of the U.S. Office of Personnel Management

During our interview, John gave us examples demonstrating why telework is such an important government initiative.

The president had called me during the blizzard this year, and we discussed that the last blizzard of similar size and magnitude was in 1996. Probably less than 1 percent of the government at that time was able to work from home. When we said the federal gov-

ernment was closed, it really meant closed in the Washington, D.C., area because technology and security didn't allow people to telework. Teleworking 15 years ago meant going to a telework center—not really working from home. People now have at their home computer or portable work station more memory capacity than those telework centers had 15 years ago. I told the president I could tell [that] during the storm just my agency and GSA—and we are getting this across the government—we had between 30 and 35 percent of our employees directly accessing the mainframe using our secure access system. Here we are: in 12 years the government has gone from 1 percent being able to do their work in a closure event [from a location other than the government offices] to almost 35 percent. What the president and I discussed was [that] our goal should really be 80 to 90 percent. That should be the standard.

—JOHN BERRY, DIRECTOR OF THE U.S. OFFICE OF PERSONNEL MANAGEMENT[2]

Berry is not the kind of person to wait for change to happen either, as we saw right off the bat when he sat down (virtually) to talk with us. He's one of the few people who have stood on both the North and South poles and he's been to all seven continents. He doesn't seem at all daunted by the telework expedition he's on. As the federal government's "Chief People Person" he is responsible for recruiting, hiring, and setting benefits policies for two million federal civilian employees. Unlike the mountain named after him, the Berry Bastion, he isn't icy most of the time; instead, he is more temperate. We found he fits his nickname, "Cool Czar," very well. In fact, just after he was sworn in as director of the OPM he declared that he was going "to put some giddy-yap into telework."[3]

And he has. Three weeks after being sworn in he announced implementation of proposed legislative provisions to expand telework in the federal government. He briefed cabinet secretaries about making telework a central part of their operations plans. Employees can now learn more about telework possibilities through a new Web site, www. telework.gov, and a Telework Talk blog with—you guessed it—the first postings coming from Berry himself.

He views telework as part of a larger work–life strategy for federal employees. He has said that advantages include employees being able to spend more time with their families and there being thousands of fewer commuters on the road. A tool to fulfill President Obama's charge to "make government cool again," teleworking is likely to attract, motivate, and retain people to public service, Berry feels.

He had started the day of our interview with a presentation at the Federal Manager's Association Convention, where he had stressed that telework is a priority. As he told them:

> *Now, you all know, in this day and age, it's not just snow that can close us down. A dirty bomb could go off in Lafayette Park at 10 o'clock this morning. God forbid. But if it does, probably about 15 federal office buildings are going to be (un)inhabitable for months, if not years.*
>
> *Well, we can't just say "we're not going to do that anymore." We're the government of the United States, by God, and we have a responsibility to keep our operations up and running. And so it's incumbent on us as managers to solve whatever the stumbling blocks or the speed bumps on this are, so we can make this work.*

Most people wouldn't think "federal government" when asked to picture aggressive, cutting-edge management practices, yet—under John Berry's leadership—that is just the direction it is heading. "When you look at the federal government of the nineteenth and twentieth centuries," he told us, "it was essentially a paper-processing, regulatory, regulation-driven operation, primarily blue-collar, lower-salaried employment place. That is no longer the case. It is not only the largest employer, it is probably the most complicated employer in the country, with challenges that range from financial regulatory systems that avoid the second Great Depression or third Great Depression—

whatever might be out there—[to] combating terrorism that is both home grown and foreign grown, [to] dealing with cyber security." Berry is insistently pushing and pulling, cajoling and suggesting, experimenting and visioning, and doing whatever is necessary "to make the federal government the model employer in the United States and OPM its model agency."

The Importance of Having the Best Talent Working for the Federal Government

Here's what Berry had to say about why the federal government ought to be a model employer:

Let's say we fall into the trap that some negative politicians would like you to do, which is use federal workers as a punching bag. Cut their pay. Beat up on them at every turn. What happens is that over time we won't be able to recruit or retain the best people. Then, with those challenges I discussed, there is no republic. There is no government standing today that was around 10,000 years ago. There is nothing written in stone that any country gets to survive forever. How do countries fall? They fall because they lose their ability to adapt and to keep people of talent and of goodwill working on their behalf. It is essential to inspire people to come into this service for the sake of our republic. I believe America is unique and it is worth fighting for. It is worth working for.

—JOHN BERRY, DIRECTOR OF THE UNITED STATES OFFICE OF PERSONNEL MANAGEMENT

▶ HOW TO MOVE THE SHIP OF STATE

When you think about it, a national government competes with every other national government on earth to be the most cost effective, the most talented, the best equipped to act, the quickest to respond to external threats, and the most strategic thinking about future opportunities. Telework is a key strategy to gain sustainable competitive advantage by attracting, motivating, enabling, retaining, and deploying top-notch personnel to accomplish critical work. If other governments are more effective at doing this, one's own national government workforce becomes comparatively less talented, less responsive, and less motivated—which becomes a decided disadvantage over time in key arenas.

In this sense Berry, then, is leading the telework charge at least in part to create and maintain sustainable competitive advantage for the United States. If you've ever tried to manage change in your own office you can imagine the challenge of trying to swing a huge bureaucracy in a different direction. Let's look at his strategy for moving the ship of state in the direction of a more mobile workforce.

First, he *walked into office prepared.* "I came in on day one with my team in place. I was the only one in federal government that the day I was sworn in by the First Lady on April 13, I turned around and swore in the rest of my team." He had decided to hit the ground running. He declared on day one what his objectives were and made sure *he had a strategic plan* for their accomplishment. One of the long-term performance goals in the 2010–2015 U.S. Office of Personnel Management's strategic plan is "by fiscal year 2011, increase by 50 percent the number of eligible federal employees who telework over the fiscal year 2009 baseline of 102,900." It's a measureable, stretch goal that carries accountability. Impressive!

Second, he *acts as a missionary for telework* by addressing employees, pushing the agenda, being an advocate with agency leaders and policymakers, and building support with key constituencies. "We've started what I call the 'Apostolic Work'" he told us, "trying to make the argument, trying to make the case, trying to convince people . . . to envision a new way. That you do through speeches and articles." He received a standing ovation after his presentation at the Federal Managers Association Convention, but he knows that moving forward won't be easy. A recent report, "Out of Sight, but Not Out of Touch: Federal Executives' Assessment of Agency Telework Policy" showed strong support for telework in the federal government and the belief that employees can be just as productive when teleworking, with benefits like employee satisfaction and continuity of operations. The largest barrier to telework, by a large margin, for those who don't telework was their manager's lack of support for it.[4] So Berry has a lot of proselytizing to do, even within his own leadership corps.

Third, OPM has or is in the process of *developing the policy infrastructure and support systems*—such as training—necessary to undergird a successful telework initiative. Check out the Web site www. telework.gov/ to find out just about everything a federal employee, manager, or coordinator needs to make the decision to go mobile. Policies and procedures, tools and resources, reports and studies can all be found there. Training opportunities, telework practices, frequently asked questions (FAQs), telework centers, and contacts to talk to are all easily accessible. You can even find the Telework Talk Blog there, where federal employees at all levels can talk about their telework experiences, potential barriers, ideas, telework challenges, and other topics. Leadership training, one of the most powerful ways to change a culture—especially when the top reason change is inhibited is management resistance—is also underway. "We are working on a training regimen and curriculum for new managers," Berry told us, "that will be including these notions and concepts. How you drill this through an organization of that size? I'm keenly aware that if it is only me saying this, it is not going to go very far, quite frankly."

Fourth, Berry is *trying things*. Steve Lamont, the president of Wifi. com, told us that an important way to build trust when moving to a mobile workforce is by using pilot tests.[5] "Pilots are a way to fail forward, because you fail quickly and learn lessons from it, [which] helps you improve it. The best programs are the ones that, through piloting, . . . get to the point that people in the pilot say that they love it and the rest of the organization says, 'We want it. When can we get it?' That is one of the best ways to overcome resistance—to turn a bunch of pilot testers into evangelists."

OPM's vision is that "The Federal Government will Become America's Model Employer for the 21st Century." Moving to a Results-Only Work Environment (ROWE)[6], which we discuss in Chapter 6, is one way to give workers options. In a ROWE environment "people can do whatever they want, whenever they want, as long as the work gets done." It's a mobile workforce strategy: employees can work at home, on the road, or in the office—wherever they choose to do so. That sounds pretty radical for government work, doesn't it? Berry has set up a ROWE demonstration project in one of the federal agencies. If it is successful, it will open up opportunities elsewhere. Pilots— experiments, really—are a low-risk way to move an organization forward. According to Berry:

> *If we achieve half the productivity increases that the private sector has done with this—which is upwards of 40 to 50 percent—the taxpay- ers are going to be impressed. As long as we are putting solid results on the board, taxpayers will support it. We'll be the first ones in the federal government to do this. I think this is the future, and it is all connected together. If we do this well, then flex-schedule, telework, women in the workplace, mothers in the workplace . . . all of these things start to dy- namically change, and we end up with a creative workplace that is fo- cused on delivering solid results that the taxpayers demand.*

Fifth, Berry has put *resources and focus* into achieving the goal of increasing telework by 50 percent in just a couple of years. One of the strategic "wolf packs" he created upon assuming office is "work–life balance," which is intended to create "more flexible, responsive work environments supportive of commitments to community, home, and loved ones." The telework initiative is a part of this overall effort. Re- viewing this Web site shows OPM's commitment goes beyond stra- tegic advantage—it extends to nurturing the people who spend their professional lives protecting the interests of our country. In a sense, it means treating people as people, not just as tools to get a job done.[7]

Sixth, Berry is *riding the wave*. Telework—or mobile work or virtual work or whatever you call it—is inevitable, as we point out in Chapter 2. While it's not always smart strategically to be a first mover, in this case it's smart to be an early adopter. Once you are behind the curve, then your competitors are going to be hard to catch. If you aspire to make working for the government "cool" or to be a "model," then it pays to jump in the water, especially with so many benefits and so few potential dangers, and "hang ten."

The federal government is the largest employer in the United States. The ability to lead the rest of the country toward true worker mobility seems like an unintended benefit of John Berry's quest. When a large organization takes on a social good that also has competitive benefits—the green initiatives of Wal-Mart or General Electric come to mind—the positive effects ripple throughout organizations large and small, not only within a country but also throughout the world. Such is the magnitude of what "increase by 50 percent the number of eligible federal employees who telework" can mean to workers and enterprises everywhere. Now, that would be leaving a true legacy!

▶ MOBILIZING FOR MOBILITY

We started this section asking how Director Berry was going to turn the ship of state in a new direction and we finished by suggesting that he hop on a surfboard—which we think is better than waiting out a blizzard. The truth is that he's in the right place at the right time, and he shows all the signs of being the right person to get the job done. The way he is pursuing it is instructive for all leaders considering the move to mobility: *he's creating a platform*.

The remainder of this chapter is dedicated to strategic enterprise leadership and considering whether moving to mobility might be a source of competitive advantage for your organization. Do you want to know how to *apply paradigm shift thinking about the mobile workforce* to your own organization?

Interestingly, mobilizing for mobility—at a strategic level—has very little to do with what kind of cell phone or laptop your workforce will have and very much to do with what *platform* it, and everything else, sits on. In the paragraphs that follow, we'll share why an enterprise executive really should be a sage from the stage *in addition to* becoming the more fashionable guide from the side.

We'll provide a manager's checklist of questions that you might want to consider in building your mobile workforce strategy or to test your progress if you already have initiated a mobile workforce. We'll share the advantages and risks associated in building and keeping a mobile enterprise team productive. Many companies believe they could not exist today without their mobile teams. This new business model is dependent on a dispersed workforce which enters into a win-win relationship with the company, which provides, in return, an appreciable work-life balance. It's a new strategy for most and a fresh way to play the game and win.

The Competitive Environment

The following are factors that need to be taken into consideration when contemplating a switch to a more mobile workforce.

THE ECONOMY

Companies are cutting expenses these days, which intensifies the need for alternative mobile workforce work arrangements, which can reduce costs. Even the government is capitalizing on savings through telework. Just ask John Berry, who told us the following:

> *I just closed 25,000 square feet of office space in Pittsburgh that was a teleconference center for retirement problems. We closed the lease out, and I'm going to save a significant chunk of change because all of the workers in Pittsburgh working with the union agreed they are going to work from*

home. I've got a huge savings coming my way because I don't have to pay a lease space to a landlord. This is already happening. We negotiated that with our union. The employees agreed to it. We've been able to define what their work product is. They are still handling the exact same case load. Now I don't have to pay for office space. It is a huge government savings. That is a huge savings to the taxpayer.

What are your competitors doing to lower costs and increase productivity in a tight economy? Do you want to be the last kid on the block to get your BB gun? The last person to wear a hoop skirt or a paisley shirt? It's time to move! Do you want to be the only one with employees still coming in to a big building from 8:00 a.m. to 5:00 p.m., Monday through Friday, while everyone else in your industry is closing unneeded buildings by matching the employee to the work, not the work to a prearranged, inflexible schedule and location?

What new opportunities for moving to mobility does this economy offer your organization?

The Employee

Enterprise cutbacks, layoffs, downsizing, and even company closings have created more opportunities for individuals to use technology outside of the office. They become more self-sufficient in using and buying computers, and in installing Internet connections and wireless technologies. That, in turn, provides them more freedom from the office cubicle and offers the potential for a better work–life balance. It's a management philosophy that turns "shared control" over to the employee. Just consider for a moment what it takes to change the decision process, polices, roles, technology, communications, security, hardware, and software to facilitate "shared control" of the employees' own work environment, which includes scheduling and independently working away from the eyes of their managers.

What new opportunities for moving to mobility do these contemporary, raring-to-try-virtuality employees offer your organization?

TECHNOLOGY

Empowering employees to work outside of the office, with secure connections and affordable mobile equipment, allows access to proprietary data, records, and information. Mobile employees, through the use of technology, can maintain high levels of productivity when working away from traditional brick-and-mortar offices because they can have personal uninterrupted focus, less travel time, and secure enterprise data access. The challenge isn't so much finding the right technology these days as it is keeping up with it!

What new opportunities for moving to mobility do emerging technologies offer your organization?

GLOBAL COMPETITIVENESS

Profit requirements often necessitate deeper penetration into regional and global markets, requiring more travel and more customer relationship building. Technology allows the remote worker to be closer to the client and to collaborate peer to peer and peer to group, when needed. Access to critical information, contacts, and connectivity are still the top tools that allow the mobile workers to compete.

What new opportunities for moving to mobility does this smaller, flatter world offer your organization?

The Path to a Paradigm Shift

Thinking of any one of the preceding factors opens up new prospects. Thinking of the possibilities at the intersections between one or more of these items can create completely new paradigms—new rules, as mentioned in Chapter 2—at local, national, and even global scales. This way of reflecting about the world, and indeed the new realities of the world, leads to roads that did not exist before. Paradigm shifts can completely change our thinking or belief systems and allow new conditions previously thought to be impossible to become possible.

The recipe for a paradigm shift in how you manage your own company starts by rethinking these possibilities. Consider how connecting people over time and space through the Internet, with VoIP, or using collaborative software and mobile devices such as laptops and mobile phones might be a completely new way of operating your company.

Let's not be naïve, though. What might some of the risks for your company be if you deployed a mobile workforce? This group of independently thinking nomads, traversing from office to office, city to city, and state to state *could add some drama to your boardroom meetings*—at least initially. Change always involves risks.

Moving to a new business strategy paradigm will also require a *trust* relationship with everyone involved. That means trust at every level of management and throughout the enterprise system. See Chapter 4 for a discussion of trust—we think it is essential for this kind of strategic shift in direction.

Being a Sage about the Stage

As much as we ascribe to the teaching strategy of being the guide from the side—that is, the mentor, coach, or expert who leads by example and support—we think you are going to have to also be the sage from the stage—a visible leader—to move this puppy forward. What does that mean? Picture John Berry's apostolic work, his aggressive agenda, and his vision for the future. To make big change you have to lead the pack, not just sit on the side and encourage.

▶ ENTERPRISE ANALYSIS OF "MOBILE READINESS"

While executives plan and collaborate on the initial phase of building a mobile workforce, it is generally the middle managers who know the immediate urgent needs—based on changing market conditions, looming competition, other threats and opportunities, as well as the particular circumstances of the members of their own workforce—which have to be considered when this new team structure is to be built.

After the initial moving-to-mobility idea has been launched, the company needs to go through an internal process of analyzing strategies and purpose. This is a big deal. It touches everyone in the company. Everybody will be talking about the new structure, because it will be disruptive for them, whether in a big or small way. Each employee and contractor will feel uneasy until his or her own role has been established.

The following is a simple checklist for success. This generalized outline can help your department think through the fundamental questions the group needs to consider. The collaborative effort required to come up with the answers will get everybody involved in the process who needs to be, and preferably early on. Those people will range from senior executives to staff assistants to the folks in shipping. Everybody involved in the change needs to be engaged, so we suggest starting with discussing the very basics needed to support a mobile workforce.

Once you have identified this initial team, the leader needs to start the ball rolling. Meet with this group and those people who communicate forward-thinking ideas and solutions. The following are simple questions you might pose, in any order, in such a meeting.

Questions about Our Company's Mobile Strategy

1. What will be the primary competitive advantage of having a mobile workforce?
2. Is there a need for change?

3. How healthy are our current customer relationships? How could having a mobile workforce build deeper relationships with our customers?

4. What is the expectation of departments that move to a mobile workforce environment concerning ROI or other performance measurements?

5. What will be the cost benefits of developing and supporting a mobile workforce?

6. What will be our real cost of having a mobile workforce?

7. What will employees want or benefit from by being part of the mobile force?

8. How will we manage the mobile workforce outside our corporate offices?

9. How will roles change for existing employees?

10. Is new training required for those who support the mobile workforce?

11. How will we match internal and external employees for maximum productivity?

12. How should a manager handle employees who are unsupportive of the mobile workforce?

13. How will the company find the talent pool needed to move to a mobile workforce?

14. How will we train and support a new remote group of employees and contractors?

15. What systems will be available to provide mobile data, access to secure content, and company information?

16. How will our vendors be selected?

17. Will IT be exclusively responsible for software selection, or will the sales organization or other departments have something to say about the selection?

18. How and to whom will IT report options regarding mobile solutions?

19. How will our IT department allow for remote connections, support remote connections, and what policies and practices for remote devices will be needed?

20. How will the company approve new hardware such as laptops, wireless modems, and mobile devices such as PDAs and smartphones?
21. How will the company support the need for software licenses extended to mobile devices?
22. How will the current systems, such as the LMS, support mobile devices?
23. What is the road map for back-end updates and migration to these services?
24. What software will be used for team collaboration?
25. What will the policies be for hardware replacement, disaster recovery, and response time?
26. How will vendor services, Internet, VoIP, mobile carrier contracts, mobile applications, and software be handled?

Whew! That's a good starter list for your team. Working through these questions as a team will develop shared knowledge and commitment to the decisions that are being made. A key part of this change process is enabling workers to discover the benefits of a mobile environment.

▶ THE PLATFORM

Peter DeNagy is an interesting chap. His degree in politics has prepared him well, perhaps better than an education in IT or management information systems might have done, for a successful career as a senior leader in major technologies corporations. He has held executive positions and led efforts at major communications and consulting firms such as Accenture, Harris, GTE, Sprint, Global Crossing, EDS, and BearingPoint. Now he is senior director and general manager of U.S. Enterprise Mobility Enablement for Samsung Telecommunications America. That's a hefty title! But he couldn't have been a more interesting person with whom to talk. We got together with him (virtually) twice—the second time he met us at the (virtual) door of his home, calling us while waiting for a repair person to drop by. And his time was money—Samsung Mobile, the division he works for, is the leading cell phone manufacturer in the United States; it had 2008 revenues in excess of $4 billion. He was the person who caused us to really think about the importance of having a *platform* when moving to mobility.

"An enterprise leader who wants to mobilely enable the work-force," he told us, "must make platform decisions first and then make the device decisions. Devices change. You need to develop the plat-form." Samsung makes devices for six operating systems, he told us, and the enterprise mobility leader needs to choose one of those, or others available, if they are going to drive value.

You can make decisions, he said, at a division level that could be good for the business unit but couldn't necessarily be leveraged by the entire organization. If you are lucky, those choices can be integrated and compatible with the larger organization. But if they aren't, he says, "What do you do?"

Starting with the platform is like building a house, he told us. Be-fore anything else, you dig the hole and put the foundation in. "The first thing you have to do is determine what the business driver is or what the business need is. Once you derive the business need, then you can go forward and look at a platform that you have high confi-dence in that [you] not only can develop today but [will] be able to develop tomorrow. . . . There'll be a very robust set of devices that will be able to achieve your goals." At the end of the day, he emphasized, the choice of devices is tactical.[8]

A platform makes every other thing that's crucial for a success-ful mobile workforce strategy—building trust, consistency, training, and providing the right tools, as examples—more possible. Building a platform includes (but is more than) choosing the right operating system and then the subsequent "how-we-do-it technology" hardware and software questions. It also includes the core "where are we going" leadership questions and the "how we work together" questions.

The Platform: Where Are We Going?

The thought of planning to build out a mobile workforce has probably already hit watercooler–type discussions within many of your departments. That is a good thing, because these kinds of complex questions should be deliberated openly. Getting this right will take a considerable amount of time, resources, and the focus of committed people. You'll want to think seriously about your plan before heading into the big strategic decision meeting. You'll want to base it on plenty of dialogue, feedback, and the opinions of key people who will be involved in the success of building your virtual team.

The first thing to remember is that moving to mobility is only part of a larger organizational success strategy. It has to complement and support the competitive direction and plan for the company. For

The Strategic Mobile Workforce Platform

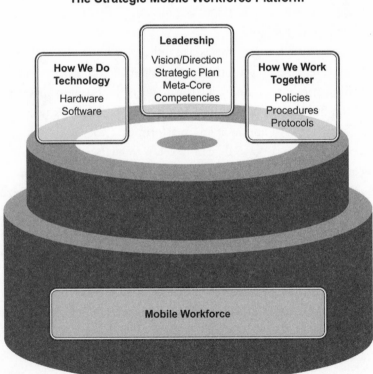

example, John Berry's telework initiative was just one part of OPM's overall vision, goal, and strategy for the federal government to "Become America's Model Employer for the 21st Century."

The question to ask is: How does having a mobile workforce further organizational goals? If you are competing on the basis of cost, how would having a mobile workforce get you to be the low-cost provider? If you are competing on the basis of any core competency, how would having a mobile workforce get you success? Your organizational vision, direction, and strategy are building blocks upon which your mobile workforce strategy must rest.

▶ TELEWORK IN SUPPORT OF AN EMPLOYER OF CHOICE STRATEGY

Here's what Barbara Wankoff, KPMG LLP's national director of Workplace Solutions, had to say about telework: "It is one of our key strategies from a business perspective. We believe that being an employer of choice and a great place to work not only positions us competitively for recruiting and retention but it also motivates our employees and allows them to be as effective and productive as they can be and to do their best work. It is definitely a competitive tool."[9] Telework fits into a much larger company strategy to attract, motivate, and retain talent. And that fits into an even larger strategy (we assume): to increase revenues, market share, and all the good things corporate owners love to see happen each quarter.

KPMG makes just about every "good" list for employees. For example, the Families and Work Institute's *2009 Guide to Bold New Ideas for Making Work Work* lists the main KPMG office and features 12 of their local offices that each share great examples of work–life flexibility. To get in this guide you have to be a winner of the Alfred P. Sloan Award for Business Excellence in Workplace Flexibility. Winners have proven to be models of innovative and effective workplace practices. Not bad.

"Telework," Barbara said, "is very interesting because we have a culture of flexibility. We really promote the idea that people can have control over where, when, and how they get their work done." KPMG offers a wide range of work options so people can select what best works for them, their job, and their lives. "For some," says Barbara, "that might be telework, and for others that might be flextime, flex schedules, or compressed workweeks." Telework is an important choice, because the workforce is already dispersed because of client assignments. Some employees never set foot inside a KPMG office. Employees have the tools—laptops, remote access, and collaboration Web sites for teams for discussions and sharing of documents and calendars—and they can get the resources and information they need from just about anywhere. "Our platform is this," Barbara told us, "and therefore sets up an environment where managers may not be working in the same location as many of our associates."

Part of the KPMG platform for mobile work involves extensive training for managers, which includes workplace flexibility. Tools on KPMG's Web site specific to telework are available, including discussion guidelines (between manager and employee), decision-making guidelines, and things to consider when thinking about telecommuting. KPMG has an *Alternative Work Arrangement Telecommuting Guide* and an *Alternative Work Arrangement Conversation Guide,* for example, which support managers and employees who are planning mobile work agreements together. Included in the guides are such topics as tips for successful telecommuting; work scheduling; performance measures, what the impacts are to the team, coworkers, and clients; and the benefits and possible costs that might result as a consequence of telework. "The key," Barbara says, "is to encourage that dialogue between the employee and the manager, to be sure to set expectations, to clarify roles, to clarify accessibility, and to communicate with those other team members or other people who need to know what the arrangement is."

▶ "HOW WE WORK TOGETHER" PLATFORM

The platform includes not only strategic decisions regarding technology, mission, vision, and strategic objectives but also key decisions about how the organization works together. That includes policies, procedures, and practices. One key arena is human resources.

Some concerns for leaders and human resource managers are related to security.[10] Establishing communication protocols, telework policies, and expectations is important, which might include how meetings are run, how timely communication needs to be, how performance will be evaluated, how time will be tracked, and how other safety or legal responsibilities of the employer and employee will be handled.

Some organizations may wish to create telecommuting policies and procedures, as OPM, KPMG, and many others have done, or assign telework coordinators to support efforts as the organization moves to mobility. As we will discuss in later chapters, training, hiring, and performance management are also key platform items for employees and managers.

▶ ROLLING IT OUT

The State of Arizona has one of the nation's most successful telework programs.[11] Starting in what could be considered prehistoric telework times—1989—Arizona now has more than 20 percent of its 21,000 employees who telework. They estimate that state teleworkers drive 5.25 million fewer miles annually, take 175,000 pounds of pollution out of the air annually which would otherwise be there, and suffer 181,000 fewer hours of drive time a year. Impressive!

Every organization will plan and execute its moving-to-mobility strategy differently, in order to meet its unique needs. We saw how John Berry and the U.S. Office of Personnel Management are kicking their program into overdrive. The ways in which Arizona's program grew is also instructive.

In 1989, before iPhones, iPads, or even iPods, four state departments partnered with AT&T to demonstrate that telework could be a useful strategy for reducing travel for both public employers and private employers. Calling it the Pilot Phase (from 1989 to 1993), they developed telework policies, a telework agreement, and a helpful guide for teleworking. The state and AT&T then selected and trained participants. After six months, participants, their supervisors, and their coworkers were surveyed. The results showed not only that travel could be reduced but also that employee productivity, efficiency, and job attitude had the potential to increase because of the improved work environment.

As a result, the state moved into a Formal Program and Development Phase (1993–1996), and at that time 13 additional state agencies joined the program. In 1996, an overall evaluation of the program was conducted. The current Mandated Program Phase began in 1996, and it continues to the present. The governor of Arizona mandated in 1996 that all state agencies implement the telework program with a goal of 15 percent employees in Maricopa County actively teleworking. In 2002, that goal was reached, and then-governor Jane Hull expanded the telework mandate to 20 percent active participation. State managers—who know a good thing when they see it—now combine telework with compressed workweeks, flextime, and other flexible workplace options in order to retain and attract employees. Business continuity is important at the state level too, and employees with critical functions are trained to telework. Full-time virtual teleworking to reduce office space costs is also encouraged.

Arizona is a role model for rolling out a telework program and an example of how moving to mobility can serve employees, the organization, and the owners (in this case, the taxpayers).

▶ SUMMARY

We started this chapter with an example from the federal government, and we end with one from state government. One is experienced, with proven results; the other on its way to making significant gains. Along the way we've shared what corporations like KPMG have done to create a platform for mobile work, and how a mobile workforce can be a source of sustainable competitive advantage. We've shared a list of questions designed to help your team discuss the issues surrounding moving to mobility, and we've talked about the strategic importance of having a platform upon which more tactical, short-term decisions related to your mobile workforce can be hung.

Isn't it time you seriously looked at moving to mobility?

John Berry Sums It Up

> *If we succeed at it, it will allow America to retain its competitive leadership. To maintain our quality of life and provide a future for our children and grandchildren— that is going to be essential. It really comes down to that. This is one of the most important things I'll get to do in my life is to help launch this. I'm hoping it is not killed in the cradle.*
>
> —John Berry, Director of the U.S. Office
> of Personnel Management

▶PART TWO

Performance Management
and the Mobile Workforce

►CHAPTER SIX

Autonomy or Not Autonomy?
That Is the Question

We are always working on several jobs at a time. It's really important to be able to—within a very tight time frame—deal with four, five, or six client issues within a very tight time frame. The only way most of us can pull it off is through all the devices we use—the ability to work from home, a cab, the airport lounge, or client site.
—JOHN HALE, MANAGING PARTNER, KPMG[1]

Performance is *getting things done.*

For you as a manager, it doesn't matter if your employees are younger or older than you. It doesn't matter if they share an office with you or work halfway across the world, if they are executives or entry-level employees, if they have a Cisco telepresence system or use Morse code. It makes no difference whether they speak another language or communicate by channeling, because your job—with one caveat—is to do anything you can to get your employees to get the most things and best things done.

The caveat is that whatever you do, it must be legal, moral, and humane. If you want to achieve high performance for a long time, you will help employees realize their full potential through doing work about which they are passionate, and doing it with people about whom they care.

As this chapter relates, mobile performance management technology has improved to the point that employers should no longer be afraid that productivity will plunge when the workforce goes mobile; they should instead be worried that they will lag far behind the competition if they don't incorporate a mobile strategy.

Performance management strategy has progressed in two equally promising, though seemingly opposite, directions. One direction involves using technology to improve performance by giving workers less autonomy, that is, increasingly assigning them tasks and scheduling their work for them; the other gives workers more autonomy, that is, increasingly giving them control over their own schedules and tasks. Technology facilitates both strategies, and it enables performance to improve. Both strategies result in an increasingly mobile, high-performance workforce.

▶ WHY WOULD ANYONE SLOW HIS OR HER EMPLOYEES DOWN?

John Hale is a true road warrior. He often spends four or five days a week on the road working in airports, hotels, and clients' offices. He's the kind of person who, as he says, can land in Salt Lake and take two conference calls while running through the airport.

His personal road has been circuitous too. He comes from a small logging town, has earned a trade as an ironworker, spent time at the U.S. Treasury office, and today provides advisory services to clients across the country. He ran KPMG's advisory practice in Latin America out of Mexico City before returning to the United States after 9/11. All of which prepared him to be the prototype mobile worker. But he's also a mobile manager. He's a managing partner at KPMG, with lots of road warriors who report to him.

KPMG LLP, the U.S. member firm of KPMG International, whose member firms have nearly 94,000 professionals in 148 countries, is one of the nation's leading providers of audit, tax, and advisory services. The firm makes sure its professionals have all the technological bells and whistles—computers, wireless cards, PDAs—they need to do their jobs and to stay connected. But, as it is for so many companies, that's just the ante to get in the performance game. After that, it takes a savvy manager like John to maximize employee performance. But if getting the most out of employees is so important, then why does he work so hard to slow them down?

At times it seems that John and his employees are "one with the road." The focus of his work is mergers and acquisitions, and his clients are mostly private equity firms. So he is dealing daily with high-pressure people who demand instant attention when needed. Technology, he says, is a "double-edged sword." Using technology has increased productivity greatly and given clients immediate access, but at the same time it really requires managers to work with their employees to deal with the reality of never being able to disconnect. KPMG hires some of the best and the brightest, and they demand much of themselves to get things done, so John has to be sensitive to his employees and to, actually, at times, coach them to work less. That's not what you'd normally think would happen at a high-flying global firm such as KPMG, but the truth is that 24/7 accessibility can actually interfere with productivity and also wear down people.

So what does John do to manage performance under these circumstances? *One key role he plays is that of "coach and mentor"* a key component of the firm's strategy to attract and retain top talent, and it's not always the big-ticket performance behaviors that he deals with. For example, he sometimes notices employees, wanting to be responsive to client needs, picking up and looking at their phones every time they buzz. Counterintuitively, being connected in this case actually reduces productivity. "You may have to take them aside," he says, "and tell them you know that they are trying to be responsive but that their productivity curve is actually flattening. It is going the wrong way because of this enhancement device." With 100 people working for him, these seemingly tiny productivity losses can reduce performance significantly.

But when clients call these days and you don't answer immediately, you'd better have a pretty darn good reason, right? They know you just looked at your messages and are now sitting on that call. "Twenty-four hours is a lifetime now," John says, "with all the connectivity." So you'd better be right on it. Right?

Well, maybe right or maybe wrong. Sometimes, as John relates, "you have to put your arm around people and tell them they need to kill their BlackBerry for 24 hours. You can see them fray." In fact, KPMG encourages people, even up to the partner level, to leave their mobile device and laptop at the office at least one week a year. "I've gone so far," he tells, "with some people to say, 'I want you to check your computer in.'" Because if they don't, they won't take a real vacation. They won't recharge, and they won't be as productive when they return. Some clients are nearly impossible to disconnect from because they are investors with hundreds of millions of dollars, but John finds that most clients are understanding, given enough notice.

▶ SETTING EXPECTATIONS

Riddle: What is 250, 100, and 150? Answer: The number of e-mails John gets a day (250); the number of those which are for information only or spam (about 100); and the number of which actually make John do something (about 150). Imagine *150 requests that need a response each day.* Each one pulling at your attention. Each new one distracting you from excellently completing the one on which you had been focused. Each perhaps spawning several other actions.

Now manage that e-mail load while taking your laptop out and shoes off while going through the Transportation Security Administration (TSA) line at the airport; or while you are taking the taxi to your next appointment; or when you finally hit the hay in a hotel that has only intermittent Internet service. As with a paintball fight, these time-sappers are coming at you from all directions—from clients, employees, your boss, and, yes, maybe you even get a couple green (envy) or red (angry) or blue (sad) ones from your family each day. Splat, splat, splat, splat . . . thud! Pretty soon, if you're not careful, you are deluged and drowning.

It turns out that *setting expectations* makes all the difference; those expectations will be different for different people. John lets his employees know his priorities and what he needs, and doesn't need, from them. In a very busy week with many priorities, he will tell his employees where they stand in that list. His expectation will be that when they send him something they will tell him what he needs to do with it and when he needs to do it by so he can prioritize his time. He doesn't expect employees to send little acknowledgement notes, because that increases his workload significantly. For example, every time someone writes back and says "thank you," he has to spend another millisecond opening that e-mail. "I tell my folks I have a presumption, having a Southern upbringing, that you are a very polite person," he says. "I know you're appreciative. I know you're dutiful. You don't need to send an email that says only 'thank you'. Likewise, I believe that if I ask a member of my team to do something they will do it. I don't need them to acknowledge their willingness to do what I asked. I only want an e-mail that tells me they *won't* do what I ask and why."

▶ AUTONOMY OR NO AUTONOMY? THAT IS THE QUESTION

It is a good thing that effective mobile workforce managers have an understanding of what motivates mobile workers (see Chapter 9) because technology is becoming so discriminating that the historic assembly line, time-and-motion approach to improving worker performance now seems pitifully rustic. Today, of course, managers can track every keystroke we make on a computer, follow anything we look up on the Internet, and peruse any e-mail—either work or personally related—we send or receive while on the job. In fact, companies today not only look at what workers *have done* and *are doing* but also are gathering massive amounts of employee data to build models to predict what employees *will do*. Big Brother isn't just watching you, sister, he can pretty much figure out what you'll do even before you do it.

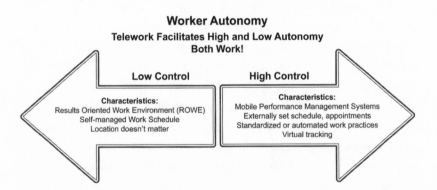

Worker Autonomy
Telework Facilitates High and Low Autonomy
Both Work!

Low Control

High Control

Characteristics:
Results Oriented Work Environment (ROWE)
Self-managed Work Schedule
Location doesn't matter

Characteristics:
Mobile Performance Management Systems
Externally set schedule, appointments
Standardized or automated work practices
Virtual tracking

The research being done now, tied to technology, will soon allow management to make traditional job task analysis seem as outdated as the early, clunky computers of the past. Organizations are becoming increasingly sophisticated about understanding how to divide each job into particular tasks and ever-minute chunks. They are also doing the same in capturing each worker's set of skills and knowledge. The analysis is becoming so discreet, and the software programs so powerful, that huge jobs can be divided into many tiny steps, which can then be linked to a workforce's set of skills and knowledge such that thousands of tasks can be divided between thousands of workers.

Stephen Baker's fascinating book, *The Numerati*, describes the sophisticated modeling that companies are now conducting to understand employees.[2] They start by breaking our behaviors into tiny pieces, and then they use software to "mix and match us in a fraction of a second, with a million, or 100 million, others." According to Baker, these organizations will be able to figure out the financial return for each skill and job category, and to compare productivity in more and more detail. The goal is to construct mathematical models that one day might track such personal characteristics as a person's food choices, friends or enemies, and even allergies—for tens of thousands of a company's workers. The task is to "depict flesh-and-blood humans as math." This work will eventually allow companies to know at a very fine level what skills and knowledge each employee possesses, to break job tasks into very finite steps that can be assigned to different employees possessing those skills, and to do that not in time chunks of days or hours, but eventually in minutes. "This virtual assembly line," Baker says, "sounds menacing. The surveillance has more than a whiff of Big Brother. For those of us who aren't $1,000-per-hour consultants, life bound to a mathematical model is sounding like abject data serfdom." Or, perhaps like good old-fashioned exploitation of workers.

The counterargument, of course, is that these tools will improve workers' productivity, document their value, improve their marketability in a more competitive talent market, and make organizations more successful. Those who cannot, or will not, perform will get left behind. Those who excel will be richly rewarded.

If you tie research about human beings into work technology, you get a pretty unbeatable combination for improving mobile workforce productivity.

▶ LESS AUTONOMY, HIGHER PERFORMANCE

Mobile workforce management systems now provide the technology that allows organizations to direct, measure, evaluate, and physically track what every employee is doing every minute of the day.

How do you get the maximum performance out of workers in multiple locations, handling more than 250 pieces of heavy equipment? A few years ago Keystone Excavating, a leader in its market out of Alberta, Canada, couldn't even handle its paperwork, like timesheets, efficiently.

It is still a leader today, however, because they now automate. Using Ranger mobile workforce technology from Mentor Engineering, Keystone now stores all data from work assignments in a central database; dispatchers schedule new jobs in the database; and field workers in their vehicles log in and receive job tasks and instructions electronically. Completed work is electronically captured, so now billing is more accurate and faster. Workers are assigned to new job sites through their Ranger mobile computer. Now the equipment is tracked in real time, so the company not only knows where each piece is but also when it was used. It can even identify vehicles that were either speeding or idling. With this system, operators get to their jobs 20 minutes earlier than they did before, staffing requirements for schedulers have been reduced, and the money the company invested in mobile workforce technology has been returned in only one year. And that doesn't include other savings in overtime hours. Because subcontractors are 30 percent to 40 percent of Keystone's business, the company hopes these companies will also automate by adding electronic devices to their vehicles.[3]

Energy companies are also finding that mobile performance management systems are improving productivity. For example, Austin Energy gave its field workers rugged Toughbooks and adopted mobility software so dispatchers could issue work orders wirelessly to technicians; they, in turn, could fulfill these orders and send them wirelessly back to the office. Previously, 25 employees sorted manually through piles of paperwork orders every day after field workers dropped them off at the office the night before. Crew workloads can now be monitored electronically, and jobs can be moved to technicians who have finished their work orders early. In fact, the computer now also schedules the work of each technician, taking into account where each person starts the day. Other benefits include saving thousands of dollars in metering fraud. Technicians who spot tampering now can notify the office immediately, and often investigators are there within an hour.[4]

ClickSoftware Technologies' software is being used by Cable& Wireless Worldwide to synchronize its engineers' schedules, taking into account the worker's skills, location, and current workload and then doling out the work in real time. The software then monitors where the workers are, allows them to be relocated to deal with urgent situations that come up, and takes work progress data and other job details that the worker records in his or her mobile device.[5] Potomac Electric Company eliminated 100,000 pieces of paper a year for just one group by introducing a mobile data system for its field workers. Performance also improves through mobile workforce technology in ways that aren't always so obvious. Now work crews working in outage situations no longer have to work from paper maps, which are hard to update; the mobile systems now used during severe weather situations take the pressure off radio communication systems.[6]

Mobile workforce management technology is also improving performance in twenty-first century water utilities, Oracle reports.[7] Software now can schedule, route, monitor, and clarify work and handle reporting for utility field workers. A 20 percent increase in productivity occurs just by having workers start at the worksite instead of at a central location. Software can analyze jobs to see what parts are needed and available, and it can send instructions about where crews can pick up the equipment needed. Tools to improve performance, such as checklists and decision support systems, instruction manuals, diagrams, and blueprints, are easy to access mobilely. Some systems even let customers schedule their own appointments, coordinate crew locations with those appointments, and inform customers about changes in the schedule.

▶ LESS AUTONOMY, HIGHER EMPLOYEE SATISFACTION

We thought the impact of "being told what to do" might have a disastrous impact on employee satisfaction, but it doesn't have to. Rick Mayer, owner of Island Aggregates, a concrete pumping company in Vancouver, Canada, assured us otherwise.[8] He now uses mobile performance management technology that has improved productivity, with potential cost savings of $100,000 per year. It has improved the accuracy of billing and invoicing, reduced data entry time, facilitated faster billing and dispatching, and overall has improved resource management.

But what about the employees? On the surface it would seem as if employees in these systems work like galley slaves, tightly leashed to their work with little opportunity for creativity or decision making. But let's dig a little deeper.

"That's not true at all," Rick told us, though making the change to this system wasn't easy. "We had long-term employees who ran this equipment in a certain way, and change was difficult. We were developing it as we implemented it, so there were some glitches. There were some frustrating moments. I won't lie to you." But over time employees have grown to value the new system. "Right now, if the unit goes down, the guys don't want to come to work," Rick says. "It has made their life very easy. We've actually been able to attract employees now from our competition because they were having to drive all the way back to the office to hand their paperwork in or they were terrible writers."

So, why is it that employees prefer *more* control over their work? It seems counterintuitive.

It turns out that mobile performance technology reduces the work employees don't want to do and don't like doing, such as paperwork, so they can do more of what they really like doing. Rick tells this story:

> *This one fellow who came to work with me in the last two years, his wife had to rewrite all his bills. His handwriting was so illegible. He would*

take his paperwork home at night with him. His wife would rewrite it,
and then he would hand it in to the office, because he was embarrassed
about it. We've taken that completely away. [Employees] don't have to do
that. It is simple touch buttons. They are all drop menus. We give them
choices that we require.

What we've found now is the drivers don't need to remember when
they started and stopped. They get in in the morning and log into their
unit. There are no arguments about timecards now, because as soon as
they log into the truck, [they are also logged in on] their timecard. They
have the ability to log off for lunch. They don't have to remember the
exact time. There is no confrontation. [The system] is transparent.

Rick told us the most unsurprising news: the younger workers
picked up the new system faster than the more experienced, older
hands. Some of his veteran workers don't even have computers at home
and are afraid of technology. To answer those concerns, Rick made
sure the system was designed to make it easy to use: touch screens;
no need to check spelling; big buttons, so accuracy and spelling aren't
issues; and four-digit secured personal identification numbers (PINs),
so no one else can take credit for someone else's work. Now, the surprising news: the older workers are now devoted to the new system.
Rick explains:

These guys, and they are still with me, don't have computers at home,
and they are very comfortable using the hardware now. It has come to
the point now where if something goes down or something is not work-
ing properly, there is a phone call right away that we need this [mobile
workforce performance management system] up and going. [The work-
ers] don't just take [time] off the job. We didn't set it that if we have a
hardware issue that it would disable them [from] doing their job. They
still have the ability to do what their job is. They've really fallen in love
with it and embraced it.

Fewer changes in daily assignments make workers feel as if they
have more control over their day. Less hassle with paperwork or trying

to communicate on the radio, less overall stress, fewer manual processes, and less rework all add up to increased worker satisfaction for customers of companies like Mentor Engineering, which offer mobile workforce performance management systems.

▶ MORE AUTONOMY, HIGHER PERFORMANCE

Consider for a moment a worker's dream result from being allowed to work mobilely. First, you don't have to drive to work. You can work right out of your house, or in a coffee shop, or you might be on the road and work out of your hotel room, or you might work in a client's office. You get to choose *where* you work. Second, you can work *when* you want. If you have to drop the kids off to school, you can do that, and then scoot back to the house to zip off a few e-mails. If you need to go to a doctor's appointment, there's no problem, and you don't have to ask anybody for permission; you just go. Later that night you're on a conference call with someone in France, or Germany, or China. Last, you get to work *how* you want. If you want to write on a yellow pad and fax it to your teammates, you can. If you want to work using the latest iPad, you can. If you like to videoconference, you can. If it works best for you to meet once a month (or once a day, or once a year), you can. The promise of mobile work is flexibility.

The question for managers has always been, "What will working mobilely do to performance?" The evidence is in, as we've seen throughout this book, that moving to mobile work very often increases performance. And, as we've seen earlier in this chapter, one approach to improving performance is to use technology to manage workers' time very tightly, which can result in impressive performance improvements. Let's now consider another strategy that also increases performance—letting employees do whatever they want, whenever they want, as long as work gets done.

▶ ROWE

Every person we've interviewed and every source we found has told us that the key to creating a successful mobile workforce is to create and set clear expectations; there must also be a focus on observable results. Best Buy has introduced a new performance management system, called ROWE, that takes that wisdom to its ultimate conclusion.

ROWE stands for Results-Only Work Environment, a human resource development practice developed by Best Buy that facilitates the mobile workforce in its purest form. The philosophy behind a Results-Only Work Environment is that "each person is free to do whatever they want, whenever they want, as long as work gets done."[9] As long as people get their work done, Best Buy doesn't care when they do it or where they do it. In fact, they don't care if workers come in at all. So what does that mean?

First, no one has to worry about calling in sick or asking for vacation. No one requests time off to go see the doctor or to take one of their children to school. Why worry about flextime, when you can go anytime you want? And anyone who wants to be a mobile worker can be, because it really doesn't matter where you get your work done, as long as it's done.

In their book *Why Work Sucks and How to Fix It*, Cali Ressler and Jody Thompson share the Best Buy story. Both authors were the key employees at Best Buy who helped the company, through fits and starts, to develop what they would come to call a Results-Only Work Environment. Let's look at the results for Best Buy.

First, both types of turnover at Best Buy are going in the right direction. Voluntary turnover is going down, as much as 90 percent, which means that employees want to stay. Involuntary turnover, on the other hand, is going up, as managers focus on performance. Poor performers don't get to stay at Best Buy. The result of that is millions of dollars of savings in reduced turnover costs, and an incalculable amount of savings from cutting out pay for people who aren't doing their work.

Second, the authors report a 35 percent average increase in productivity when organizations move to a Results-Only Work Environment. That's not bad, especially when managers may not even know where their employees are half the time.

Third, all the soft issues you might anticipate in a show-up-when-you-want-to environment prove to be nonissues. In fact, most employers feel that the interactions with their managers in a ROWE environment stay the same or improve, and the same goes with their team members and clients. Even better, 72 percent of employees migrating to a ROWE environment at Best Buy felt their connection to the organization was strong or very strong.

ROWE results are impressive with other organizations as well, which report higher productivity per employee, greater job satisfaction, higher organizational commitment, increased accountability, more work–life balance, and higher wellness indicators.[10]

The Creators of ROWE—Cali and Jody

Cali Ressler and Jody Thompson developed ROWE—Results-Only Work Environment—while working at Best Buy. Today they run CultureRx, a company that shows companies of all types and sizes how they can establish a ROWE. Find more information about Culture Rx and Cali and Jody at http://gorowe.com.

We asked them if there was any situation where ROWE isn't the best solution, and they assured us there was not[11]:

ROWE works well in any situation where there's a job to be done. It's important to remember that ROWE is not a Remote-Only Work Environment but rather an environment focused on employees determining the most efficient, productive ways to get to their outcomes.

In a ROWE, employees are where they need to be when they

need to be there. In a hospital, a surgeon needs to be in the operating room to perform a procedure. In a zoo, employees need to be physically present at certain times to feed the animals. In a retail store, customers need to be served. In these cases, if people aren't in the right place at the right time, that's a performance issue.

Interestingly enough, the default "management system" should be one where there isn't an assumption that just because people are physically in one place, there's work getting done.

Organizational citizenship behaviors (OCBs) occur when people go above and beyond the call of duty to support the organization, help other workers, and do things for which they are not directly accountable.[12] Employees don't have to do this—rather they take the initiative to do them. We wanted to know if ROWE, in which the only requirement is "as long as the work gets done," discourages OCBs in the workplace. Cali and Jody assured us that ROWE and OCBs are totally congruent, telling us:

ROWE absolutely encourages OCBs in the following ways:
1. ROWE liberates people. Employees go from feeling "owned" from 8:00 to 5:00 Monday through Friday to feeling like they are in control of every second of their lives. They view ROWE as a gift and a chance to live life to the fullest. In return, they'll do much more to support the organization, their coworkers, and do things they're not directly accountable for.
2. No Sludge. In a traditional work environment, people judge others for how they spend their time. "10:00, and you're just getting in? Wish I had your job!" "There goes Kim at 3:30 to get her sick kid from daycare again—wish I had a kid!" "Banker's hours again?" In a ROWE, this language is called "Sludge," and it's not tolerated. Through the ROWE migration process, teams learn an Environmental Sludge Eradication Strategy, and they work together as a "smart

mob" to rid the environment of this toxic language. Being Sludge free fosters more genuine, respectful relationships among employees.

One issue we worry about is "performance expectation creep"—when organizations set higher and higher goals for employees when they improve their results. Sooner or later people crack because it is impossible to achieve expectations even if people work every waking hour. Doesn't ROWE encourage this type of superhuman organizational expectation, we wondered? Cali and Jody assured us it does not:

During the ROWE migration process, managers learn the importance of rewarding efficiency. If you reward efficiency with more work, people will stop being efficient. Period. As goals are reached, managers and employees work together to set the bar in a different place. More often than not, employees are coming to managers and saying, "I can do more" vs. the manager initiating the conversation.

Regarding working all the time: In a ROWE, you set your own boundaries vs. having the clock or calendar doing it for you. You might sleep in on a Tuesday, work from 11 a.m. to 1 p.m., walk the dog, go to the office for an hour for a meeting, go grocery shopping, make dinner, and work again from 10 p.m. to 2 a.m. Work is already 24/7—ROWE just gives you control to handle that.

▶ ROWE AND THE MOBILE WORKFORCE PERFORMANCE

In a Results-Only Work Environment people show up when they decide to work and do it where they want to. Work is considered differently, Cali and Jody say, in a ROWE. Work isn't a *place you go*, they say, it's *something you do*. People at every level stop doing things that waste time. No one just puts in their hours, sitting in assigned cubicles, going to a central location because that's what's expected, or wastes time in rush-hour traffic. Sounds a lot like a mobile workforce doesn't it?

Cali and Jody give the example of one employee named Trey who has worked in a ROWE for two years. A typical day for him, he says, starts by waking up when the sun is too bright for him to sleep any longer. Then he checks his e-mail for pressing issues and watches an episode of *South Park*. Then he walks over to the grocery store and buys some breakfast. After breakfast (which is really closer to lunchtime), he works in front of his television with ESPN in the background. He might go to the office then, or work from home or maybe not work at all. He may work later that night if he needs to. He says, "I'm never *not* accomplishing anything. I always do what's expected of me." And the funny thing is that since his team went into a ROWE environment its productivity has increased significantly. As long as the work gets done, Trey says, his manager is happy. "This year alone," he says, "I traveled through Europe for 19 days following my favorite artist from Paris to Brussels, Amsterdam, Prague, and Cologne." He goes on to describe his trip, which included camping, water parks, and more concerts. "I basically do what I want, when I want, all the time. I do my work, for the most part, when it's convenient for me. Since I always get my work done, I can enjoy life to the fullest while working for a great company." Now, that's the essence of a great mobile workforce.

When you really think of it, however, a Results-Only Work Environment isn't all that revolutionary. Business owners are free to do whatever they want, whenever they want, as long as the work gets done. Consultants are free to do whatever they want, whenever they want, as long as the work gets done. Artists are the same. Farmers are the same. The challenge for managers is to figure out the best environment to provide their own mobile workforce. Is it the highly controlled environment of mobile performance management software? Is it a high-autonomy workplace of a Results-Only Work Environment? Or are those two compatible? Regardless of how the environment is set up, one of the keys will be to have the right support systems set up to do the work. Just because Trey is gallivanting all around the country doesn't mean that his performance won't be hurt if he doesn't have the right kind of mobile device, access to information, and collaborative tools that he needs to do get the work done. He'll need those whether he's sitting in a park, catching a concert, or sitting at his breakfast table.

▶ SUMMARY

How many times have you wished for more autonomy and less micromanagement? How many times have you wished that you didn't have to waste time completing tasks that didn't make the best use of your skills and expertise? In this chapter we've discussed the two, very diverse, different directions organizations can take to move their workers to mobility. One stresses more control over workers and the other, seemingly, gives workers total control. In reality, these aren't mutually exclusive alternatives. The answer to determining the kind of environment that is best for your organization is to carefully think about your own performance management system as it relates to a mobile workforce, as we'll see in Chapter 7.

CHAPTER SEVEN

The Mobile Performance
Management Process

Reducing the Distance between Manager and Worker

Managers are kind of like an orchestra conductor or a sports team coach. You've got a whole team that is moving in and out of the foreground and background doing different things and handling different life events. It is your job to see that they get what they need when they need it.
   —KATHIE LINGLE, EXECUTIVE DIRECTOR OF THE
   ALLIANCE FOR WORK-LIFE PROGRESS (AWLP).[1]

Hiring is going to be one of the most critical jobs of a manager but then comes understanding how to coach to get the most out of that individual. The first step is you have to align putting the right person in the right role and then, considering the behavior, how do you coach that person for optimum performance?
   —LORI CORUCCINI, FOUNDER/CEO OF PREDIX INC.[2]

The truck driver listens to the last strains of Patsy Cline, slaps a quarter on the counter, winks at the waitress, takes one last sip from his coffee cup, and strolls out into the baking sun. The diner, located at the crossroads between nowhere and somewhere, is surrounded by . . . nothing. Endless blacktop heading east and west. A quiet gravel road meandering north and slanting off to the south. Grassy, rolling acreage stretching in every direction. The man slips a cigarette out of the pack, taps it on his jeans, brushes the phosphorus-tipped stick across the matchbook, lights it, and takes a draw. He circles his dusty rig, checking for any signs of trouble, and then swings into the cab. He clicks on his AM radio—there's Patsy Cline again—turns the ignition, struggles into gear, and pulls out onto the shimmering highway. He puts the hammer down, grinds into second gear, and he's on down the road, leaving only a trail of diesel smoke behind.

This is the iconic truck driver of the middle of the twentieth century; successor to the milkman or produce deliveryman of the early 1900s, and predecessor to the GPS-navigated, satellite-entertained, Internet-managed driver of today.[3] The modern trucking industry has had one main purpose from its early start-of-the-1900s' beginnings—to transport goods. Today that freight ranges from concrete, to nuclear waste, to heavy equipment to, naturally, milk and produce, and just about anything else that can be moved.

Tyler Ellison is the president of Con-way Multimodal, and before that he was the senior vice president of the Global Group at Schneider National, a $3.7 billion trucking, logistics, and intermodal services company that conducts business in more than 28 countries worldwide. He has degrees in history, engineering, and law, the kind of eclectic education that is likely to prepare leaders for the global, highly connected economy of today and certainly the future. As we talked with him it was easy to see that he has a more comprehensive perspective of the complex interworkings and future needs of the trucking industry than one would expect. In the past, it was easy to conceptualize the business: (1) get a truck, (2) get people to ask you to move something with your truck, (3) take it where they want it to go, (4) bill them. After talking to him, we realize it's not so simple anymore.

Today's trucking industry is a multifaceted whirl of technology, competitive strategy, and basic mechanics, all tied together by one person: the truck driver who moves the freight. Until the day when trucks can be driven remotely (and we're not saying it couldn't happen someday) there will always be someone needed to get behind the wheel and put the vehicle into first gear. As with the truck driver of yesteryear, today's also works long hours behind the wheel, often driving 11 hours a day with another three hours of paperwork, fueling, or other activities such as inspections tossed in. Truck drivers account for the highest total number of all work-related deaths, 12 percent, and if you are one, you are five times more likely to die on the job than the average person. Unlike those of the twentieth century, today's drivers can't disappear when ferrying a load from one location to another. Operator performance—including location, fuel usage, amount of time driving, engine idle time, speed, gear optimization, whether the truck is loaded or empty, and which direction it is heading—can all be tracked mobilely. So there's no hiding out at the diner anymore, because—who knows? —they might even know what kind of pie you're eating.

Con-way's mission statement says that "our employees are our biggest competitive advantage," and so it should, because not only are truck drivers the *sine qua non* of the trucking business, they're hard to get and to keep. There were 1.8 million heavy truck drivers in 2006, and a good number of them are expected to retire soon. In 2005, there was an estimated shortage of 20,000 long-haul drivers, a number that is expected to grow to 111,000 by 2014. "Retaining and attracting drivers is obviously a key differentiator in a tight workforce," Tyler told us. The need to attract, develop, motivate, and retain talent is a top priority for trucking industry leaders such as Tyler. Due to the nature of their business, most performance management has to be done mobilely.

"The typical truck stop cowboy that everybody has in their mind is not the case anymore," Tyler says. "They're very sophisticated businesspeople; more of a skilled workforce than I think the general public gives them credit for." At Con-way, a $4.3 billion freight transportation and logistics company operating in 18 countries with 26,000 employees, even little performance improvements can make a significant difference.

Tyler's piece of the business is multimodal services, which takes supply and demand for transportation and finds the best mode of transportation—whatever it is, even if it's using a competitor's assets—so the freight can move most efficiently. He's a broker of transportation services and has employees scattered across the country. At Schneider he managed thousands of drivers, so he is well aware of the challenges of leading people at a distance.

The performance management job of a leader supervising mobile workers in Tyler's organization is to *provide a value proposition that transcends the physical work structure.* His leadership team continually *asks how they can be equally responsive to employees who aren't physically colocated, and they look at it in terms of processes.* What are the issues related to giving and getting feedback? Or how about training? "What's the process to engage folks that are out in the field so they're not cheated on leadership development?" Tyler asks. Most of the answers, he says, come through a combination of technology and process.

Employee development is an especially challenging issue for mobile workers. Tyler has invested heavily in a Web-based curriculum. The process starts with understanding the skills or attributes that employees need in order to succeed in a particular role. Sometimes a mobile worker may need some different skills or attributes than someone located in a central office. As training proceeds, feedback has to take place. Often that happens at weekly one-on-one meetings to discuss business results and at a monthly one-on-one meeting to give developmental feedback. Once a quarter the employee participates in a 360-degree feedback process, which benefits both the employee and leader. Perhaps quarterly or once a year the leader meets face to face with that employee or group of employees, as well as monthly via videoconference, and weekly via a conference call.

An important key to performance management is *keeping people on track by giving and receiving feedback,* and Tyler's organization takes advantage of technology to do that regularly with mobile workers by keeping track of load status and important milestones in real time. Satellite communication, e-mail, and mobile phones are all used to track progress. At Con-way they are even considering using Twitter to dispatch trucks.

"My gut reaction," Tyler says when we asked him if there was anything different about the performance cycle for mobile workers, "is that how it's carried out has to be a little bit different, but the tenets are the same. How you go about executing that [performance management cycle] is probably different." Just for starters, the generations communicate differently. A 21-year-old may have a different style than a 40-year-old, and how that person wants to be communicated to may be different, and Tyler's leadership group is trying to get a better understanding of how to accommodate a differentiated employment relationship with differing generations. He shared an example with us. One of Con-way's younger workers committed a terminable offense for not making a vacation request during the holiday. But it turns out the person actually sent the request via text message and the supervisor never looked at it.

The same holds true for meetings. How to run an effective meeting remains the same, but when there is a staff meeting, leaders need to make sure the mobile workforce is involved and included in the meeting. *For performance meetings it's not "out of sight out of mind."* Says Tyler: "It's setting up conference calls for the weekly one-on-one and results reviews. It's having the discipline and method to be able to

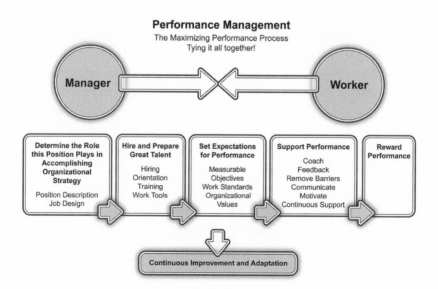

Performance Management
The Maximizing Performance Process
Tying it all together!

| Manager | Worker |

| Determine the Role this Position Plays in Accomplishing Organizational Strategy

Position Description
Job Design | Hire and Prepare Great Talent

Hiring
Orientation
Training
Work Tools | Set Expectations for Performance

Measurable
Objectives
Work Standards
Organizational
Values | Support Performance

Coach
Feedback
Remove Barriers
Communicate
Motivate
Continuous Support | Reward Performance |

Continuous Improvement and Adaptation

keep the worker as close to being in sync as if he or she were physically colocated."

Again, the question Tyler challenges his organization to ask is, "Are our human capital processes robust enough to give the worker in Ann Arbor or Anchorage or wherever everything she would get if working out of the main office—from leadership development, feedback, and everything that employee deserves?"[4]

▶ THE PERFORMANCE MANAGEMENT PROCESS FOR THE MOBILE WORKFORCE

First let's examine what performance management is. Performance management is the process of setting, working toward, and achieving organizational goals. Performance is evaluated, rewarded, and, in a continuous improvement culture, adapted. The two key players involved are usually the manager working with an employee, but they can also be the board of directors with the CEO, a self-managed team looking at itself, or a parent with a child. When it's a manager and his or her mobile worker, the goals are organizational goals, and a key strategy is to use the process to reduce any perceived or real transactional distance between them.

This process sounds simpler than it actually is, and it is often made more complicated than it needs to be. We won't go into detail about performance management in this book, as it's been discussed in much detail elsewhere, but will focus on keys to success for the mobile workforce.

The Beginning: A Very Good Place to Start

The above reference to lyrics in a song from *The Sound of Music*[5] represents just the *opposite* of what great performance management is for mobile workers. Rather, Dr. Stephen R. Covey's dictum, "Begin with the end in mind,"[6] will get you much better results and make life easier for you. *The most important thing you can do as a performance manager is to visualize where you want your organization to be and what goals you want to achieve.* Then, as with any strategic planning, execution in large part comes from your employees. To achieve those organizational goals, you'll have to consider the kind of employees you are going to need. What knowledge, skills, and attributes will be required by your workforce?

What's the Job That Needs to Be Done?

Now let's talk about specific jobs. Before you hire anyone, ask yourself what you want that person to achieve. Before we even get into people, let's look at the desired results. Let's look at the very *ending*. It's a very good place to start.

As a manager, your organization has certain results it's been asked to achieve. When you imagine those desired results for a particular job, think in terms of behavior and measurability. At the end of the day what does the person in this job need to produce? Is it sales? And if so, how many sales, bringing in how much revenue? Is it analytical reports? And if so, what quality indicators tell you it's the kind of report you want? Is it increased press coverage? In which case, what kind of stories do you want to see, in which media, and written by whom? Even better, what kind of behavioral responses—votes, trips to the zoo, Internet searches—do you want those stories to produce? Go through any desired results in your organization and ask yourself those questions. What will it look like when it's been successfully accomplished?

What Are the Goals for This Position?

Once you know the results you want, they can be translated into written, measurable, observable, deadline-driven goals. These goals can be daily, weekly, monthly, annually, or much longer term. Some people might call these "objectives," others "goals," but it really doesn't matter as long as your organization uses the same language. Organizational goals may change slowly, but the goals for a particular job may change with more regularity.

Job Design

At this point, we need to achieve those goals, and generally we hire people either contingently or permanently to fill a job designed to do just that. Then we can start being more specific about how workforce mobility fits into this scheme. In the past, most organizations designed jobs to be located in one place. But, as we've seen, especially with more sophisticated technology, location is less restricting than ever before. Indeed, being able to locate workers anywhere gives the organization additional degrees of strategic freedom, which can be a source of long-term competitive advantage.

So, when redesigning a job, rethink any assumption in your head that has to do with location. Just because you once used to have a document center, why can't you put all your files in a cloud and let your document workers access it from anywhere they wish? Your administrative assistant has always sat right outside your desk. Why? Many excellent assistants work in completely different parts of the country from their bosses. Rethink those constraining assumptions—for all your jobs.

In fact, why not think about this in terms of tasks instead of the whole job, which is really a set of tasks organized for one person? Which tasks can be completed mobilely and which are tied to a specific location? Think about that a lot, because some tasks that require a physical location today might not in just a few short years, months, or even days. For example, today we think we need bank tellers to be available for customers. In a few short years, when most people have some form of telepresence right in their own homes, there may be little or no need for a retail bank location. How about emergency medical teams—those we need to be right there on the spot for sure, right? If we think far enough out and use our imaginations, however, do you think there could ever be a time when emergency support could be given via telemedicine? Heck, maybe we'll be teleporting one of these days and won't even be driving cars. It could happen. Just ask those people who thought we'd never step on the moon.

So think of any task that could be automated, communicated, tracked online, developed into a computerized work tool, or virtualized in any fashion. As we've seen in the previous chapter, more and more performance management systems are doing just this. Some tasks aren't ready to be mobility enhanced quite yet, but you may be surprised at how many are.

Now bundle those tasks into a job, or redesign jobs that you already have to represent these new, mobility-friendly tasks. Remind yourself that these tasks—many now to be executed at a distance—should enable the work to be completed as least as efficiently, quickly, and cost effectively (or use any other organizational result measure) as it was before. Ideally, they should improve productivity, and usually they will, by a lot.

Providing the Work Tools

Before you hire anyone or reassign anyone to a job, you'd better be sure the mobility tools needed for success will be in place. Are you going to need an Oracle (or Reflexis, or Mentor, or . . .) mobile workforce performance management system for your field workers? Or will a mobile phone and a netbook do? Will you need a knowledge management system for that hardware, so your workers can share, update, and track information either synchronously or asynchronously? What about collaborative tools? There's no need to buy a bunch of gadgets you don't need—but you'd better have what you do need to facilitate performance instead of obstructing it. You are, after all, the "Human API."

We've now considered the results we want from this job, the tasks that will be required to get those results, which of those tasks we can mobilize, and what kind of hard- and software support your employees will need to get the job done. But we'd better think about what kind of people we'll need to fill that job too.

Hiring

Now it's time to think about hiring people, though in most organizations it may be that you are either redeploying people or retooling them for this kind of mobile work. We'll examine how to hire and prepare great mobile talent in Chapter 8, but for now the thing to know is that *if you want high performance you have to hire high-performance people.* You want people who won't quit until the job is done, workers you can count on, people who will keep themselves up to date with changing organizational imperatives and technology and their profession. As Cali Ressler and Jody Thompson relate in Chapter 6 about their experiences with Best Buy, performance is everything—you can work anywhere and at any time, *as long as the work gets done.* Or *you* are done. Having high-performance people is essential to maintaining a winning organizational culture.

Orientation

Once you've hired people you want, the best way to get them locked into your organization is to give them a sound grounding in your company. Some organizations spend just a little somewhat informal time with orientation, and some spend weeks and have a very formal orientation, giving employees exposure to different parts of the organization, but good organizations find a way to share the culture and the "this is the way we do things around here" with new employees. Mobile managers we interviewed often make it a point to meet personally with new mobile employees when the workers first start. Some, such as Greg Lowitz of RipCode, or John Gentry of Virtual Instruments, spend a good deal of face-to-face time with new employees at first, making sure they know the ropes. Greg goes on sales calls with his workers until they feel comfortable with the information and company processes and can be successful. For mobile workers this orientation time is particularly important. Getting them off on the right foot is essential. They will get a real sense of organizational norms and, more specifically, how you like things done as they begin to work with your team, other organizational members, and you. Too many people have been lost because managers have had a sink-or-swim culture. Too many talented people sink in that kind of environment, when a safety jacket would have buoyed them up long enough to start dog paddling. That brings us to training.

Training

How can you expect employees to improve without training them? We think that training is important and we devote a chapter to it (see Chapter 8), but let's think of it in terms of performance for a minute. It would be easy for leaders such as Tyler Ellison to just let his mobile crew do their jobs and to let it go at that. After all, pushing widgets is what we pay people for, isn't it? But providing training does at least a couple of things. First, it lets mobile workers see that you care about them beyond the immediate job. When you invest in them they are more likely to become emotionally committed to your organization. Second, you build organizational capacity. The more your workforce knows, the more it can do. Tyler makes sure that every mobile employee gets the same leadership development opportunities as every other employee gets. As a manager of a mobile workforce *you have to be intentional*, like Tyler, in assuring that mobile workers get every opportunity to learn just as others do.

John Gentry—Road Warrior and Manager of Road Warriors
"Thanks for the note. Very fitting that I am typing this e-mail from 30K feet aboard a jet from Chicago to Toronto. This week I will have traveled to Phoenix, San Diego, Toronto via Chicago, and Atlanta. I have employees working for me in all these locations, and am also coordinating corporate resources to join in the fun, either in person or via 'GoToMeeting' online conferencing. "

That's the e-mail we received from John Gentry when we asked if he would be interested in being interviewed for this book. Yes, he's a true "road warrior." We finally caught up with him several weeks later and got a picture of what it's like to be a road warrior managing a team of road warriors.[7]

John is the senior director of Worldwide Solutions Consulting for Virtual Instruments Inc., which is a small, rapidly growing company that offers storage area network optimization, specifically focusing on virtual infrastructure. He's responsible for a team of solutions consultants operating worldwide.

His largest problem, he told us, is maintaining a connectedness to the corporate initiative and direction while maintaining consistency in message and work products. "I have 12 employees," he says. "I don't have a single employee [who] is in an office. Every single one works remotely from home. Oftentimes, remote employees can feel like they are stranded on an island. It is keeping them well tethered to the mother ship via information repositories, online applications like salesforce.com (which we use extensively), and GoTo-Meeting–based Webinars and conference calls. It is creating a virtual office space for a bunch of remote individuals."

To do that, he maintains consistent communication, with weekly worldwide calls with team members and supporting functions. He also has assigned management objectives to the team. "We have five overarching MBOs [Management by Objectives], each of which is very specifically designed to align the resource behind common goals." Those goals include giving consistent feedback to marketing about such things as success stories or usage cases; providing feedback to engineering requesting feature enhancements or additions; and taking responsibility for developing a particular area of expertise that will be valuable for participation in the development of proposals, customer meetings, and cross-educating one another.

He measures performance through a combination of qualitative and quantitative measures. Quantitatively, he gives minimums (for example, the number of cross-regional calls or proposals). Qualitatively, he judges the value employees deliver to the larger organization (for example, helping others as a subject matter expert). "It is a personal priority for me to make the MBOs meaningful in that I never grant 100 percent achievement because, if I do, I lose an opportunity for coaching. Even someone who is hitting their goals may hit 90 percent, but I will give them some constructive feedback for how they could improve or how they could have invested more. I believe you have to have a qualitative element to make it meaningful and to make it specific to the individual and their current place on the learning curve or place in their own personal professional development. Quantitative measures tend to lump everyone into a common bucket of capability. I'm obviously managing a very diverse team."

He hires only what he calls "A players," in a highly competitive market for talent. His workers execute their jobs without much direct oversight, and that gives John the ability to provide leadership and direction for overcoming challenges, inspiring them to look for unique or creative ways to solve problems.

He talks about leading in the spirit of the upside-down paradigm: "I tell my people I work for them. They don't work for me. My job is to get what they need from corporate to be successful and to protect them and be their advocate in facing the company. Between those two you hope that you create a very healthy work environment that people will choose to be a part of. I think we've been quite successful with that." He sets the goals high to stretch his employees and then provides the support they need to achieve them.

He is on the road three of four weeks—meeting with each of his employees at least once or twice a quarter, including Europe, because, he says, nothing takes the place of meeting face to face. He meets with his employees to coach them, leveraging the opportunity to get into markets to demonstrate expertise, approach, presentation style, and the value captures he wants from each employee. John gave us a specific example:

I have a resource in Atlanta. . . . I flew into Atlanta [at] midnight on Wednesday, and yesterday [I] spent all day with that person in a series of customer meetings and a series of interviews for their sales counterpart. They sat with me in all of those meetings and provided their color commentary specific to [the] market. But I really took the lead in presenting to the customer, asking the questions, shaping the responses. . . .Then we spent time in between the meetings—in drive time—talking about what just happened, what we learned from it, what we think the challenges are going to be, and what the next steps are. It is really about focused presence in [the] market, side by side with that resource, to provide that mentoring and also offer them the opportunity to provide that feedback. One of the things that came out of that day yesterday was my resource there had an idea for something they would like to see added to the product—one of their MBOs. . . .We had an opportunity to really discuss in detail why they thought that was a good request, who might be the right person to put that request in to, and how they should phrase the request and the associated business justifications. It really provides both an opportunity for leadership by example and a conduit for feedback to the company and to myself.

The situation with training is the same: John starts new employees with a minimum of three days at the corporate location with fairly intensive in-person training. They then go back to their markets for a week and dig through and read the library of content they have online, which is extensive. John drops in to see them in their market the third week, and they both go on a series of customer calls so the new employee can see John execute them firsthand while they listen and observe. Then, during the fourth, fifth, and sixth week the new person shadows one of the professional services people as they deploy a customer solution or execute a service engagement with that new customer.

What's it like to be a mobile manager? How demanding is it? As John relates:

You certainly have to have a very profound work ethic and be willing to work hard. However, I would say it is equally important to work smart and to be sure to carve time out to give back to yourself, and in my case that is often in the form of time with my family. When I hang up with you guys today I will be done. I'll spend the rest of the afternoon playing with my son, watching the Olympics, and really winding down from the week.

I'd say the ability to multitask [is important for a mobile manager]. It is interesting: We have notes repositories on all of our clients . . . but I really hold all of the most active opportunities in my active memory so I can get a call at any time from any resource and be very present with their specific concerns without having to go shuffle and search for the relevant content. It takes a certain mental capacity that is really more inherited than learned, although you can learn effective strategies and so forth.

Expectations

How important is expectation setting? How about for a Results-Only Work Environment? Can you imagine one of those fancy mobile performance management systems being effective if the workers weren't held to high standards of execution? But if you've done your homework, this part of the process is much easier. If you know ahead of time the results you expect (you started at the very ending after all, didn't you?), then you know what goals to negotiate with each of your workers. In fact, difficult, specific, committed-to goals are the most motivating, we discuss in Chapter 9. Make those goals observable and you have a real basis for evaluation at the end. Make them mushy and subjective and you are moving out of a high-performance management system and into a negotiable, political management system. And don't forget to set expectations for supporting and living organizational values. A good way to do that is to model them yourself. If you value integrity, act with it. If you value cost consciousness, don't spend lavishly on yourself. With mobile workers, values have to be emphasized heavily, because those workers aren't around to observe how people act in the corporate environment or at the service center. They'll only see how people behave virtually, and they will have to infer expectations more than others do.

The same holds true for organizational standards. If collaboration is expected, describe what that looks like. If communication is important, be sure to let your employees know what that means. For example, how often and in what ways should the worker communicate with clients, coworkers, or the manager? Once a day? On the phone? With summary data or full reports? Only when there's a crisis or at the weekly meeting? Be specific and up front about what you expect. Then you can be precise when evaluating results at the end of the period. Road warrior John Hale, discussed in Chapter 6, makes it clear that he doesn't need or want messages containing thoughtful pleasantries such as "Will do!" when he has 250 other e-mails coming in each day.

Support

Once you've agreed to the goals for the year you can breathe a big sigh of relief and go about your business until it's evaluation time again, right? *Wrong, wrong, wrong.* Now *you work for your employee* as he or she sets out to achieve those ambitious goals. You don't take responsibility for his or her work, but you are there to remove obstacles when needed. You'll be a coach and an encourager at times, and you'll be there to give valuable feedback to help keep performance on track. Sometimes you'll need to go out and get resources—new technology perhaps, additional staff or volunteers, maybe just a three-hole punch—that they'll need along the way. Maybe they need to learn some new skills or to develop relationships with new people. You might have to pony up for some training or a trip to meet with them. Your job now is to help them get to the finish line.

Evaluation and Reward

When you set goals and other expectations with your employees you will also need to be clear about how evaluations will be made and how each person will be rewarded based on the performance you have both agreed to. That is the time to make sure your employee understands completely what is expected. You should make sure you have plenty of time to talk these expectations over with your employee. Encourage questions and discussion, because you don't want to set the employee's performance expectations in a vacuum. You need to know the reality your employee faces and to be open to learning something that might affect something that you both agree to.

With this kind of setup, performance evaluation is a relative breeze: you both go down the list of accomplishments and expectations point by point. You'll be able to say with confidence whether each has been accomplished or not. Reward according to the commitment you made when you set goals.

Sometime, perhaps after your annual evaluations, sit down with employees and think about what would improve performance for the next cycle. Are there some business processes that are broken that just get in the way? Are there some broken relationships that need to be mended? Are you giving the right support? Is the employee right for this kind of work? Candor, even though difficult and sometimes hurtful, is your most valued asset here, and will build a climate of respect between you.

Then you can start the whole cycle all over again. Seek excellence in your own management growth. Your own performance management goals should be clear. One of them should be learning how to develop and sustain a high-performance environment for your mobile organization.

▶ AUTONOMY OR NOT AUTONOMY? THAT IS *NOT* THE QUESTION

We posed a false dichotomy to you in Chapter 6. The solution is not one or the other: autonomy or not autonomy. What's required is to do what the job and the person calls for. Some jobs are more conducive for automation; some just aren't. Some people fit right into a more structured environment and like it better, and some want to set their own structure. As we say in Chapter 9, everyone is different, and everyone is the same. Not all jobs can be treated the same way either, so you'll just have to figure out what's right for you.

That's, of course, why you get the big bucks.

Right?

▶ SUMMARY

Performance management is the heart of managing mobile workers. It's where the rubber truly meets the road on a daily basis. It is the litmus test for managers—if you can do this well for mobile workers or for any worker, really, then you are much more likely to succeed in seeing your team meet truly high-performance goals. In this chapter we have covered the basics of performance management, commencing with goal setting and continuing through evaluation, from the perspective of managing a mobile workforce. In Chapter 8 we will go into more detail about hiring and preparing high-performance mobile talent.

►CHAPTER EIGHT

Hiring and Preparing Great Mobile Talent

Getting the Right People on the Virtual Bus

Every position in a company, including the mobile workforce, has a particularly behavioral job demand to it. There's really no such thing as a generic job model that would tell us exactly what the behavior needs to be for a mobile worker. The absolute key is to be able to integrate what somebody is made up of. For a manager, it's critical to understand their drivers and the motivators of a mobile worker so you can coach them appropriately. It's key.

—LORI CORUCCINI, FOUNDER/CEO, PREDIX INC.[1]

As Jim Collins famously said, getting the right people on the bus is critical for organizational success.[2] The same is even more true when taking on new virtual employees. Hiring and training a mobile workforce, that is, finding and developing great talent who you may not physically meet with very often, is the focus of this chapter. This isn't a small challenge—lots of your employees will be home-based or on-the-road workers sooner or later. Let's review the facts again.

In May 2004, the *Los Angeles Times* featured a story about JetBlue.[3] Seven hundred JetBlue reservation agents worked from home at the time—that's all of them—with company-supplied second phone lines and personal computers. Of course, that's just one of many companies with home workers. The article also reported that, at the time, 70 percent, that's almost 100,000, of Hewlett-Packard's employees worked from home part of the time. Work at home reaps tangible benefits too. AT&T, for example, reaped over $180 million in operating benefits from telework. In fact, the article reported that the number of U.S. company employees working from home at least part of the time grew from 11.6 million in 1997 to 23.5 million, or 16 percent of the American workforce, in 2004. Can you imagine the numbers now?

Today there are few barriers to doing many jobs from anywhere. JetBlue and others are leading the way to break location-based work paradigms. The air carrier finds that as the work–life balance improves, turnover goes down and there is higher employee satisfaction. In fact, JetBlue's founder and CEO, David Neeleman, estimates that productivity of employees improves by 25 percent when they are home based. Not bad.

Hiring and training mobile workers isn't as easy as all of that, of course. The people reporting to you might be located across the street, across the country, or at *un petit bistro* in Paris. Here are some questions you might want to ask yourself when contemplating taking on a teleworker or two.

1. What type of individual would you hire to work from home? What type would you trust to travel from one hotel to the next, or from one client to another, day after day?
2. What tools and advice will you seek when looking at the knowledge, skills, abilities, and attributes of potential mobile employees?
3. What are the functions and responsibilities the employee will be expected to perform?
4. What resources exist to support your mobile employees? What will they need to be successful?
5. Are the managers trained to supervise mobile workers? Do they

know how to motivate people whom they seldom see, and can they resolve conflict, communicate clear objectives, build teamwork, and hold them accountable? Do they know how find the right balance between face-to-face discussions and virtual meetings?

6. How does your company train employees for the mobile work environment? What are the safety and health issues, for example, that people on the road need to know about and to prepare for?

Hiring is difficult; for many companies it's the biggest investment and most important decision they will make. Think about the cost to recruit, hire, train, motivate, retain, maintain, promote, and eventually retire someone. What if that person is a total dud? Or what if he or she is a constant grain of sand in the teleworks? As John Gentry shared with us, he hires only A players.[4] You don't want to be hand-holding or putting out unnecessary fires; if you hire right you can rely on your own A players to solve issues.

Our best advice is to make sure you have top-notch human resources professionals helping you. They'll need to support the learning curve your organization will go through, to identify the pertinent policies and legal issues affected. You'll need them to add their best organizational development expertise to the mix in order to position and execute the successful change management process for moving to mobility, customized to the needs of your organization.

The most important consideration will be to know the purpose and roles of your mobile team. Executive support, organizational investment, and your own personal commitment must be all aligned with the culture and direction of the company and with what you expect behaviorally from a remote employee. You need this close match to mitigate your risk and increase your odds of success. *You'll start things on the right foot by knowing what is expected of your mobile employees and then managing to those expectations.*

The work–life balance equation is real; people are eager for it. Employees are likely to give their loyalty and commitment to organizations that provide it. Hiring people who fit your culture and understand your expectations—with the skills and abilities to produce—makes all the difference. One person we interviewed has vast experience and depth of knowledge in this arena: Lori Coruccini.

▶ THE BEHAVIORAL SIDE OF HIRING

We were fortunate to interview Lori Coruccini, Founder/CEO of Predix Inc., a strategic consulting company that helps its clients to better understand job modeling and how to match employees to the roles and performance expectations of their company.[5] Lori has been the executive of personnel and talent management and training companies for 20 years. She knows what it takes for a manager to build trust and a skilled mobile workforce.

Lori deeply believes that understanding behavioral expectations is crucial for hiring, training, and then managing success. "Every position within a company," she told us, "including the mobile workforce, has a particular behavioral job demand to it. There's really no such thing as a generic job model . . . that would tell us exactly what the behavior needs to be for a mobile worker. Each company is going to drive its own culture and its own behavioral needs based on [its] leadership and also based on the culture that's within the company." Her thoughts are congruent with the theme we've been following throughout this book—the principles of hiring and training mobile workers are no different than they are for any other kind of worker—it's the application of them that may differ.

One of the first steps for hiring, she believes, is to identify the *behavioral job demands*. The second step is to understand how to coach and manage that behavior, and to really understand what drives an individual's interest.

Lori explained that within the hiring process there are four critical steps to bringing someone into a mobile workforce: "First you need to have *role clarity within the job description*. You need to be able to *set expectations, manage the role, and coach to it*. Then you need to *identify behaviorally what that position requires*, considering especially what the company leadership and culture stand for. Third, make sure *the person's values match company values*. Last, but not least, you need to *hire the skill set*—which is the component among the four that is teachable. This method works for the CEO down to a frontline person—mobile worker or not."

Knowing and identifying the exact behaviors specific to the job specifications for which the company is interviewing and hiring is critical. It is important to know that the profile of an at-home worker might be completely different from that of a road warrior or a corridor mobile worker. We'll describe those differences in the sections that follow.

▶ TECHNOLOGY ENABLES THE WORK

To hire and train a mobile workforce, managers who drive the business model and business objectives for the company first must be well organized and in alignment with departments such as sales, customer support, technical support, and marketing. The effort to achieve these objectives may place heavy demands and expectations on the IT department. Establishing clear expectations is an absolute priority before hiring anyone who will be conducting business outside your offices and basically on the Net.

Think about it. Everything has to work together. The network, hardware, and the software all support the customized work of every individual mobile worker wherever and whenever he or she needs to be on the job. They interact together. It's a true technology–human ecosystem. Like the chicken-and-egg analogy: it doesn't really matter which one you start with—all are essential to get the work accomplished.

Managers don't have to be IT experts to hire, train, or lead mobile workers, but they should know, through experience, the challenges their new teleworkers will face and the pitfalls for which to watch. All the issues regarding the planning and deployment of hardware, software, and security policies, including both public and secure Internet connections, need to be addressed so that, for the mobile worker, the ability to communicate and share information is seamless, easy, and intuitive. Technology can't be the stumbling block when finding and preparing the right people to move the profit line higher and higher.

Training a mobile team is not a new idea. Certainly the methods vary from company to company, but all employees within the organization, whether onsite or on the road, need to be on top of their game no matter where or what they call their office. Trainers need to take into account that more and more employees, not only in sales but also in tech support, customer service, and even at the executive level, are increasingly able to choose where and when they want to work.

Employees are no longer leashed to the desk or to a brick-and-mortar office, and that makes coordinating training sessions a strategy game. Advances in mobile technology give trainers a new set of opportunities and requirements to consider, ones that open up an entirely a new dimension in how business training can and should be conducted. The best training departments in today's top companies have evolved from a little room with a few desks and old hand-me-down computers. They are now well equipped to manage the required knowledge infrastructure to build smart teams and to help them to do their jobs more effectively on a global scale and in a way that measures performance. The companies that stand out from the crowd are creating innovative training units that deliver immeasurable value to the long-term health and prosperity of the enterprise and to every member of the organization.

There is a higher level of urgency today for training management to react to the fast, competitive nature of business. The question for your organization remains, "How can we educate our mobile staff in an engaging, interactive, and inclusive manner that is just as, or more, effective than if they were in the office every day?" Let's find out.

Doug Harward is respected for what he has brought to the training world as a global director at Nortel. He works from his beautiful offices in Cary, North Carolina, just off of the I-40 Interstate, tucked into an upscale business park, surrounded by a never-ending string of lush green trees and sitting next to the immaculate corporate grounds of SAS headquarters and other impressive corporate giants. From the early days of Nortel, Doug earned the responsibility to lead as a global manager responsible for tens of thousands of employees on a global scale, including the early formation of mobile business units and dispersed employees. He is the founder of TrainingIndustry.com and the Learning Content Network.

When I (coauthor David Clemons) met Doug, we had face-to-face meetings that were facilitated through Greg Kaiser of the International Speakers Bureau. The two-hour meeting with Doug and Greg was with two of the sharpest and most creative minds I've met. They know how to take ideas to fruition. I was sitting in Doug's office listening to these two talking about business strategy while I was just trying to focus and keep up! Things move fast around thought leaders within this industry.

Doug brought up a big idea for the enterprise training manager: "When we think about the distribution of information to a mobile device, I'm really trying to study the difference between push/pull. For me to push content to somebody on a mobile device, it is 100 percent about opt-in because of the invasiveness people would perceive. In an enterprise world, I don't have to worry about it, because they are my employees and I'm going to tell them what information I want them to have. In the public world, the B-to-C [business-to-customer] market, we've got a whole different set of implications. I think about the societal implications of using mobile devices we haven't even learned very much about yet. I push about two million e-mails a month to our members. I can't do that to a mobile device unless they tell me they want it."

Being mobile and using mobile technology are two legs of a three-legged chair, he told us; the third leg represents the users and how they want the content pushed to them. This notion of "opt-in," in a redefined way, will most likely play an important part in employee training in the near future. Employees will select the Centers of Excellence that are being pushed to them by their company. Some information will be obvious requirements, but some will be selected by the topics employees choose to pursue, engage, and collaborate in. The information available to employees on their mobile devices will be as vast as what the Internet provides on any day. This is going to become a bigger training portal than most people think today. It is predicted that by 2020, the mobile device and the networks that drive it will be the solution to instant global communications in every sense of the word.[7]

Trainers have an ever-increasing need to reach the wide array of employees, contractors, partners, and strategic customers who touch every department and business unit. Whether you are the vice president of corporate training and education or the one person who makes up the training department, you serve the needs of a disparate set of offices and individual road warriors, corridor mobile workers, and home-based mobile workers, many of whom will be located in international settings. Your work has to be coordinated across sprawling corporate campuses, language barriers, and time zones. Your audience of trainees often has far less face time with peers and managers than virtual time. They have an ever-increasing directive to do more with less. *Their training must be designed around their mobility* to give them the best choices of learning opportunities, and to take them when and where they can. With the right people, training this workforce can become a source of competitive advantage.

▶ THE PROFILE OF A MOBILE WORKER

Every manager knows that the perfect employee doesn't simply appear. Rather, he or she is discovered over time as that person tackles a series of tasks and projects. Training each mobile worker with a unique plan that meets the individual needs of the employee can be a a hit or miss, if you aren't careful.

Different sources categorize mobile workers differently. For example, an interesting Cisco study classifies mobile workers as On-site Movers, Yo-Yos, Pendulums, Nomads, or Carriers.[8] We thought it would be helpful to think about a training strategy for mobile workers by considering three main types of mobile workers. That will help to understand their primary working habits and styles. Although every individual has a unique personality and set of preferences, each group has distinctive roles, use of technology, and geographic locations.

▶ CORRIDOR MOBILE WORKFORCE

Generally, when we imagine the mobile workforce, we think of the typical traveling executive or salesperson, popping from city to city into busy airports, rental cars, and hotels. However, not every mobile worker travels outside of the physical structure of a corporate building or a large factory, or even a campus. We were surprised to learn about the size of this particular group.

The best description we found for these people was given to us by Brent Lang, the president and COO of Vocera Communications.[9] Brent told us this is one of the largest groups of employees, whom he calls "corridor mobile workers." These employees use their *leg power* to move from office to office and room to room, through halls, and between buildings. Corridor warriors are people who might work in a hospital, warehouse, or retail store. They are generally not sitting behind a desk waiting for the phone to ring, but often they are on their feet moving from location to location for many purposes and needs. In the best situations they use real-time technology to handle critical and noncritical communications. If they are lucky, they might use Vocera voice-activated badges to communicate in real time. If they are unlucky, they might have to scurry down a hallway or to another building to find people or to share information.

This type of mobile worker can be tough to communicate with or locate without a well-thought-out mobile technology and workflow plan. Out of view for them means out of sight in five seconds flat, even when they have urgent roles and responsibilities that require urgent communications to do important work such as saving lives. Brent pointed out that, as a manager, "you can't always see the person you urgently need; therefore, you have to use a real-time technology to locate, communicate, message, or call *rather than yelling down the hall!*"

Typical Profile: Corridor Mobile Worker

Here's what a typical profile looks like for an average corridor mobile worker:

- ▶ *Office.* Has a shared fixed office location or office to work from but seldom is in the office
- ▶ *Movement.* Office to office, aisle to aisle, or building to building, connected by corridors and/or the close proximity of buildings
- ▶ *Role types.* Nurses, security, IT technicians, factory plant supervisors, facility managers, plant superintendents
- ▶ *Mobile technology.* Push-to-talk, voice-activated handheld mobile devices, laptops with wireless capability, cell phones, walkie-talkies
- ▶ *Tech savviness.* Generally dependent on IT to manage Internet connections and mobile hardware
- ▶ *Delivery of Learning.* Instructor-led courses, team collaboration, and online

▶ AT-HOME (HOME-BASED) MOBILE WORKFORCE

Technology empowers small- to large-sized businesses alike to conduct business from the homes of their employees. They do it by establishing secure, trustworthy communication and information-sharing capabilities between the office and where employees live. This could be via a mobile device or VoIP phone, laptop, or desktop computer that has a secure connection. This group talks to clients and staff, creates documentation (such as customer service records), conducts and attends conference calls and online meetings, and fulfills roles such as dispatch or accounting. The primary communication is not through face-to-face meetings but through direct customer and team contact through use of technology or as an individual contributor. This is a virtual employee, one who spends the entire day within the digital environment and has developed skills that help boost credibility and deliver information effectively, and who trusts that the Internet connection and the reliability is always on.

Typical Profile: At-Home Mobile Workers

Here's what a typical profile looks like for an average at-home mobile worker:

- ▶ *Office.* Both has a fixed office in the home and uses wireless modems to connect in many locations within the home
- ▶ *Movement.* Home to office, occasionally some city-to-city traveling
- ▶ *Role types.* Small business owners and managers of large companies, customer service agents, online sales agents, technical support agents
- ▶ *Mobile technology.* Laptops with wireless capability, wireless modems, PDAs, smartphones with e-mail, SMS, and some file storage, virtual private network (VPN) for secure access

▶ *Tech savviness.* Generally capable of solving issues such as those relating to connection and hardware

▶ *Delivery of Learning.* Online, collaborative team meetings and on-location training for face-to-face contacts

▶ MOBILE ROAD WARRIORS

The remote digital nomads known as mobile road warriors are, in every sense of the word, *mobile.* They stay connected through technology, regularly hunting and seeking the next Internet connection. They are often extroverted, and must be organized and highly adaptable to the environment they travel to and work from. They like to rely on technology and support from the corporate training, marketing, and IT departments or groups within the enterprise. These employees and businesspeople are on the road and away from home and the office a majority of the time. Their role is to move around to get new business, maintain relationships, and represent their company's offerings in a professional manner. The need to deliver results keeps the road warrior busy. This is a very capable, independent thinker who likes the challenges presented by traveling and being constantly on the road. The mobile road warrior can solve many issues and knows when to ask for help.

Typical Profile: Mobile Road Warriors
Here's what a typical profile looks like for an average mobile road warrior:

▶ *Office.* Has an office within the enterprise or at home but stays connected with work the majority of time from different locations

▶ *Movement.* Home or office traveling office to office, city to city, and internationally

▶ *Role types.* Employees of small businesses to Fortune 100 companies, territory salespeople, enterprise managers, executives who work from home and travel regionally and/or internationally, employees who are extremely specialized based on training and skill who need to provide services to various offices or clients

▶ *Mobile technology.* Laptops with wireless capability, wireless modems, PDAs, smartphones with mobile e-mail, SMS, and some file storage, VPN for secure access

▶ *Tech savviness.* Knows whom to connect with when the time-to-solution is an issue; has an internal champion whom he or she can call on; likes working with a few trusted software programs and hardware devices

▶ *Delivery of Learning.* Call conference, Web-based conference, and occasionally in-office training; use of laptops, earphone plug-ins with microphone or use of mobile device or laptop for inbound calls, including VoIP

Training managers have to consider how each of these groups is most likely to access learning opportunities. If the worker is home based, will online learning systems, accessible from a desktop computer, suffice? If the worker is a road warrior, will podcasts and video or audio streams, provided to a mobile phone and caught while he or she is waiting at the airport, be the best way to learn? Is it best, as John Gentry does with his road warrior team, to bring them in first for intense, several-day, face-to-face training sessions and then give them access to virtual knowledge systems? Each group of workers takes a customized training strategy. Each organization has different tools available for them.

▶ THE FUTURE OF MOBILE EMPLOYEES MAY START RIGHT IN OUR PUBLIC SCHOOLS

Mike Cook is the executive director of the Educational Services and Staff Development Association of Central Kansas (ESSDACK), which is a nonprofit educational service center.[10] As an educational research and development organization, ESSDACK helps school districts in the state and on a national level to establish programs that are collaborative in nature and thus more efficient and cost effective.

Mike speaks the obvious, powerfully, about where talent and technology connect. We all know that students will need to be better trained and equipped to be competitive in a global talent market. Businesses will need to have a supply of technologically savvy talent around which to build their corporate visions. According to Mike, "When you talk about a mobile workforce and the tools that they use, the first thing I see is that we're not developing the skills kids are going to need when they get into jobs that don't yet exist. It's really interesting to see larger institutions that have been around forever struggle to capture and maximize some of these tools. The part that scares me the most is business is demanding we use them and schools are demanding we lock them out."

Mike told us about his early development as a child, growing up on the farm. His father taught him to look at something, analyze it, tear it apart, and put it back together, fixing the issue. He learned by doing. He states that the focus today is to get content scores and basic memory recall. The real skills that are needed, he feels, are simply not the priority.

For example, he thinks students at the high school level are not engaged in their schools because they are losing the ability to be creative and innovative, and to learn while using their hands and brains in solving problems. Students are fully engaged in Twitter and Facebook, but those things aren't allowed on many school campuses. Why, he wonders? Those are the learning tools of student choice, and the future, and schools don't use them.

Such youngsters are the road warriors and corridor warriors of the future. Are they getting the skills they need today, and the metaskills they will need in the future, to continue to advance through careers that will be constantly changing?

"In my professional background," he told us, "I was a biology, chemistry, physics, and anatomy teacher. I was a major control freak. I would say, 'This is where, when, and how you are going to learn biology.' Today you don't need me for any of that. Education has to become accepting of the fact that the learner is mobile. The information is mobile. I don't need a 900-square-foot classroom. I need access."

Manager Alert! Who Is Generation Y, and What Is the Impact on the Mobile Workforce?

The Generation Y (Gen Y) group won't be entering the training room of yesteryear very much. Also known as millennials and the iGeneration, these new employees like to use technology, expect their employers to provide technology-based training and resources abundantly, and are multiculturally savvy.

How does your training strategy cater to this Gen Y group? What is the competitive difference your training department offers that will attract and keep its Gen Y trainees engaged? Mobile technology and features such as mobile e-mail and mobile texting, as well as mobile applications such as online communities, social media, and instant messaging, are used ubiquitously by this group. You're missing the boat if these tools aren't in your virtual training toolbelt. And there's a bunch of them, as everyone knows.

These people grew up using electronic technology. They can search for answers, whip out questions to large numbers of people who use social media, and tweet up to solve problems anytime they want. There is no one way to train this audience—or any other one—but if you want to attract and then engage this particular group, you'd better be using some nifty apps. They know how to track down information better than you probably do. Why not put them to work creating your strategy for training and learning? Otherwise, watch the best ones

SMS themselves over to job openings in more tech-savvy organizations. And the idea of working or training mobilely, for this group, isn't a decision so much as it is reality. Why in the world would they even consider being chained to a desk when a netbook would do?

These folks aren't going to need the basic technology (remedial training, really, for most of us of a certain age), because they'll have all that. That gives you the opportunity to really challenge them with cutting-edge tools, technology, and applications. That's what will grab their attention—not SMS 101. This is the most educated, technology-savvy group on the planet. So let them use technology and social media to communicate, and forget the podium and the lecture when you can. Give them quick, bite-sized, downloadable learning opportunities for their cell phone, and, instead of you giving the feedback to them all the time, ask for feedback often from *them*. You'll be surprised what you learn.

▶ MOBILIZING YOUR TRAINING DEPARTMENT

The paradigm of work is changing, and so is the paradigm of training to meet the needs of now-mobile workers. Think of the mobile workers in the field; what are they asking for? What do they urgently need? Is your enterprise content mobile enabled? Can mobile users find your content on their laptops and other mobile devices on demand? Is the content you've been pulling out of three-ring binders for the last 20 years repurposed or reprovisioned so your mobile team can access it?

▶ TECHNOLOGY BASELINE

Every training department should create a strategic content plan that serves the needs of both your mobile workforce and also those who aren't mobile. This integration plan should tie in the existing LMS, CRM, and CDN systems and infrastructure that already exist within the training department and the IT departments. The issue today is how accessible the content is for *all devices, wherever they might be* when a request for content is made.

If your goal is to produce content, then the question that needs to be addressed is how accessible and searchable that content is. Today, content is distributed primarily in the form of Word documents, Excel documents, PDF files, MP3/MP4 audio files, and 3GP/WMV/FLV video files, which are accepted by laptops and most mobile devices.

Blended learning occurs when different learning approaches—traditional and distance—are mixed together. Collaborative learning (for example, when teams or peers learn together) is a blended learning arena where mobile content and the mobile Generation Y will merge. The baseline technology of online learning hasn't yet moved far away from those *who are sitting within the corporate walls* (office to office) on fast broadband connections. However, learning management systems will be requisitioned to provide mobile components to the laptops and mobile devices of the mobile workforce.

This mobile strategy is a small game changer. Enabling laptops and other mobile devices to have access to learning management systems will change how management thinks about, plans, and develops policies and practices dealing with how content is accessed and distributed. For the best mobile team results, have very clear expectations and objectives in using and accessing content. That will drive use and increase team performance. We suggest lowering barriers to access and providing the content that is needed regardless of the device used when possible.

It's not an easy task to manage training for an entire organization. In most cases there is an unlimited amount of requests for content, and this can be a large burden on several departments. *"And now corporate wants us to create a plan for training the mobile folks?"* Providing this kind of training requires more work and more responsibility, and it creates new issues for the managers.

Those companies developing training strategies for the mobile workforce or evolving their existing training platform are very deliberate in answering tough questions regarding leadership, policy, direction, staff priorities, software and hardware technologies, and overall goals for growth. The ecosystem of departments, managers, and technologies will then drive training department initiatives and point them in the direction to meet everyone's needs. If the corporation is investing heavily in a mobile strategy then the training department will also have to receive the support it needs to train faster, more efficiently, with urgency, to solve the needs of these mobile workers.

To motivate employees to want to learn, there should be a clear path of reason and value which answers key worker questions. "Do I, as a mobile worker, have time for any training?" "Will I get some measurable benefit out of it?"

Training must be woven into the culture of the company. Companies need to staff their learning organization with people who are passionate about helping employees be their best. More knowledge and leadership, not less, is an essential part of the equation that the mobile workforce requires. Like ongoing communications, it takes more effort and time to prepare to train and then to actually train a mobile worker.

A picture of the training rooms in the 1980s, 1990s, and even in many industries today, would show training being facilitated through use of a few desks, a few whiteboards, and a computer or two that has access to a highly guarded network which is tough to access. Remember those days? What about the early of days of mobile devices? Were you one of the early adopters who purchased a Motorola DynaTAC mobile phone, otherwise known as the "Brick"?

Fortunately, technology has taken over as we use more online training and virtual classrooms, and we're now getting training via mobile devices such as netbook computers and smartphones. Corporate knowledge bases are accessible by secure VPNs. Mobile employees are likely to recognize the value of training and how it provides the opportunity to perform their jobs at a higher level of results and for advancement within the company. The culture and tone of the mobile team is a direct reflection of the initial training programs offered to all new employees.

The practice of transferring knowledge into the workforce comes down to operating effectively with less face-to-face communications and leading with business objectives in mind. The ROI delivered by the training department is based how well it prepares the mobile workforce to manage and solve issues, many of which are related to the human element and relationships.

Profile of a Mobile Leader

We interviewed an executive from a national insurance company. He is a market claims manager with their national event and catastrophe team, and is responsible for hundreds of mobile workers; at any one time his responsibility could scale to a thousand field agents working within a community that is recovering from a disaster such as a hurricane or some other big destructive event. His teams are called on at a moment's notice to assess damage and help people put their lives back together again. According to him:

One thing that could be constantly improved is how we communicate down to our frontline. You can send an e-mail to everyone, but you don't know if they read them and understand them. It is difficult to measure how well people are getting that type of information. The reality is, if we don't do our jobs right, we put the company at risk. We put the local agents and their relationships with their customers at risk. There is a lot riding on this, so we've got to do it right.

We've got hundreds of people in this mobile workforce, and they are all assigned in small groups. It is kind of like the army. You've got a small group assigned to a sergeant, or what we call a "front-line performance leader" or a "front-line manager." What tends to happen is [that] as we send people out we're analyzing the events that happened to a local market. What could easily happen is a local market needs either a few . . . resources or a great number of resources. . . . While an individual adjuster would report to [his or her] front-line manager, all of a sudden, we want to send the right number of people to the right place, and many times . . . smaller groups get broken up. Immediately they could be assigned to a location where there is no one else from the team—maybe it is a zip code or a small area of a city—the agent represents the company as a lone representative. Maybe now you are working with people from other groups [whom] you've never met before, but you've got to service the customer and account for the work that is being assigned. You've got to do that in a very short period of time. Of course, it is hard to work in a vacuum. It is much easier to work when you've got resources you can rely on. There are folks you've never met before, but they are handling the same type of damage in the same city.

This mobile workforce leader and his company consistently train from the classroom, in the field, and with one another when engaged in an urgent project. This training ecosystem depends on the social component that each person provides, regardless whether she or he is an employee or contractor. Knowing how to access knowledge and then how to use it is the key to solving urgent issues.

Training a mobile workforce to handle a catastrophic situation can minimize the risk for the company and save lives. Agents and managers have to use technology daily to deploy and communicate with teams. They have to develop training policy and procedures so their agents and managers know how to perform their jobs effectively even in dire circumstances. The expectations must be set clearly, as workers often have to work independently at many points during disaster recovery. In such a situation, as in the example that this manager gives, what's essential for these mobile workers is not just the book learning, it's knowing how and when to seek advice from others and how to communicate in a specific environment where the connection to knowledge at times can be very limited.

Are your workers trained well enough to make critical decisions when they are needed in a crisis mode such as insurance agents face often? That's a lot of responsibility placed on the training department. In each disaster event that is faced, such as a hurricane, the need to control expense is very important to companies like these—but the reaction time to provide recovery solutions to customers is *essential*. Training for the entire mobile workforce is critical, measurable, and rewarding to those who solve these often desperate situations.

▶ DEVELOPING TRAINING MATERIALS

Even though we can turn off the dings and buzzing for which our mobile devices are notorious, we know that a barrage of e-mails and text messages, alerts, and reminders—these urgent needs and priorities of business—are awaiting us when we log back in. Your training can get lost in the deluge.

Training people across time and distance poses challenges, perhaps the biggest of which is connecting people and knowledge in a way that makes training stick. The materials should be delivered with clear expectations, as with any training. Motivate the mobile workforce to engage in the training by scheduling time for it when they are on the road; perhaps training can be done during a break, when mobile workers can browse through the latest mobile presentations you have created and sent to them. So, what is engaging mobile training content like?

The Building Blocks of Mobile Training:

The following are the core building blocks for mobile content, as well as questions you need to ask yourself.

- ▶ *Content.* Is it of high quality, short, concise, relevant, and easy to find?
- ▶ *Levels of urgency.* How does the content break through the minutiae? What makes it urgent?
- ▶ *Modality.* What forms are required on the handheld vs. laptop vs. other forms?
- ▶ *Delivery.* Will content delivery be through a mobile network carrier, public or private WiFi, or public Internet connection? Will mobile applications be used or enterprise secure e-mail with dynamic links, SMS text messaging, VPN? These are elements of a baseline strategy that is unique to most companies. Is the content "stand alone after being downloaded or does the content require a connection at all times, or partial?
- ▶ *Frequency.* How and when is this content connected to an existing LMS, CRM, and/or CDN? What is requested or automatically updated?
- ▶ *Feedback.* What is the strategy for real-time user feedback regarding increasing the quality and delivery of content?
- ▶ *Integration.* How does content that reaches the mobile workforce get produced when budgets are already at a minimum?

Challenge: Drive Time

Steve Franklin is the national manager of learning development for CoBank, the largest bank in the Federal Farm Credit System.[11] In rural America, farmers and agricultural cooperatives need stable sources of funding. CoBank finances agricultural cooperatives along with telecommunications, energy production and distribution, and water systems infrastructure projects. He discussed with us how his mobile workforce makes efficient use of their driving time:

Our salespeople are very mobile. When they go out in the field, they are driving for hours through rural America meeting one customer, then the next, through the day. So there's a whole lot of "windshield time." We're trying to find more ways to deliver training for them, to take advantage of that time. The first thing we've done is sign up with an organization that offers the biggest management and leadership in sales titles on audio CD. It works a lot like Netflix, where [customers] can put . . . [audio materials] into a queue that they are sent one at a time. It has been a really good way for them to get some training. So, one of the challenges is . . . to be able to deliver more of our training in that audio format so that [workers] can [take] advantage of that time. We're still working on how to do that.

▶ TECHNOLOGY AND SUPPORT TO CONNECT AND ENGAGE

Here is some good news. All of the required technology to build the supporting infrastructure needed to sustain a mobile workforce is already here today. It will advance profoundly tomorrow. And it will keep advancing daily to protect systems, secure content, and allow for seamless uninterrupted global connections to content and people. Sure, connectivity isn't perfect today: we operate knowing that we might get cut off on the subway or in a hallway, or will have to survive without Internet access on the plane. But our current technology has enough reliability, capacity, and capability to provide the mobile worker with powerful options for conducting business. The learning initiatives and the value of learning within the enterprise today have many different and unique possibilities.

New considerations, with new rules and boundaries, present challenges to existing styles, formats, and even personalities. The mobile workforce is engaged over different time zones, cultures, languages, and Internet connections. Changes are necessary for everyone who touches a mobile team. A mobile support staff quickly learns that their training needs are very different from those who work outside of the brick-and-mortar offices—they certainly are more urgent. The communication style for coaching and helping remote workers solve issues related to security issues, connection and VPN issues, accessing various files, and/or setting up rights management is foundational. It all seems the same—until you realize that many of the issues now involve and are made more complicated by having mobile workers. There is also more responsibility on the shoulders of the mobile worker to solve his or her own issues and to be resourceful enough to do it with efficiency. IT departments are also learning to communicate more effectively—coaching, listening, and helping to solve problems faster.

▶ MANAGERS OF MOBILE WORKERS: HOW TO MANAGE THEIR TRAINING AND GAUGE THEIR NEEDS AND STYLES

Leading members of a *trusted enterprise global team* is a calling, an opportunity, and a challenge for you as a manager. The weak will shiver at the idea, but the confident and strong will embrace it. Leading mobile workers requires doing more, moving more, and engaging in more collaboration than what used to suffice during five-minute meetings. The challenge is to take the time to become the carbon copy of what you expect in the field. Be remote yourself, use the technology, travel, be mobile, be collaborative, and resolve issues 24/7. Then go back to leading.

In 2010 a well-advertised television series debuted, called *Undercover Boss*. On the show, the company CEO "anonymously" showed up in the workforce in the guise of the Average Joe. The workers were completely unaware who the CEO was, and they had no idea of the identity of the new recruit. The objective was to get the head honcho out of the boardroom and into the field where the company operates every day, and where the heartbeat of progress really lives. This deep immersion of the executive into the workforce provided great value to the company, giving the leader a real, appreciable understanding of how difficult jobs can be and what it takes to complete the tasks employees face every day.

What if the training department were to go undercover to see how well the available training is delivered and how the value of the department is scored? This question is interesting for a training department, because often its employees do not come from the departments they serve.

It's an essential accomplishment with measurable results for any training department and company to put training in place for all of its employees, and to meet all of their unique needs by investing in those programs that hit the bottom line.

▶ SUMMARY

Training has transformed in many directions during the last 15 years. In the office, blended learning now includes not only instructor-led training (ILT), but also distance learning delivery. On demand, search and find now, knowledge at your fingertips—these qualities are all essential for the mobile workforce. It's easier than ever to connect and to set up a secure connection to access company systems. With this *paradigm shifter* in place, the mobile worker finally has the opportunity to learn on the go. The mobile workforce will use knowledge not based on a set schedule but will need training, rather, on just-in-time need. And that will take place at the coffee shop, in the airport, on a train, or during drive time when moving from client to client. These changes will take more effort from everyone—but will produce beyond what anyone could have imagined just a few short years ago. The need to hire people who are technically savvy and then to continually prepare them to perform excellently through the coming changes has never been more important.

In this chapter we discussed the need to hire people with the potential to be high performing mobile workers. We described three different kinds of mobile workers—corridor, home-based, and road warrior—and how their training profiles compared with each other. Then we talked about the realities of training mobile workers and how the field of play has and is changing due primarily to the evolution of technology and its application to learning. We finished with appreciation for the demands upon training departments and also their critical role in the future success of the mobile workers of today and tomorrow.

CHAPTER NINE

The Eight Principles Model
Motivational Tools for Mobile Leaders

We use a personal touch as much as we possibly can.
—MCKAY CHRISTENSEN, PRESIDENT, MELALEUCA[1]

Do you really think that simply setting challenging goals and then paying your workforce to achieve them is enough of a motivational strategy for your organization over the long term? It might work in the short term, especially in a tough economy when people are desperate for work, but in the long run if you just depend on a pay-for-performance plan you'll lose your best workers to those who can pay just a little bit more, and you won't get the most out of those who remain. That is especially true in a virtual environment, where your best employees and contractors can find work anywhere in the world.

Just think about it. What do you really want from the people you hire? You want their most creative ideas, right? You'd like them to be loyal, and committed to your long-term success, even in arenas in which they aren't directly being paid to produce. You want them to help others in your company when those people are struggling.

You don't want them to bad mouth the company when they are with others or to sabotage your efforts, right? Are these behaviors important to you? Wouldn't you want the best workers to come to you first when they have employment choices? When employees go above and beyond the call of duty they are exercising what are called "organizational citizenship behaviors"—OCBs—and it takes more than money to earn them from your employees.[2]

What is different about motivating mobile workers from motivating those who are located together? The answer: not much in content, but lots in magnitude. People are human, and what naturally motivates them won't change just because they are using a mobile device. It doesn't matter where we are located, most of us like recognition for our good work, doing what we find meaningful and interesting, and collaborating with people who are fun and from whom we can learn.

Most people become demotivated when they aren't rewarded for their work, when they are in a toxic work environment, and when they don't have the tools to get the job done. Obstacles to completing our work—exacerbated by working at a distance—cause motivation to plummet. We are all the same in what gets us going and what stifles us. Working at a distance just makes it harder to provide the good stuff and to banish the bad. Managers need to take more—not less—time to build the right motivational environment. As Steve Lamont, the CEO of Wifi.com, told us, "I've seen a whole bunch of failed experiments where companies put the wrong technology in the hands of people who weren't ready for it or the job, and it all crashed and burned."[3] How motivating do you think those organizations were?

So, people are motivated and demotivated for many of the same reasons no matter where they are, and therefore it's critical that managers know what those causes are. The mobile workforce is no different than any other group of working people except that distance means that managers are going to have to be even better at applying those motivational principles, and also more committed to applying them on a much larger basis.

▶ THE EIGHT PRINCIPLES OF MOBILE MOTIVATION

Much of this chapter is based on Michael's book, *The Manager as Motivator (MAM)*.[4] It describes seven timeless principles that even the most noncharismatic leader can use to create positive, highly motivating work environments. Since these principles are timeless, they should apply equally well to managing the mobile workforce, right? Well they do, and we share them here with a focus on how they relate to your mobile workforce. We also added a principle, building trust, which is the essential glue that ties all the motivational principles together and is even more important for people working at a distance. Of course, technology supports all eight of these principles in a mobile environment.

Summary of the Model and Eight Principles

There are two important motivational arenas that managers can affect every day. The first is *setting the environment,* and the second is *setting and pursuing goals*. Why do we care about the environment for motivation if we have clear goals, accountability, and rewards? Shouldn't that be enough? The answer is no.

Have you ever worked in a toxic work environment, where people didn't trust each other? How motivating was that? Have you ever felt

The Eight Principles Model
Motivational Tools for Mobile Managers

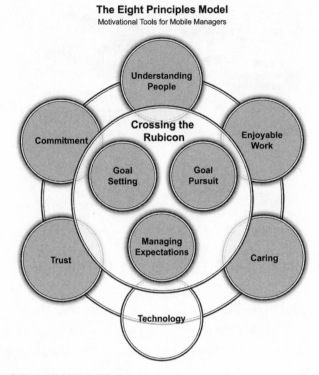

Adapted from *The Manager as Motivator*, Kroth, 2006
Copyright © 2007 by Michael Kroth. Reproduced with permission of ABC-CLIO, LLC.

micromanaged or abandoned? How motivating was that? Have you ever felt as if your organization was treating you like an object—a tool to be used—and didn't care one thing about you personally, or your family, your hopes, or your dreams? How motivating was that? We all know that goal setting is one of the most powerful ways to motivate workers, and we will discuss the keys to goal setting and pursuit later in this chapter, but setting a climate for building long-term, sustainable motivation is equally important.

The first three principles are the *foundational principles*. They set the stage for every other motivational principle to be effective. Our first principle is, *Trust Is the Glue*. We think trust is so important that we have written an entire chapter about it (see Chapter 4). It is all important. It holds all motivational things together, builds synergy, and makes relationships seamless. The second principle is, *The More You*

Know, the More You'll Know What to Do. What it really means is that to be a great motivator you have to understand human nature deeply, and also to understand each person's situation thoroughly. Without that awareness, you will just be shooting in the dark when it comes to trying to get the most out of the people who work for you. The third foundational principle is, *The More You Care, the More They Will Care.* If employees believe you really are concerned about them as people— beyond their worth to you as a tool to get things done—then you will be able to tap into their loyalty, commitment, and dedication to you, the cause, and the organization.

Principles Four and Five are the soil in which motivation is nurtured. Principle Four, *Do What You Love, the Motivation Will Follow,* draws its title from Marsha Sinetar's book, *Do What You Love, the Money Will Follow.*[5] We know that, when people enjoy their work, the motivation comes from the work itself, and the manager has to do very little except support his or her employees. The trick, of course, is to be able to figure out and then provide work that people love to do. Principle Five, *Create Organizational Commitment,* is the last piece needed to set the organizational climate for highly motivated work. Making the commitment to do something is very powerful, whether it is for an organization, for goals, or for a leader. This principle demonstrates how leaders can build powerful commitment to their program, department, or organization.

Creating a highly motivating environment for sustaining motivation through Principles One through Five is just an important start. Creating the milieu without clear, challenging goals that support your organizational success is like building a Corvette and not taking it anywhere. Principle Seven, *Set Challenging Goals,* gets things going. Setting difficult specific goals is one of the most useful, motivating things the manager can do. But setting goals isn't enough. To be successful you have to pursue them even during difficult times. *Crossing the Rubicon* refers to stepping over the edge—making a commitment to goals that are set. Principle Eight, *Build Willpower,* shows how managers can help members of their workforce build the fortitude not to give up. Finally, we know that when people believe in themselves they are more likely to persist longer, give more effort, and set their goals higher. Managers using Principle Six, *Manage Expectancies,* help employees develop a belief in their capability to achieve challenging assignments.

Technology and Motivation for the Mobile Workforce

Lousy technology is extremely demotivating. Have you ever wanted to scream when your fax machine went on the blink? Have you ever pulled your hair out—perhaps literally—when your printer spewed out blank page after blank page after . . . ? Have you ever lost everything on your computer, as we have? Does that make you want to cry like a baby? Weep like a willow? Wail like a banshee? We feel your pain.

We've all been there, and know the consequence of tech troubles. The previous examples are egregious, but little day-to-day obstructions are even more wearing: downloads that take way too long; audio conferences that strain the ears just to make out every other word; videoconferences that seem like convenience store crime tapes (slow-motion blurs with a five-second delay); software that is three upgrades older than your client's. Bad technology erodes energy.

When workers have poor technology to support their work, every piece of the motivational puzzle starts to fall apart. First, no employees believe the organization cares about them or understands them when the tools provided are mismatched dinosaurs. Second, enjoyable work deteriorates into an endurance contest involving long suffering; employee delight is replaced with techno-blight. Third, coping with tools that don't work can sap self-confidence. Fourth, when the equipment doesn't work, performance can be spotty even for the most proficient performers; therefore, trust is eroded—you just can't depend on anyone. Fifth, people are less likely to shoot for the stars and to seek excellence when they know they are going to be dragged down by (or have to drag along) the ware—hard or soft—that's supposed to be lifting and supporting them. Shall we go on? When technology is a drag, so is work.

Alternatively, great technology is exciting. It connects mobile workers seamlessly, provides needed information instantaneously, and supplies virtual work tools at the touch of a keyboard. It makes one feel powerful. It increases the scope of one's knowledge, skills, and abilities. It stretches the realm of possibility—impossible performance plans become promising. It shows that the organization and its managers know what people need to do the work at hand. You want to go fast when you're driving that Corvette. You want to win the gold medal when you have the lightest, fastest, most aerodynamic equipment. There is something about having the best tools to do the job that's inspiring.

Technology comes between the mobile workforce and the job to be accomplished in either a supportive or destructive manner.

▶ SET THE ENVIRONMENT FOR MOBILE MOTIVATION

Principle One: Trust Is the Glue

Think how motivating work would be without trust. You wouldn't believe it when your boss promised a reward for completing a task. When your boss didn't trust you to be working at home instead of goofing off, you'd say, "Okay, I *will* goof off." Twiga Foundation president Patricia Kempthorne says that trust is a key issue with telework. "One of the challenges we hear about telework," she says, "is how to trust somebody, how do I really know they're working if they're not sitting in the office?"[6]

On the other hand, a high-trust environment is the organizational bonding agent that enables motivation to flourish. "There is nothing that motivates, or inspires, people like having trust extended to them," say Stephen M. R. Covey and Rebecca Merrill in their book, *The Speed of Trust.* "When it is, people don't need to be managed or supervised; they manage themselves."[7]

Principle Two: The More You Know, the More You'll Know What to Do

Have you ever tried to find a restaurant without an address or a map? Ever tried making a new dish without a recipe? Without a map or a recipe it's almost impossible, right? Well, then why in the world do you think you can motivate employees without having a deep understanding of them and their needs?

If you really want to motivate people, you need to have a profound understanding both of human nature and of the human situation. Everyone has the same human nature. We have desires, wants, hopes, and dreams. We fear, we avoid pain, we like to belong to a community, and we want to be a part of something greater than ourselves. Great leaders understand human nature. They know that people like recognition, to have fun, and to be rewarded for their work. They know that most people have a need for achievement and autonomy—and that they hate to be micromanaged or to do meaningless work.

Understanding the virtual workforce is even more critical, because you aren't in a position to observe behavior. Bill Avey from Hewlett-Packard knows the value of really understanding his employees. "You need to have [technology] in order to be successful, but then the determinant of whether or not it is successful is whether or not, from a leadership perspective, you somehow bridge that gap and create . . . personal relationships."[8] Those deep relationships form a foundation for understanding employee goals, insecurities, hopes, and personal challenges.

Great leaders also understand that every single person is unique. We have different personalities, are facing different circumstances, and enjoy different kinds work. A young husband or wife with children might be struggling to make ends meet, and so they would be more motivated by immediate rewards. A person closer to retirement might be more interested in more time off or having more social time at work. Some like to sit in front of a computer all day, and some like to work outside. The point is that if you don't know each of your employees, and what his or her motivational needs are, then you're shooting in the dark. Lori Coruccini says, "It becomes very important to understand what's motivating [mobile workers] to do what they do every day and how to increase their performance and productivity by understanding what's driving them and working with the motivators. . . . Everybody is motivated by something different."[9]

You wouldn't try guessing what your customers' needs are, would you? In fact, you probably spend a lot of time surveying your customers, conducting focus groups, tracking their buying habits, and gathering any kind of information you can to determine what will motivate them to purchase your product. Why wouldn't you put the same effort into understanding what would cause your employees to buy into your leadership, your vision, and your company?

That's the reason this principle is so important: *it leverages every other motivational decision you'll make.* Spend time here and you'll know what kind of work your employees enjoy, what kind of goals will excite them, what kind of rewards are most meaningful, and how far they can stretch without giving up. Come up with a generic motivational plan and, sure, you'll do better than if you didn't have one, but you will leave so much potential on the table.

Principle Three: Caring—The More You Care, the More They Will Care

Caring has been studied in the fields of nursing and education but less so in the field of management. Caring, like trust and understanding, has an effect on every other motivational principle. When your employees believe that you care about them, they believe that you have their best interests at heart. They're more likely to want to work for your company, even if they don't have to.

But what does it mean to be caring? Clearly, it is more important to actually care than just to go through the motions, but there are some important competencies managers can develop to demonstrate caring. Co-author Michael Kroth and Carolyn Keeler recently developed what they call the Recursive Model of Manager-Employee Caring.[10] Caring managers, they say, exhibit four important behaviors. First, they *Invite* employees, by being receptive and fully available to them. They pay attention, they show interest, they accept the employee, they're open to new ideas and possibilities the employee suggests, and they're empathetic.

Second, caring managers *Advance* employees. They have a real desire to help employees succeed. They are real advocates for employee success and promotion. They protect employees. They look for employee opportunities to move ahead or into new areas. And they make the employees' goals and plans a high priority.

Third, caring managers *Capacitize* employees. That is, they see the potential in people and help them grow and learn. They give helpful feedback, they encourage employees to grow, they believe in them, and they teach and mentor employees.

Fourth, caring managers *Connect* with employees. Over time, they develop relationships of trust, mutual respect, and an emotional connection with each other.

Virtually Passionate at Citrix Online

Citrix Online sells products such as GoToTraining and GoToMyPC, and its niche is to provide "services to work from anywhere with anyone," from small to midsized businesses. We like Citrix's goal: "We believe in creating products that we ourselves want to use." One of its most popular products, GoToMeeting, is what we used for most of the interviews we conducted for this book, and it worked like a charm.

Mike Mansbach oversees Citrix's global sales and field marketing, and since he joined the company in 2004 the business has grown nearly 200 percent. Fittingly, the company's products enable companies around the world to engage their employees in telework, and Citrix has a mobile workforce itself. "Built into the product set," Mike told us, "is the ability to work from anywhere as productively as if you were sitting in a physical office." Just because its products help mobile workforces around the world doesn't mean that leading its own mobile workforce has been easy for Citrix. In fact, increasing the company's own mobile workforce has been a learning experience for the organization. It has employees who work from home offices and on the road, all over the world. So how does Mike keep his team energized? He explains:

Can you keep a sales team as motivated virtually as if they were physically colocated? Yes, and it's hard. It is harder because you can't look them in the eye. It is harder because they can't look you in the eye. Passion is something that many people need to take them to the next level. To stay motivated. To grow. To stay in the job. Passion is something that is more difficult over distance. You can hear it, but it is much more powerful if you can see it. Those visual clues are very powerful clues. The way we have overcome that is we have put together a series of communications. We have balanced virtual, online meetings, online Webinars, and world-wide .com calls with a set of physical and personal meetings that are anchors for the year. Everything else is done to support that kind of visual, passionate push when we are physically together. Then you get together on an annual basis as an entire group.

The other point Mike emphasizes about motivating a sales team at a distance is "communication, communication, communication." The organization has constantly analyzed and refocused the content of communication and the how of communication. "We can meet globally," he says, "virtually every month. We use our own tools to do that."

Principle Four: Do What You Love, the Motivation Will Follow

When people are doing work they enjoy, the motivation to do something special flows from the work itself. The manager doesn't have to do much more than to make sure the worker doesn't exhaust himself or herself. Ask yourself why people spend hours at hobbies for no money at all. It's because the work itself is motivating—and in fact that's what work should always be but often isn't. When people are doing the work they love they get into a stream that just carries them forward.

It is when people are doing work they don't like because they have to that leaders must design costly incentive programs, conduct hard-nosed performance appraisals, and force acceptable behavior. So let's think what makes work enjoyable for mobile workers.

Mobile workers like work that is challenging and innovative and that gives them a chance to develop their ideas. (Funny, so do members of the traditional workforce.) Mobile workers find it enjoyable to try out new technology, to learn something, and to grow personally and professionally. (So do most people who work across the aisle from their bosses every day.) Lots of mobile workers like to work with caring people with whom they can build professional and personal relationships. So do traditional workers. Mobile workers want to do work that is meaningful and makes a difference. Well, who doesn't? Mobile workers like to laugh and have a sense of play, curiosity, and self-expression in their work. 'Nuff said—have we made the point? Everything that makes work enjoyable to the onsite sales force applies to a sales force operating globally. Everything that makes an accountant jump out of bed in the morning pumped to head to the office does the exact same thing for the accountant jumping out of bed 2,000 miles from her corporate headquarters.

Principle Five: Create Organizational Commitment

When people are emotionally committed to your organization, they want to be there. They're excited about the future, they feel a strong emotional bond with their leaders and coworkers, they have a sense of pride in their work, and they feel that the organization cares about them. There is a sense that they would volunteer for this organization even if they weren't being paid.

Employees can also feel committed to an organization from a sense of obligation. They feel as if they ought to continue to work there, perhaps out of a sense of duty.

Finally, employees remain committed to organizations they don't care about, and about which they don't feel a sense of duty to, because they'd lose too much by leaving it. That loss could be money, benefits, relationships, or even accumulated vacation time. When people feel that they have to stay with an organization simply to avoid loss, they're motivated and committed, but not as much as they would have been if they'd had a strong love of the organization.[12]

Technology changes constantly, but you want your employee loyalty to transcend the latest software update or new gadget. How to do that? Richard Morris, the director of learning technologies for Mission Aviation Fellowship, says you have to depend on deeper qualities:

> *I think the problem is a changing world. [It] makes the importance of a commitment to a vision, the mission, more important. Because, particularly for us, where we're in technology (a part of what we do), it's constantly changing. So I can't make any commitments on things I've done, or things I've built, or products that we've developed, or whatever. We can't hang on to those things. . . . [We need to] focus much more on the people we're serving and their needs and the calling that we have rather than on stuff.[13]*

Principle Six: Manage Expectancies

It's interesting. Two people with exactly the same talents and skills will react differently to a similar challenge. One will set low goals, not try too hard, and give up early. Another will set stretch goals, put tremendous effort into achieving them, and will persist beyond what anyone would expect. One of the biggest reasons the two behave differently has to do with what psychologists call "self-efficacy."[14]

Self-efficacy is the belief an individual has that he or she can do a particular task. If that belief is high, a person is more likely to go to the mat to achieve the goal. If it's low, that person is more likely to give up. So it's in your best interest to help your employees to build it. In that sense you are an "expectancy manager." Your job is to move someone with low or marginal self-expectations to the belief that he or she can climb mountains. You can see sports coaches do that all the time. The talented team doesn't believe in itself, and it just keeps falling on its face every game. A key player expects to drop the pass in critical situations—and so she or he always does. It can take some time, but great coaches move people from feeling helpless and hopeless to peak performers who believe they cannot do anything but win the championship.

Many of your mobile workforce will be very confident. You hired successful people to start with, didn't you? Maybe some are computer jockeys, cocky as all get out. But some won't be. And a person might be confident in one area but not so much in another. That's when you come in. People develop self-efficacy by developing mastery—by learning how to do something well, by watching and learning from successful people with whom they can relate, and by getting encouragement from people whose opinions they respect. Whatever you do, don't just let your employees sink or swim. You might just see some valuable people drown who didn't have to.

Principle Seven: Set Challenging Goals

Goal setting has been rated the most important management theory by organizational behavior scholars. In fact, hundreds of studies have been conducted to increase our understanding of what kind of goals are the most motivating.[15] Almost every human endeavor—sports, career success, relationships, exploration, health—has a better chance of success when the right kinds of goals are established. Without goals, people and organizations meander; with them, amazing accomplishments can be achieved.

It turns out that specific, difficult goals that people are committed to and believe they can accomplish are the most likely to get the most out of your folks (more effort, focused on something that matters, for a longer period of time). Easy goals simply aren't very motivating. Confusing or vague goals aren't either. And people who don't believe goals can be accomplished (they think: it's too much of a stretch to get there, there's not enough management support or commitment, resources are too limited, goals are conflicting, my own ability is in doubt, as examples) give up earlier than they would if they thought they could achieve them.

Goals are organizing mechanisms for the mobile workforce. They keep people focused and working together even when far apart. And they are essential in a ROWE (Results-Only Work Environment). Cali Ressler and Jody Thompson, the authors of *Work Sucks and How to Fix It*, told us why:[16]

> *It's not just one person here and there trying something "outside the norm"—it's large groups of people moving toward one common vision. . . . Team performance is encouraged through the autonomy that's given to employees in a ROWE. Everyone receives the same reward for being efficient—time. Everyone wants their colleagues to experience that reward, so people start cross-training and assisting each other to meet team goals. This all happens naturally through the change—it doesn't need to be forced.*

In a Results-Only Work Environment, if you hit your goals, you can go home; or, if you are already home, you can go play. In a mobile work environment, where people are evaluated by results, goals are even more important motivators than, perhaps, they are in a colocated environment, which tends to evaluate performance more subjectively.

So it's your job as a manager to calibrate these variables for your mobile workforce, given your organization's goals. You may be given fuzzy goals yourself. If so, you have to make them motivating—clear, challenging and yet doable, important—for your own workforce. Whatever you do, don't assign goals that people can't control. Don't give goals related to the weather, to interest rates (unless they can influence them), or to how their boy(or girl)friend will react to anything. Letting the group set its own goals can be a possible plus and a possible minus. People might be more committed to goals they help set, but they tend to set lower goals than a leader would.

Crossing the Rubicon

Between goal setting and goal accomplishment lie commitment and willpower. The stronger the commitment to the goal, the more likely it will be achieved. I can set specific, difficult goals of all sorts until the cows come home, but if I'm not committed to put forth the effort to achieve them, it won't make any difference. Sure, on January 1 my goals are to grace the cover of *People* magazine (why not?), get a date with Angelina Jolie (it could happen), or win the Masters Golf Tournament (who knows what Tiger and Lefty will be up to this year?), but they are irrelevant unless I plan to put the effort (do something wacky to get a magazine cover, get on my hands and knees and beg for a date, invent Flubber-irons for my golf clubs) to accomplish them.

"Crossing the Rubicon" represents the emotional and cognitive leap people take between goal setting and goal pursuit.[17] In 49 BC Julius Caesar's decision to cross a small river called the Rubicon, thereby breaking a Roman law and therefore risking death, has come to represent the process of making an irreversible commitment. After traversing the river he had to move forward, seeking a military victory, because he was already marked for death. Setting goals without committing to them is practically worthless.

Principle Eight: Build Willpower

Willpower takes over when the attractiveness of the goal wears off and the real work begins. Sure, I pledged to do something wacky to end up on the *People* cover, but do I really want to ruin my reputation to do it? Absolutely, I'll beg Angie for that date, but it will take lots of effort just to get past the security guards to get close enough to do that. Yep, I want to win the Masters, but I'm not all that keen on practicing that same chip shot for six hours a day when I could be practicing my beverage-drinking skills.

So even when your employees start out committed, their willpower may wane. They might give up in the face of other goals competing for their time, the adversity they face, or just because they lose interest. That may be okay for them personally, but a manager missing targets for very long will be deadly to the organization. If you are the manager who fails to make targets, your career plans will be short-circuited.

Willpower, also known as volition, is strength of will.[18] How hard will your employees fight to get the job done, to make their targets, or to beat the competition? How much of their soul will they put into thinking creatively, taking personal or professional risks, or stepping outside their comfort zones? There are a number of strategies you as a manager can execute to sustain motivation to get things done.

First, do everything listed in Principles 1 to 7. To the best of your ability, create an environment where your employees are understood, feel cared for, are doing work they enjoy and find meaningful, and are committed to your organization. Provide the kind of support that helps employees believe in themselves and goals that are challenging but doable. This will reduce the need for volition—pure willpower—because there are so many reasons to accomplish it.

Second, get your organization and your employees into the habit of being successful. Start wherever you have to—perhaps baby steps at the beginning—and get people into the habit of expecting to achieve goals and to believe that failure is not an option. Keep your own promises. Habits, over time, become just "the way we do it around here." Develop a culture of accomplishment, not failure, and your employees will fight to achieve the goals that have been set. Mediocrity cannot be an option.

Third, give strategic feedback. There's nothing like being given a goal and then finding yourself flailing away—lost and alone—trying to reach it. Without feedback—reinforcing praise, constructive criticism intended for improvement—motivation nosedives. Each person is different and needs and wants different kinds and amounts of feedback, which is another great reason for spending time on Principle Two, *Understanding*, but everyone needs to know how they are doing. Tracking progress is critical for helping people to keep focused when distractions are all around.

Fourth, support your employees. Encourage them, remove obstacles and distractions, be positive and optimistic yourself, be a good listener, have your antenna out to detect how your employees are dealing with challenges and life, make sure they receive awards along the way, and celebrate successes.

McKay Christensen, president of Melaleuca, Inc., has a motivational approach that very simply incorporates much of what it takes to motivate and to sustain motivation for workers of any kind, mobile or not.

Motivating by Helping People Reach Their Potential

At our company we've found a simple leadership formula that works at all levels of the organization is to create a servant mindset with our 2,500 employees. It involves three steps:

Step 1: Clearly set the vision.
Step 2: Help each associate understand their stewardship role in that vision, and establish a way for them to regularly account for that stewardship.
Step 3: Focus almost exclusively on helping others reach their full potential.

Don't be fooled by the simplicity of the formula. It's extremely challenging to create this type of culture. Once you do, however, your organization, family, or group will never be the same. Imagine being an employee where your manager focuses almost exclusively on helping you reach your full potential. Wouldn't that be energizing?
—MCKAY CHRISTENSEN, PRESIDENT, MELALEUCA INTERNATIONAL[19]

▶ MOTIVATION, WORKPLACE FLEXIBILITY, AND TELEWORK

In 2003, St. Luke's Episcopal Health System in Houston converted its entire medical record payment systems coding staff to a group that works at home. Coder productivity rose 20 percent, and it has remained there since. Supervisors and managers also have flexibility to work at home at times when not needed in meetings. Absenteeism is reduced, recruitment and retention has improved for these high-in-demand workers, and weather emergencies, including flooding and hurricanes, have not interrupted service.

What's your image of accounting firms? Harried accountants and their support staff working unholy hours during the tax season? BDO Seidman decided it would be a strategic business imperative to use workplace flexibility to respond to economic and business cycles; it developed "BDO Flex" so the company can manage more strategically how and when work gets done. Now teams in markets such as Austin, Phoenix, and Nashville work from home and client offices, saving office space costs while at the same time increasing client service. CEO Jack Weisbaum views such flexibility as an opportunity to build business during both up cycles and down ones, and the company views it as a strategic business imperative.

Capital One is one of the 10 largest banks in the United States. At Capital One, employees can choose to work in the same office each day, work at home one to two days a week, or work almost always at home. To be productive at home, they get all the technology they need. Managers have several programs to help them supervise a mobile workforce, including an online Virtual Team Toolkit, and Flexible Work Arrangements Conversation Guides help supervisors discuss requests for workplace flexibility arrangements.

St. Lukes, BDO Seidman, and Capital One are each recipients of the Alfred P. Sloan Foundation awards to organizations that demonstrate business excellence in workplace flexibility. You can find more about these organizations, and many more examples—including countless great ideas for your organization—of workplace flexibility in Sloan's *2009 Guide to Bold New Ideas for Making Work Work.*[20] The Sloan Foundation, in partnership with the Families and Work Institute, the Institute for a Competitive Workforce, and the Twiga Foundation, sponsors a national initiative called "When Work Works." The idea is that workplace effectiveness and flexibility enhances global competitive advantage for the United States, and helps both employees and employers. It's a great win-win.

They have all sorts of data which shows what we already know intuitively: flexible workplaces are more likely to have employees who are satisfied with their jobs, who will stay with their employer, be more engaged in helping the organization succeed, and improve productivity, in an atmosphere of respect, support, learning, and challenge. Flexibility isn't just a benefit for employees, these organizations say; it has real competitive benefits. Take a look at the Twiga Foundation (http://www.twigafoundation.org/) or When Work Works (http://www.whenworkworks.org/) to find much information about flexible work.

Twiga Foundation president Patricia Kempthorne has example after example of how workplace flexibility increases productivity. She believes the principles of motivation work exactly the same for both colocated workers and mobile ones, *except that you have to try harder when working with teleworkers.* "It's not as intuitive," she told us, "when you're not walking by somebody." She says that picking up a phone or sending an e-mail, checking with mobile workers, asking how they are doing, telling them that they are doing great work, and sharing that great work with peers on a consistent basis is critical. "Sometimes out in the field you can feel disconnected," she says. Rewards systems are very important for motivating at a distance, she says, and can be done verbally or through video conferencing.[21]

▶ SUMMARY

In this chapter eight principles for motivating your workforce were outlined and specific applications to mobile workers were illustrated.

The Eight Principles Model was presented, based on coauthor Michael Kroth's book, *The Manager as Motivator*, adding to it the principle of trust and the relationship of technology to motivating mobile workers. In Part 3 of the book, which we move to next, you'll find chapters covering how to keep up with the "phoneses" and how to develop "virtual teams."

▶PART THREE

Technology, Tools, and Teams

CHAPTER TEN

Keeping Up with the Phoneses

Using Metaskills to Keep Pace with the Increasing Evolution of Hardware and Software

The human body is capable of renewing itself in extraordinary ways: wounds heal, brains learn, hands master new skills. All in all, humans adapt in amazing ways to challenges and opportunities. But what about groups of humans working together toward common goals?

Continuous renewal is, in fact, a distinctive feature of the most successful organizations. But why are some organizations so much better at renewing and refreshing themselves than others? How can some companies face the same set of external conditions as their competitors, "changing customer patterns, competitive threats, revolutionary technology developments," but produce something clearly superior?

—JANE LINDER, *Continuous Renewal: Managing for the Upside*[1]

When we chose the title for this chapter, "Keeping up with the Phoneses," we thought we were being pretty clever. After all, it was a nice play on the phrase "keeping up with the Joneses" with a smart mobile technology twist. So after we were committed to the title and had written about half the chapter, we happened to do an Internet search for it. Naturally, we found the Wikipedia entry for "Keeping up with the Joneses," which reconfirmed for us the connection between that phrase—which means keeping up with your neighbors—and the importance of keeping up with your competitors when it comes to mobile technology. (We, of course, also ran into the entry for "Keeping up with the Kardashians," which we hadn't expected, but should have. Research sometimes turns out to be more interesting than you might think.)

We couldn't believe it when we came across a 1996 *New York Times* article called, you guessed it, "Keeping Up with the Phoneses,"[2] so we weren't being as original as we'd thought. The *New York Times* scooped us, which is of course what they get paid to do. And it was a 14-year-old scoop at that.

But let's think a minute—if you *hadn't* kept up with the Phoneses— that is, updated mobile technology in your business or organization along the way, what would you be using today, while the world is walking around with smartphones?

Well, for one, your employees would be lugging around very heavy, clunky mobile phones, if they had them at all, and (if your employees hadn't updated their own personal mobile skills over the years) the odds are very small that they would even know what a text message is. And forget about hooking up to a Wi-Fi hot spot in an airport— your employees would more likely head over to a telephone booth (which, of course, they couldn't even find today) to check in with the office. When they got to the office, your employees would head to the library to look up information that had been printed—if they are lucky—sometime this year, because they wouldn't know anything about Google, which actually began in 1996. Internet searches? Web pages? Blogs? Laptops? Forget it! Your employees would be helpless competing against those in companies that actually did "keep up with the Phoneses."[3]

Like the Joneses next door, businesses down the street and across the seas are doing more than trying to keep up with technology you are using and plan to use. *They are trying to get ahead of you.* If you're thinking about your current idea, most likely so are they. There aren't a lot of technological secrets out there for the average organization. Everyone, with the exception of the technology inventors, sits on a level playing field. We all can use the same technology to help us make decisions, improve processes that help us predict outcomes, communicate with customers, and lower our costs—through, perhaps, a mobile workforce strategy—so that we can improve our ROI. We are all able to communicate faster, across every boundary and barrier, than could have been imagined just two or three years ago. And two or three years from now we'll all be on the same playing field again, just doing things much better, faster, more creatively, and effectively—through the latest toys—than we are today. It is an endless cycle.

That's why we continue to contend that it's not the technology, *it's the people* who can give you the competitive edge. It is true that some organizations will be able to buy research, tools, and systems that others can't, and that will yield competitive advantage for awhile, but it all comes back to your workforce.

It becomes the ultimate virtual video game of technology—a race to who can find the people who can work with technology that is stable and scalable, and that "plugs in." The companies that can define their needs, set their goals, and do their due diligence are the ones that will be the Joneses and reap the ROI first. Often we see the "shiny new wheels" and how, so easily, they can persuade us to action. Your enterprise technology strategy has to be backed by a needs assessment and has to have team buy-in to succeed.

As we send this book off to the publisher, the new Apple iPad is just coming onto the market and all the buzz is whether or not it will be putting Amazon's Kindle out of business. The Apple iPhone changed the smartphone market—and paradigm—not too long ago, and the latest BlackBerrys, Droids, Nokias, and Samsungs are gracing the belts, purses, and pockets of mobile workers worldwide. In the short six months between now and when this book hits the bookstores, the technology will have changed again. It is difficult to give thoughtful advice about which devices to track. Our friend, Kit Brown-Hoekstra, and her coauthors did a great job in their book, *Managing Virtual*

Teams, of listing and comparing the various categories of tools that are available to follow. They include collaborative software, meeting and communication, information broadcasting, information sharing, Wikis, RSS feeds, and "Push" technologies. They describe, in detail, issues related to installation, customization, security, and basic information about the specific tools and how they are used. We highly recommend you pick up a copy of her book for this kind of run down, because it has lasting value.[4]

But do you imagine that some new devices and software have come on the market since their book was published in 2007? Yep, they sure have. How, then, do you Keep Up with the Phoneses? The answer lies in developing mobile technology "metaskills" as a core competency in your organization.

▶ STEPPING OFF THE PLATFORM

What's needed is a strategic platform. Peter DeNagy, general manager of Samsung, put it most eloquently in Chapter 5. He contends that the most important step for an enterprise that is building a mobile strategy is to decide on the platform that will be used as the medium for long-term solutions; that platform will serve as the foundation for strategic mobile workforce decisions. While the mobile device you are using right now will mostly likely be outdated and replaced with something else that's announced in next quarter's press release, the strategic platform continues to serve as a reliable constant in the midst of swirling technological change.

That idea rings true for many of us who have been through this decision tree during the last 20 years over and over again. We get excited about the shiny new wheels, and we always seem to want to move fast toward the things that will change more quickly than we want them too. We need a strategic platform, well grounded, to help us stay the course.

▶ METASKILLS ARE THE KEY TO SUCCESS IN THE MIDST OF CHANGE

Metaskills "transcend any particular job, task, or career."[5] Six of them, for example, which can help to prepare people for careers that seem, these days, to be continually reinvented over one's lifetime, were identified by coauthor Michael Kroth and McKay Christensen in their book *Career Development Basics*: adaptability, learning to learn, the ability to anticipate, creating, problem solving, and interacting. Metaskills are used when everything else—mobile technology, for example—changes around you. They can include knowing—by autonomous learners—how to "access, glean, select, review, and integrate" content into their personal knowledge.[6] They can link what people learn to real problem solving.

These are the kind of metaskills that will also serve mobile workers well. In addition to training your deployed workers in the immediate content—facts, how-tos, latest updates—you need consider developing their meta-competencies, which will have longer-term payoffs.

Organizations develop core competencies, which are sources of sustainable competitive advantage.[7] Smart organizations develop those employee metaskills, or meta-competencies, that stand the test of time. The ones your organization decides are strategic may be different from those of other organizations. At this point we'll look at a short list of competencies that we think are important for organizations that wish to adopt a mobile workforce strategy.

▶ METASKILL ONE: BECOME A LEARNING ORGANIZATION

LearnKey, Inc., is a Utah-based company founded by John Clemons in 1987.[8] The world of learning via VHS video was essentially jump-started by this company. Can you imagine hearing the news in 1992 that Sony and Phillips were set to introduce the write-once optical media CD and player, a technology that would combine the use of audio, text, and graphics and basic navigation logic? (Note there is no mention of *video* even at that point.) So, to stay ahead of the "Joneses," LearnKey was one of the first companies to invest in building and distributing CD-ROMs into the learning market.

The catch? The PC manufacturers had not yet fully embraced the technology. The learning curve was steep with the CD-ROM publishing software, and it took months, in 1992, to actually create content and repurpose the video media that would play back on the PC boxes with Windows 3.1. Showing real-usage case studies was also a challenge. LearnKey found that being an early adopter (three years early, in fact) by charging ahead into the CD-ROM technology game could be both expensive and risky. But once CD-ROM caught on in the mid-1990s and became the default medium and playback device for audio and video media, the investment paid off. In the twenty-first century, technology changes a lot faster, format wars rage on vast battlefields, and the chances of making the wrong choice in technology to support your organization are higher than ever.

Keeping up means making an effort to continue educating your staff and moving the company technology and process forward. In the LearnKey scenario, innovation started the company and pushed the company forward for more than two decades. Early adoption of new technology slowed its pace, as it did with most companies, but it never halted. The need for innovation to move the company forward has kept the company in a strong financial position. A simple film clip showing how technology adoption progresses might start with capturing video content to VHS, then moving to CD-ROM, then to DVD, then to online learning portals, and now to what John Clemons calls "the next big idea," which is delivering the content to any device with complete mobility. It is now a reality that the ability exists to bring content to wherever your "mobile self" is currently located.

Stories from many others are similar to the LearnKey story, and buying technology is only a portion of the expense to keep up with this ever-moving technology shell game. Early adopters are the true risk takers, and sometimes they are credited for bringing new and improved solutions to the world of enterprise.

Every new product must be seasoned by the heat of trial and error. Without this, new ideas would never become the standards that Bluetooth, mobile e-mail, SMS texting, voice recognition, sales force management software, and many others have become. Not every company is willing to take risks, and timid companies generally follow second or third in line to those who know the benefits of keeping up with technology. Keeping up means making some degree of effort to continue to learn and grow. This can be true and gutsy leadership.

If you want to keep up with the Phoneses, you'll have to become a learning organization.[9] What does that mean? How about taking risks? You can't learn without trying. You'll never know if a mobile strategy will work without at least trying pilot projects. To keep up with the Phoneses, president and CEO of Wifi.com Steve Lamont recommends that the mobile workforce conduct pilot tests to integrate people with technology.[10] Tests give the enterprise a good impression of what is involved when trying out a new technology. It's a manageable and reasonable approach to being innovative. Steve says, "The most important thing to get right is the pilot tests. The ones I've seen go the best are the ones that have isolated a group of people who are going to be part of the experiment. By limiting the focus, there are ways to limit the total cost invested and ways to involve people on the front lines in a lot of the design and decisions. *Pilots are a way to fail forward, because you fail quickly and learn lessons from it that help you improve it.* The best programs are the ones that, through piloting, . . . get to the point that people in the pilot say that they love it, and the rest of the organization says, 'We want it—when can we get it?'"

So constant learning, trying new things, learning from those new things, capturing that learning and sharing it across the board, reassessing, and moving forward is a metaskill. Trying new software, testing a new application, deciding to hold pat in one area but to extend in another, all lead to learning. You can't keep up if you're not getting better.

▶ METASKILL TWO: RENEW YOURSELF

If constant learning helps you improve, grow, and move forward, renewal refreshes your organization. Best Buy, the company that began the Results-Only Work Environment (ROWE) experiment that is spreading to organizations exponentially, is also an example of renewal.

Bala Chakravarthy and Peter Lorange outline a four-decade process of evolutionary transformation that has allowed Best Buy to move from a small audio components store in Minnesota to a chain of superstores, then to a low-price consumer electronics warehouse, then to a hybrid low-cost/high-end electronic merchandiser, then to modular stores with knowledgeable in-store consultants who can handle complicated transactions, and then to an organization with a customer-centric and segmented approach, a reengineered customer experience, and more employee responsibility for decision making. Talk about renewal! Best Buy doesn't attempt revolutionary change; instead, it aims for continuous renewal, looking for new opportunities while building new capabilities. Best Buy experiments, explores opportunities, stops experiments that don't work, revises the vision—re-visioning continuously.[11]

Organizations that keep up with the Phoneses are self-renewing. They reinvent themselves. They renew their resources. They refresh their workforce. They not only learn, they innovate.

Innovation is back. Tools are evolving in faster cycles, replenishing old technology with weekly and even daily automated updates. This time frame is much faster than in 1987, when LearnKey got started, and measurably faster than last year. This is a sign of fast, dynamic, on-the-fly technology. Innovation such as this will drive the mobile workforce too. Collaboration technology used on the mobile laptop along with the mobile devices will be synched and able to interchange data on the fly, and automatically. The real private network is the one between our own devices that will connect and share with each other, saving time and effort to keep up with information. How about the *mashup networks* (look up what these are—as part of your own learning organization process—if you don't already know) that supply a combination of high-speed online software that lets us access information anywhere the mobile worker will spend the hours of his or her day?

We are required to have the right *metadata skills*, those necessary to navigate through the computerized technology jungle, to understand the basic components of how to log in to the network, search for data, pass data, sync data, and build data. Mobile workers, as independent as they often are, need these skills to get by when their IT professional is 2,000 miles away. Innovation, renewal, and transformation enable organizations to keep up.

▶ METASKILL THREE: COLLABORATION

Finding executives who can tell their stories regarding designing, using, selling, and producing innovative technology has been a rewarding experience for us and those on our team. Throughout this book project we were able to interview executives who have made a significant contribution to the mobile industry on the technology side and the process of the mobile enterprise.

One of these, Steve Lamont, who we mentioned above, is a well-respected business leader in the space of mobility, broadband, and cellular communications. He follows technology and, as the president and CEO of Wifi.com, he knows how the mobile workforce and the average consumer is living her or his days connected into a wireless world. "I believe that the next big breakthrough is going to be in the area of collaboration," he told us. "Not only do we have dispersed and mobile workforces, but we have the need to solve problems with people that perhaps cross-function within a company, perhaps international, perhaps a mix of customers, vendors, and suppliers. Collaboration is going to be the next big breakthrough."

The collaborative tools, Steve feels, are going to get even more important, but so will the people skills. "We've got to bring the people side of it along with the tools and methodologies," says Steve. "I'm involved in a number of businesses, and when people don't understand how to collaborate, it doesn't matter what the tools are. [Collaboration is] the next frontier."

It makes sense. If you want to keep up with the Phoneses in a virtual world, you'd better know how to work with each other, with outside others, and with others who are across the desk or across the continent.

▶ METASKILL FOUR: CONSILIENCE

Consilience is the idea that there are methods to unify the sciences and humanities.[12] But for Phoneses, consilience represents the convergence of mobility and mobility technology with differing or unusual others. Brian Dolan is the cofounder and editor of MobiHealthNews, an online daily trade journal covering the emerging wireless health space. Right now he's observing the uniting of two industries: the wireless industry and health care. "Every day we are taking the pulse of convergence and keeping an eye on it," he told us.[13] The mobile workforce is uniquely positioned to harvest this idea of pulling disparate ideas or groups or interests together because of its flexibility, the requirements for ever-new and applicable technology, and we already know that the Hewlett-Packards and the Ciscos of the world are studying the human interface with technology. The combination of hard and so-called soft sciences is being played out through the development of commercial products such as telepresence.

To keep up, though, means that your organization has to think creatively, nonparadigmatically, and opportunistically all at once. Who and what can benefit by "jumping together" in new ways? You can bet that your competitors are looking at every possible combination that will move them to the top of the heap.[14]

▶ METASKILL FIVE: ASSESSMENT

We'll end with this skill, because it often gets underestimated (possibly because people and organizations don't have good assessment skills?). Hone your cost/benefit analysis skills so you can make good purchase decisions about adopting new mobile devices or buying into new applications. Sensitize your abilities to review critically all the new devices the marketers are trying to sell you. How well do they fit your long-term platform? What's their life cycle? Learn to do this deeply but also quickly, like a rancher buying cattle. You need to be able to make quick decisions based on solid assessment of the pros and cons involved.

Technology has infiltrated our companies through our employees' interest, through our phone systems, mobile carriers, Internet providers, hardware vendors, and software licenses, just so we can compete and stay current. Ten years ago we only had to worry about the software version that would get us started, such as operating systems and software for word documents and spreadsheets. Today there is a blend of technology that updates *on the fly*, automatically, pinging us to tell us what the software is going to do. We have a choice; we can say "no," but eventually the software is back asking again, just like the cable guy who knocks on your door to sell his service of cable—eventually everyone has cable. You have to be able to assess and decide based on long-term benefits, not just because something looks sexy at the time.

▶ KEEPING UP WITH THE PHONESES WITH UBS FINANCIAL SERVICES

With the recent focus on the financial nerve centers around the globe, we were interested in interviewing a global company that reaches into many areas of financial concerns within business and consumer fronts. We met with Steven Erickson, the global program head of leadership and management development programs for UBS Financial Services. The company has over 70,000 employees in over 50 countries representing wealth management, retail, and commercial banking services. Steven works in the UBS Business University, which is on track to become a virtual university across the globe. We met in person at Steven's office in Stamford, Connecticut. We also interviewed him by phone, e-mail, and by Web conferencing using GoToMeeting conferencing tools. We were particularly interested in knowing how UBS is adopting mobile management processes and the policies that drive a global company.

Steven shared his ideas and concerns about the security of data and how mobile workers access proprietary content: "Because IT security is such a huge issue for our firm, we have really tight security policies. You can't even access popular video sites like YouTube from your computer here within our offices; many sites are blocked. Because we are a financial services firm, we are very careful [about] who and what we allow into our network." Steven pointed out that this type of policy runs at odds with some of the younger people coming into UBS, who are already used to having information at their fingertips. "We often have to get those sites cleared so that they can get access to it or put the video on a site that they can access without having problems. It does take a little more work. I think we're not the only ones in our industry with this challenge."[15]

It is clear that UBS is staying ahead of the technology game by taking careful steps concerning the security and policies that drive its mobile business component.

▶ KEEPING UP BY KEEPING ON

The ability to execute, with persistence and character, is a metaskill that we didn't mention above but that we want to end with. The ability to succeed, over time, depends on sticking it out—like LearnKey did during its difficult, risky forays into new technology during the 1990s. It means having the character to stick to the platform and the strategic direction when short-term, attractive technology choices glitter, demanding you buy them when you know they are fool's gold. It means carrying out a strategy for developing metaskills such as learning, renewing, consilience, collaboration, and assessment.

You can keep up with the Phoneses, the Joneses, and the Kardashians, if you want. You just have to have a strategic plan, a platform, and keep on keeping on.

▶ SUMMARY

Keeping up with the Phoneses has more to do with the metaskills that will serve you over time, than with making sure you have the latest technology. In this chapter we shared five metaskills—out of any number of others you might find advantageous—that you may wish to consider integrating into your mobile workforce strategy. Metaskills are a key part of your platform—they are anchors for you when everything else is changing, and they allow you to evolve strategically, rather than pell mell.

In our next chapter we cover virtual teams, and we start out by comparing them to massive online games like *World of Warcraft*. It's time to saddle up your avatar and get into the mix. Talk about collaboration—we're just getting started!

CHAPTER ELEVEN

Developing Your Virtual Team

Reconfiguring the Process

We spend a lot of time playing video games and really enjoying it.
—Zev Barsky, senior manager of Customer Support,
LEGO Universe[1]

If you've ever played the online game *World of Warcraft* (known as *WoW*), you know the potential of virtual teams.[2] *Addicting* is a term one can use to describe *WoW*. Another is *fun*. Another is, dare we say it, *collaborative*. When you join *World of Warcraft*, which has millions of players, online, all over the world, you create a character avatar, which you control. You enter into a fantasy world where you engage in combat with other players, explore new territory, gain skills and abilities, develop expertise in your profession, and often team up with other players to pursue more challenging goals than you could by yourself. You might create an alliance with another avatar (who in reality is living in another part of the world, who you will never meet). You might go into battle with an entire group of people from all over the real world acting through their *WoW* avatars. Does this sound anything like your job?

With over 11.5 million monthly subscribers, WoW has around 62 percent of the MMORPG market. What are MMORPGs, you say? It stands for massively multiplayer online role-playing games, which have become a worldwide phenomenon.

These online games often have tools to facilitate player communication and require varying levels of teamwork during parts of the game as players protect others from dire situations or help them build wealth, skills, or community. Relationships between players can range from short meetings to highly structured and organized groups. So fascinating is the nature of these virtual relationships and interactions between players that they have led to academic research by psychologists and sociologists.

Massive online games don't have to be for adults, however. Remember playing with LEGO bricks when you were younger? LEGO bricks are little interlocking plastic blocks of various colors such as red, yellow, or blue that kids can put together in various ways to create creatures, buildings, people, or other imaginary situations. Now the company is creating a LEGO massive online game, targeting a much younger eight- to-thirteen-year-old audience than games such as *WoW* have.[3] Zev Barsky is a key player on the team LEGO has put together to create this virtual universe. Interestingly, he leads a virtual team himself.

▶ ZEV BARSKY

Zev is no stranger to the world of commercial communication technology and performance management. Earlier in his career he managed a team for an electronic entertainment company, AirPlay Network, Inc., which designed and produced interactive mobile and Web games for organizations such as Sony, CBS, NBC, the National Football League (NFL), the National Basketball Association (NBA), and Facebook. At the same time he was building a complete customer support organization for the company. He's also been a senior manager for America Online, heading up interesting initiatives and teams responsible for developing performance management metrics for AOL's 6,000 internal call center employees, creating and implementing a new management structure at seven internal and two international call centers, and developing a leadership process program for call center management staff.

When we caught up with him, he had assumed the leadership for the design and implementation of a strategic customer service approach for LEGO Universe, which is an entirely new business model for a company started 94 years ago in the shop of a Danish carpenter named Ole Kirk Christiansen. The word *LEGO* is an abbreviation of two Danish words that together mean "play well." The company of 2010 hopes the youth market will soon spend a lot of time *playing well* in the LEGO virtual global online community.

Zev has operational teams on three continents in six locations. "I report to a woman who sits in London. I'm experiencing both ends—managing remotely and being managed remotely," he points out.[4]

His role is to manage the consumer services experience in its entirety for the game. How does he build his global team? "We spend a lot of time playing video games," he told us, "and really enjoying it."

It turns out that building community is a key leadership role for virtual teams, and it involves setting expectations and the tone for building those relationships. Zev, located in Colorado, made sure, for example, that everyone in the LEGO Universe who needed to be invited to his team's holiday party was included in the festivities and the holiday presents even though they weren't physically there. He encourages social network communication not directly related to work. For example, his team has a sharepoint location called Fun and Funny, where they can post stories, anecdotes, and pictures from the Christmas party. "It's a matter of making that space for the social networking side of it and creating some personality behind the people you don't see directly, face to face, very often," he told us. The key is to build remote relationships as much as possible, and the trick there is to facilitate personal interaction.

Sometimes the simplest things build a team and emotional commitment to it. At LEGO there is a bucket of LEGO bricks at every table, and people are encouraged to play with them. So they do. During meetings everyone's hands are in the buckets while they are talking, and they are putting bricks together. Having a sense of play increases community.

It helps to have a strong and beloved brand. "When people come in," says Zev, "they see the company through the eyes of themselves as a child and the really positive experiences they had growing up. LEGO has made a point of taking that positive image externally and making sure that internally they mirror the same tenets like quality and creativity. When people look at the company and want to develop an emotional attachment, the corporate identity—our brand internally—is really solid and strong." So, folks at LEGO play games.

Collaborative communication builds community and trust. But how to do that? "It's easy to start off with a generic answer of keeping communication lines open, and that seems like the obvious starting point," Zev says, "but what I've found to be really successful is taking that principle and actually finding real-life tools to use to open communication channels—especially the digital channels."

The basic starting point for Zev's team is video conferencing. People can get together and see each other's faces during those hours of the day when their times overlap. Having shared workspaces, which are team based, is also important. Communication opportunities that don't depend upon being online at the same time gives everyone the opportunity to put their ideas out and get a reaction to them, a process that matures as a team develops over time.

As the team evolves, creative problem solving can become easier. Zev tells about a particular process that wasn't functioning very well. The team started tossing solutions around via e-mail, but they found that approach wasn't working. Then they went to their sharepoint location and used it like a message board. Messages could be posted and everyone's replies could be seen. The team started a brainstorming thread, looking at solutions, and in three days that brainstorming process solidified an effective strategy to develop a new process from a very loose set of ideas and goals.

Zev thinks of these kinds of communication processes, supported by shared workspaces, as a process for developing a kind of *shared thinking space*. Organizational development consultants try to develop creative solutions to problems by "getting everyone into the same room." Managers such as Zev can now do that virtually by using video conferencing, shared desktops, and electronic communication tools such as whiteboarding.

And, about face-to-face meetings, Zev thinks it's important to have them even if they're only held once or twice at the beginning of the relationship. "It really changes the interpersonal contact that you have with people once you have a little bit of shared physical space," says Zev.

▶ BRIAN HOFFMANN

We visited Brian Hoffmann, Hewlett-Packard's (HP) R&D project manager, at the HP facility in Boise, Idaho.[5] As we were leaving the meeting room, he took us across the aisle to the HP Printer Museum. We walked around the room, looking at the earliest printers the company had developed at the Boise site, and it was easy to remember how difficult it was to print just a few years ago what seems so simple to print today. Somehow it seems easier to let go of outdated appliances or vehicles or office equipment than it is to give up outdated organizational models. If anything is true today, it is that today's fanciest LaserJet printer will be a relic sitting in HP's printer museum five or ten years from now. If anything is true today, it is that our ability to work virtually in teams will be different five or ten years from now as well.

Historically, organizational innovations have come from the observations of gurus such as Peter Drucker, from business leaders such as Alfred Sloan of General Motors or Jack Welch of General Electric, or from entrepreneurs who have developed and used technology to facilitate change. Now, it seems as if the inventiveness of high-tech organizations such as HP and Cisco, which provide organizational solutions that business leaders can't even imagine, and the adaptive, viral nature of other shared forms of interaction such as social media (enabled by emerging technology) are the drivers fueling new organizational forms.

Brian, like the baritone sax he loves to play, can support the overall ensemble of his team's work, or he can take the jazz soloist role—setting the pace and improvising the tune for others to follow. He's an R&D project manager leading both a Boise colocated architectural and technical team, and a virtual team of more than 25 onshore and offshore people responsible for delivering programming code for HP projects. Have you ever tried managing software engineers in the same building, much less managing those sitting in Bangalore, India, halfway across the world? We, the authors, haven't, though David has a team he leads that is located in Lithuania. (Michael has trouble leading a horse to water, much less making her drink.) Brian—who is a veteran virtual team leader with a long track record of stellar productivity—excels at it. The following are some of the ways he does it.

Strategic Communications

Bangalore's time zone is 11½ hours ahead (12½ hours during winter months) of Boise's, so team meetings generally split the time difference between the two locations. There are two extended team meetings between the two locations every week, and Brian also has a meeting just with his manager, for additional coordination. He also meets with two very key people at ten o'clock the night before the management team meetings, so they are prepared for key conversations; while Brian is sleeping, these folks can be working on anything that emerges from that meeting. That's the minimum, as he is also often in contact with them online through instant messaging.

He calls it having multiple channels of conversation. He might have an extended, public team meeting, followed by a private, managerial conversation. When all else fails, he says, "the third conversation that we employ is to grab them by the shoulders and say, 'You need to get them to understand this.' I would call that a family conversation." So he is very flexible and communicates often to keep the team on track. "If I need to absolutely ensure that a message needs to be communicated," says Brian, "I will seed all these channels intentionally, purposefully, because I know they're effective. Or I'll use them to varying degrees." He is a veteran, successful manager who uses every possible communication tool he can, and in a savvy way.

Relationships

Another strategy Brian has learned from experience is to spend extended colocated work time together with lead people. Because HP has long-term projects, the relationships between people and their understanding of the project require long-term development. One of Brian's most important people is a technical lead who works in Bangalore. This person worked over two years on site in Boise, and now he's worked seven to ten months intensively with the team; Brian thinks he's high-potential management material. "You form a way of being able to communicate effectively to know what the other person needs to be most effective. It really is about effective communication, not necessarily quantity or frequency."

It's common, he told us, when working with contractors, for people to rotate assignments quickly within a year or two. For HP, long-term relationships are critical, because it takes 15 to 18 months just to develop the knowledge and competencies needed to understand and to be effective in a software environment involving millions of lines of code and five or six operating systems. "A year for us is barely getting started," he says. So issues of trust and respect have a huge impact on the team's ability to be successful. In fact, Brian believes that his contractor team is most successful when all parties consider their relationship to be a partnership.

Partnership

HP has been working with the vendor for nine to ten years, which provides contract employees for Brian's team. "It's not a contract," he says. "It's a partnership. What's the distinction? For us, a partnership means that if we encounter unanticipated difficulties, we have to challenge each other to lean in and help each other at whatever the need or time may be and on any level, be it program, technical, financial. We have the kind of relationship that we are willing to flex our respective corporate parameters in order to get what we need done." A partnership is a deep commitment to each other that involves respect, mutual support, and a desire for each other's success over the long term.

Put It into Gear

"We have normal gear, first gear, and high gear, which is working around the clock when we have problems," Brian says. The nice thing about having teams in different parts of the world is that people can be working on a problem for 12 hours and then kick it over to the other team for two hours, so they can sleep. So some group of people is working on the problem continuously for 24 hours until it can be solved. One advantage of having teams located on the opposite sides of the world is that work can be done all the time, if necessary. "When we work around the clock—I call it . . . 'throwing the football back and forth every 12 hours'—is really better not face-to-face because it's really clear what you start with and what you need to return. There's no confusion."

Keeping the Team Focused

On projects as long-term and as complicated as the one Brian's team works on, it's easy to get sidetracked. He spends much of his effort making sure that people are spending time on the right things. He says, "I try to make sure that they have a list of operating priorities they can ask themselves throughout the day: where is this I'm working on in terms of the overall value to this program this month?" He is continually recalibrating where the team is and where it's going. At the end of every four-week cycle they check progress and decide if they need to modify what people are doing. That way, they don't get way down the road and find out that people are on the wrong track.

▶ THE VIRTUAL TEAM CONTAINER

A "container" is the environment most effective for producing dialogue, according to Peter Senge, the author of *The Fifth Discipline Fieldbook* and other seminal works in the field of organizational learning.[6] The container encircles all of the qualities necessary for people to focus group attention, suspend their assumptions, and to seek understanding. It holds "human energy so it can be transformative rather than destructive."[7] Another metaphor he uses is that of a cauldron, which takes potentially destructive molten steel and surrounds it so that it might be transformed into something useful. Similarly, William Kahn uses the term "holding environments" to describe the close relationships that help people during difficult times.[8]

Teams, whether they be colocated or virtual, can also be considered to be held within a container. Traditionally, a functional work team has resided in a central, physical location. The accounting department is all on the fourth floor, for example, and engineering is on the sixth floor.

The container in those cases, quite literally, is the building itself. The team can move within physical boundaries, has designated lunchrooms where people can congregate, perhaps gym facilities where people can work out, and meeting rooms for, well, meetings. Everything is held inside the container, like water in a jar. In this container, relationships are more likely to develop with people who are located closest to you, and even working on a different floor means working relationships are likely to also be more distant, serendipitous, and connections less likely.

The container for a virtual team is much different. There is no physical shell to constrain where people interact. In fact, distance has no impact on relationships at all. Instead, like the atom, other natural forces keep energy contained and powerfully focused. Like the atom, when the balance is off, destructive results can occur. Like the atom, the possibilities for interaction and new combinations with virtual teams are almost endless. It's symbolic that it's the electric charge of the atom and the electronic technology of the virtual team that helps keep each together.

What Contains a Virtual Team?

At the center of a virtual team is its purpose. Everything revolves around that. Close, trusting, synergistic, and interactive relationships targeted at measurable results keep the team from spinning off in dif-

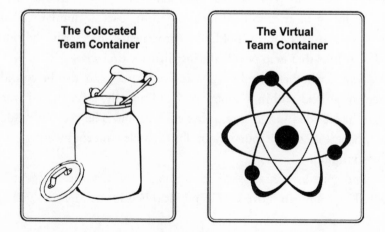

ferent directions. Trust is the glue that keeps it all together, and technology is the lubricant that keeps everything spinning. So what holds a virtual team together is analogous to what holds an atom together—an electric charge pulls everything together by enabling the telecommunication needed to build bonds between people located perhaps half a world away, to share knowledge among those team members, and to energize performance.

▶ THE VIRTUAL TEAM DEVELOPMENT PROCESS

As the use of virtual teams becomes more and more pervasive, researchers and practitioners have increasing experience and research to help us understand how to facilitate their development.[9]

Bruce Tuckman's time-tested and oft-cited process—forming, storming, norming, performing, and adjourning—has been easy to remember and to use as a reference when leaders consider how to facilitate the development of high-performing teams.[10] Virtual teams, however, are relatively new as a widespread phenomenon and provide new challenges for leaders. While the basic team development processes remain essentially intact, leaders of virtual teams need to emphasize different things at different times. In fact, to be effective, leaders should consider starting the virtual team development process *before* the actual team is formed. The virtual team development process described here can be considered a way to call attention to key tasks of virtual team leaders.

Tuckman has said the team development process starts with forming and proceeds through adjournment. We'd like to suggest a reconfiguration—or at least different emphases—for the successful development of virtual teams. We start with "norming."

Norming

Effective team leaders who are creating teams in any situation may begin the norming process well before the team is even formed. Tuckman

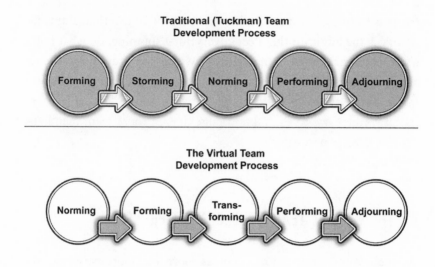

Traditional (Tuckman) Team
Development Process

Forming — Storming — Norming — Performing — Adjourning

The Virtual Team
Development Process

Norming — Forming — Transforming — Performing — Adjourning

has said that the norming process occurs as new standards evolve, new roles are adopted, and cohesiveness develops after the team forms and storms. That's true, but team members often begin to understand team expectations even before joining the organization. Good leaders often set standards before accepting a new member into the team. You know what you are getting into when you decide to join the Navy Seals, for example, and you start to change or adapt your standards of performance well before you ever step foot on the base.

Starting the norming process for virtual teams is even more important. Often virtual teams come together very quickly for specific purposes, and leaders must be prepared to be specific about expectations for communication and collaboration, including frequency: when to use particular types of communication, such as e-mail, voicemail, instant messaging, collaborative tools, or video conferencing; what the quality and timing of deliverables will be; how conflict will be resolved; how meetings will be run; and what processes the team will use.

Team performance expectations also need to be set before the team is formed. During that time the leader negotiates with management about what the specific mission of the team will be, what is to be accomplished (those decisions have to be set before the team is created), and how success will be rewarded. Now choices can be made about the type of tasks that will have to be accomplished; a plan of work; the size of the team required to meet those goals; and the knowledge, skills, and abilities that will be needed from team members.

Leaders of colocated teams should consider these issues too, but the emphasis on norming for virtual teams should be considered right at the very top and first part of the list. As leaders think through these issues, they will also be considering how to implement their choices. For example, if the leader wishes to use a particular meeting protocol, he or she should prepare that before the team is even formed. With particular communication expectations, the leader should have the protocols, equipment, and software ready and available before the team is even formed. Unlike a colocated team, where leader might be able to fake it for a while, a virtual team can get stuck, lost, or hopelessly behind very quickly if it doesn't start right.

Forming

The norming process continues as members are selected for the team and are introduced to other members. The virtual team leader selects team members (either hiring, contracting, or assigning them) based on what they can contribute to accomplishing the team goals. As in all organizational work, this selection process is critical. Having considered norms and expectations, the team leader can then consider members who are likely to fit. Do they collaborate well? Are they dependable? Do they share work values that will support team standards? Do they work effectively with people who speak different languages (if that's a criteria)?

When interviewing potential team members, the team leader can share expectations right up front, thus starting the norming process before people are even selected. When negotiating for time commitments, the team leader can share the schedule and deliverables, the tools that team members are expected to use, and how performance will be evaluated.

Most, but not all, people we've interviewed and everything we've read or experienced tells us that having face-to-face meetings at the start of developing a team is crucial. Some people, such as Brian Hoffmann, think that spending extended time in the same location is important, especially for teams that are going to exist for several years. Others believe that an initial meeting in person, with face-to-face meetings on some regular basis later on, is enough. Sometimes virtual team members never meet, and those teams still work out very well.

Author Kit Brown-Hoekstra, who has significant experience both observing and leading virtual teams, (see "Keys to Developing Virtual Teams" page 240) thinks the kickoff meeting is critically important. Even when that meeting can't be done in person, which is the preferred method, getting everyone on the same page is essential. Asking all team members to introduce themselves and talk a little about themselves and their role in the team seems like a small thing, but it helps people know whom to go to and for what purpose, lets the manager know if the person understands her or his role, and begins to build relationships. Tuckman has described the forming stages as one of orienting to the team by testing boundaries and establishing relationships, which is consistent with how we look at forming in the virtual team development process.

Transforming

As the team begins its work, the process of moving from a group of individuals to a team begins in earnest. It is really a "re-forming" process through which a group of individuals are transformed into a team whose members consider themselves to have a shared identity. As the team works together, the norms that the team leader pre-established are practiced and evolve as the group settles into a way of interacting that works for it. This is, essentially, then also a re-norming process—taking the leader's expectations and transforming them into group expectations. Processes are adapted, delegation of responsibilities and timelines change to fit the growing maturity of the team and the changing external situation, and improvements are made as the team learns new ways of accomplishing tasks. When things go well, the team develops comfortable habits of working together. It's the team leader's job to keep performance habits at high levels.

The more experienced the individual team members are in working virtually, the more able they are to contribute to this transforming process because they have had occasion to work in many situations. Therefore, there are more contributions (ideas and examples) they will be able to make to improve team effectiveness. In such a situation, an experienced team leader will find ways to encourage more experienced members to mentor, or at least be role models for, members who are less experienced. And every good team experience provides opportunities to learn for all members.

Perhaps the most important crucible for transformation comes from having challenging goals that the team can only achieve by working together. It is by crossing difficult waters together that a group of people becomes something much more.

Keys to transformation are relationship building, communicating, organizational learning, problem solving, and beginning to develop a team identity. The team leader needs to make sure that everyone feels included and that no one is isolated. After a while, members of the team will take over that role for the team leader, and he or she will only have to support and occasionally facilitate member inclusion and participation. Relationship building involves building community, interpersonal relationships, and trust; it creates bonds between people that will well serve the team during times of crisis, and will last in many cases long after the team itself has disbanded.

The importance of communicating is an important theme in this book, and it is essential for team development. Experienced managers of mobile workers, such as Zev Barsky and Brian Hoffmann, are constantly communicating with their virtual team members, and in a variety of ways. Communicating helps team leaders who may be thousands of miles away to anticipate problems that may be emerging. Communicating helps team leaders provide feedback and keep members on track. Communicating reinforces important norms such as collaboration, respect, and initiative taking.

A big part of team development, which virtual teams can sometimes do much better than colocated teams, is learning together. By using virtual offices, knowledge management tools, and virtual problem-solving tools, such as whiteboards, that colocated teams may underuse, virtual teams can communicate better; align themselves more quickly; be more transparent; and track, build upon, and save knowledge more effectively than people on the same floor are likely to do. By developing shared knowledge, virtual teams begin to develop an identity of their own, because they now have something they've created together, along with the experience of having created it.

The transforming process also includes what Tuckman calls "storming." This is when, as the new team is being developed, conflicts arise for whatever reason—power struggles, miscommunication, personality differences, or incompatible job assignments. These can wreak havoc with any team. Virtual teams can be more vulnerable to this storming, because people aren't always immediately available to resolve the problem early on, and people can misinterpret communications coming through a medium such as e-mail, voice, or even video communications that is less rich than others. Sometimes, even with the best of intentions, team members have a difficult time because they are working with people from entirely different cultures, backgrounds, or experiences. If you have established very clear expectations up front, many of these problems can be dealt with readily. If people have already established a level of trust, and know people not just as tools to get the job done but as real people, then understanding becomes easier and more intentional.

The nature of virtual teams, which are generally set up to share information transparently, with explicit behavioral results for individual members (making it impossible to hide or goof off while everyone else is pulling the cart), can actually mitigate this storming phase.

The notion that virtual teams can be more effective than colocated teams goes for problem solving as well. Shauna Wilson, author of *InterneTeaming.com: Tools to Create High Performance Remote Teams*, told us that a face-to-face environment is actually worse for problem solving than a virtual team environment.

Problem solving can be easier for Virtual Teams

Shauna Wilson is the president of Amazon Consulting, Inc., and conducts quality management system audits for companies all over the world, including Europe, China, and across the United States. She was one of the first to do so online. After working at Hewlett-Packard for 18 years, where she developed her expertise in quality management, she formed her company and is an expert in working with virtual teams. One of her particular skills is helping virtual teams solve problems, and she has developed a suite of simple tools that teams can use. She even thinks—contrary to what conventional wisdom suggests—that problem solving can be much easier in a virtual setting than in a face-to-face environment, and she gives a great example.

"This is a group of people who have worked together for 20 years," says Shauna. "They don't like coming to their face-to-face meetings. They've got two people who really [have dominated their meetings]. They haven't heard from different people—ever—because they just get overrun by these two people. I put [this group of people] into a virtual meeting and got more information out of them than I've ever gotten before."

One of the tools she used with this group was something she calls a "daisy diagram," which is a structured brainstorming tool used to generate ideas. (You can download one from her Web site at www.interneteaming.com.) The meeting turned from a content dump, where everyone sat passively, into a collaborative process, where people were now sharing information. "Now you hear from those silent people. This team actually finished their project in half the time and had twice the results they expected, because they heard from those other people. It worked out great." The interesting point is that during this process this team was in the same building at the same time, sitting at their desks, but they were using Shauna's virtual online tools.

She has taken tools used for quality processes and redesigned them for virtual teams. One of the mistakes teams make, she thinks, is that they bring their old meeting habits into a virtual environment. She uses tools to make the meetings more active. Some collaborative whiteboards, she says, allow everybody to write at the same time, for example, so everyone is participating in drawing diagrams, flowcharts, and whatever is needed to get people actively working in the meeting itself. Another tool she uses is something she calls GROW, which stands for Gap Analysis, Research, Organize, and Wealth. The process is a simple one for the team to figure out what they want to take away from their meetings. Having effective meetings is very important, she says, and she has created tools to use for effective online meetings, including sample meeting agendas and online meeting competencies for virtual teams.

Her book, *InterneTeaming.com*, is a handbook for virtual teams, and has tools and processes that cover everything from assessing team needs, to developing a team culture, to problem solving.

When you talk to her, you can tell she is a true believer in managing virtually. She says: "If you've got a virtual relationship, we're to a point now where you have friends that you like better online than you do in person." [11]

Performing

The process of transformation occurs while the team performs its tasks. At this time the relationships are formed, understanding is achieved, problems are solved, and goals are accomplished while members are working both independently and together. Team leaders aren't just focused on developing a team, but develop that team for a purpose: getting things done. When the team and the leader have done a good job of setting, evaluating, and adapting goals, processes, and ways to work together, performing becomes less a matter of harnessing the horses and more a matter of just keeping everyone pointed in the right direction.

As the virtual team works toward its goals, team leaders have especially important roles in being gatekeepers. Team members' attention, because they are separated physically, can be easily diverted to colocated projects. Other managers may assume they can impose on team members' time just because they are sitting in the same building as the managers, even though the team is currently working on a project 1,000 miles away. At this point the team leader earns her keep, acting to remove obstacles in an individual team member's way, making sure the team has enough resources and the right kinds of ones to do their job, and keeping team members focused on the task at hand.

Performance management is particularly key here. Both electronic mobile performance management systems and Results-Only Work Environment systems (ROWE) (see Chapter 6) help keep leaders on top of how the team is doing and reduce concerns about not making targets. As performance becomes more and more related to results and less to just showing up, the leader's time is dedicated more to supporting the team and its individual members, in its effort to reach goals, and less to monitoring their time. Feedback, which is important for motivation and for keeping people on track, is essential to manage performance; it is facilitated with explicit desired results, which include intermediate target deadlines.

When rewards are for team performance, as well as for individual performance, then there are incentives for working together. Collaborative work is an important norm, if a team is going to be successful; it has to be established for the team early, before the team is formed. This is done concretely in the preteam stages, when rewards are set up to support this kind of behavior.

Adjourning

One of the goals of any organization—and any leader—is to build organizational capacity. Therefore it's important for teams that have completed their task to learn from their activity and also to continue building the opportunity for future collaboration. In a virtual environment, teams can be formed and disbanded quickly, and you never know when you'll have the opportunity to work with someone again. So it's in everybody's best interest to maintain relationships, even after the team has adjourned.

▶ KEYS TO DEVELOPING VIRTUAL TEAMS— KIT BROWN-HOEKSTRA

Kit Brown-Hoekstra has worked with virtual teams all over the world. She is an award-winning author and recently coauthored *Managing Virtual Teams: Getting the Most from Wiki's Blogs and Other Collaborative Tools*. Her book is a "how-to" that gives detailed instructions on everything from project planning, to collaborating in troubleshooting, to conducting reviews, to evaluating virtual team tools. We asked her what was most important for leaders to know about managing virtual teams.[12]

You Can't Be Expert in Everything

Technology is changing too fast for anyone to keep up with all of it. "The key is [to surround] yourself with people who are savvy in certain areas and who have the knowledge that they can take and extrapolate into a strategic perspective," says Kit. Social media may be the hot button now, she thinks, but that will change with the next big thing. Managers, especially high-level ones, need to know what the tools can do, and what their limitations are, so they can manage their team more effectively. Nevertheless, they should trust the tools gurus on their teams to create an effective virtual work space.

Have Good People Skills

"I think it is a [misconception] that people who are on a virtual team don't need to be people people—don't need to have good people skills. Really, the people skills are even more important because you're not seeing these people face to face, and you're not getting visual or auditory cues as to how they're feeling or what is going on in their minds that day. As a manager, the challenge is to be able to quickly evaluate people on their team for the strengths, weaknesses, and capabilities. Then, be able to establish rapport with [every] person very quickly, because you may only have one face-to-face meeting or you may never meet him face to face." The ability to manage the people side of the process is critical, because it doesn't matter how good the technology is if the people side doesn't work. Ultimately, the people determine the success or failure of the team.

The leader's role has to be one of a generalist, and really being a coach. Leaders are there to facilitate communication and to remove corporate or technology roadblocks. "The manager's job is to be checking in with people all the time," says Kit. "Not to the point of being annoying, but making sure they've got a good handle on who their people are, both professionally and personally, so that you know if someone has a sick mom at home and [he or she] might be distracted. Those are the kinds of things you would notice right away if you were in an office sitting in the cube right next to the person. You might not notice it on a virtual team unless you are paying really close attention. That's why I say that managers of virtual teams have to be really, really excellent people people."

Strategic Thinking

The ability to take team objectives, goals, and tasks and to understand how they support the overall corporate strategy and the bottom line is essential. So too is the ability to communicate the vision to team members. It doesn't matter if you're a middle manager, director, vice president, or president, those things are absolutely necessary.

Leaders have to understand trends and what the real problem is, and then be able to communicate that. "You are forcing people to work in a different way than they are used to," says Kit.

Have the Confidence to Trust Your Team

"Gone are the butt-in-chair days, where if your butt was in your chair, your manager was happy that you were working," says Kit. With a virtual team, the question is, what are you producing, and are you producing it on time and under budget? The manager's role is to be proactive, to remove roadblocks, and to be strategic about how the team can contribute to the company. Virtual managers, Kit believes, have to have the skills and confidence to hire people who are smarter than they are, surrounding themselves with people who are capable, and then working to bring out the best in people.

Getting Started

Doing things right from the start makes a big difference. Just thinking about the need to spend time early on getting to know each other will help leaders realize that different people on your team need different things. For example, some cultures require more relationship building than others do. "If you're working in Asia, where you have a high percentage of Asian team members, you're going to have to spend more time with the personal rapport building," she says. And it's not just cultures. Engineers might need less rapport building than the marketing people or the salespeople. Introverts might need less than extroverts. "You have to know not only the cultural milieu that your team is coming from but [also] the personal frame of reference that they have," Kit says.

Equal Access to Technology

Kit told us about an experience she had several years ago when she was working in the United States with a team in the Philippines. They had to burn CDs and ship them overnight because the Internet speeds into the Philippines were so slow, even though bandwidths within Manila were fine. "To FedEx something from Fargo, North Dakota, to the Philippines took 48 hours," she says. "It would've taken them a week to download the files with the bandwidth available at the time." In a more recent example, her husband was working on a mine site in a small African country, and the mine had to shut down for a day so that there could be enough electricity available in the country to broadcast a major soccer match. Leaders have to really think about and consider the availability and robustness of technology, especially when working globally.

Time Zones

It seems such a small detail to remember that members of the team are in different time zones, but often leaders, well, zone out. If the team has people in India, England, and the United States, there is about a three-hour window when everybody is awake, and it's not the best of time of day for everybody. Kit thinks it's important that everybody share the pain. Just because there is only one team member in India doesn't mean he or she is the one who should be getting up at three o'clock in the morning every time there's a meeting, or that someone should stay at work until nine or ten o'clock at night if she works in Great Britain. Rotating meeting times so that everybody gets both the good times and the bad is important. Kit is of the opinion that "you will build a great rapport with your people if you make it clear that everybody shares the pain and everybody is on equal footing." Otherwise, people will feel as if they are unimportant because they are the ones always having to make the sacrifices.

Set the Expectation That Communication Is Proactive

People have to believe that there is no such thing as too much communication. People should be communicating constantly. Even video conferences are easy these days because Webcams are so inexpensive. So there's really no reason not to do a video unless there's a reason not to (such as it's early in the morning and you are still in your pajamas). "When I am working on a virtual team, if my clients have access to messaging, I just leave it on all the time," says Kit. "It's like a water cooler. It's like popping your head up over the cube wall, especially if people are paying attention to and managing their status button."

▶ **SUMMARY**

We had a lot of fun writing this chapter. Whenever you can start by playing the World of Warcraft and end with virtual teamwork in your pajamas you know you've been on a learning journey. In this chapter we've shared what experienced virtual team leaders like Zev Barsky and Brian Hoffmann do to develop high performing, global virtual teams; we've offered a virtual team development process that differs, in emphasis anyway, from what most people have viewed the steps to be; and we have presented what experts like Shauna Wilson and Kit Brown-Hoekstra have found work with virtual teams worldwide.

Our journey, as a writing team of two coauthors, started with a bike ride and bagels, and has continued as we have developed our own little virtual team and friendship. We can vouch that the process works!

▶ NOTES

▶ INTRODUCTION

1. "IDC Predicts the Number of Worldwide Mobile Workers to Reach 1 Billion by 2011," *BNET.com*, 2/15/08, http://findarticles.com/p/articles/mi_m0EIN/is_2008_Jan_15/ai_n24230213/?tag=content;col1 (retrieved 3/24/10).

2. "Benchmarking Progress on New Ways of Working and New Forms of Business across Europe: ECaTT Final Report," *ECaTT.com*, 2000, 10–11, http://www.ecatt.com/ (retrieved 7/20/10).

▶ CHAPTER 1

1. Peter DeNagy, personal interviews with the authors, 12/16/09 and 12/22/09.

2. http://money.cnn.com/2010/01/05/technology/apple_app_store/index.htm

3. Sources for this section include Omniture Extends Web Analytics to Mobile, Jessica Tsai, July 22, 2008. http://www.destinationcrm.com/Articles/CRM-News/Daily-News/Omniture-Extends-Web-Analytics-to-Mobile-50025.aspx, retrieved 8/30/10; IDC Predicts the Number of Worldwide Mobile Workers to Reach 1 Billion by 2011, 1/5/2008. http://findarticles.com/p/articles/mi_m0EIN/is_2008_Jan_15/ai_n24230213/, retrieved 8/30/10. Harnessing the Mobile Internet: An executive guide to the new world of mobile communications. Eliot Weinman, published by Yankee Group Research, Inc. http://www.trendsmedia2.com/4G-WORLD-2009/HarnessingMobileInternet-Intro.pdf. Retrieved 8/30/10. Number of Mobile Devices Accessing the Internet Expected to Surpass One Billion by 2013, According to IDC. 12/9/09. http://www.idc.com/getdoc.jsp?containerId=prUS22110509. Retrieved 8/30/10.

▶ CHAPTER 2

1. Brent Lang, personal interview with the authors, 2/12/10.

2. Sharon Allen, personal interview with the authors, 2/09/10.

3. Jodi LaBrie, personal interview with the authors, 1/27/10.

4. Cathleen Benko and Anne C. Weisberg, *Mass Career Customization: Aligning the Workplace with Today's Nontraditional Workforce* (Boston: Harvard Business School Press, 2007), 3.

5. "100 Best Companies to Work for 2010: Best Benefits: Telecommuting," *CNN Money.com*, 2010, http://money.cnn.com/magazines/fortune/bestcompanies/2010/benefits/telecommuting.html (retrieved 3/18/10).

6. Thomas L. Friedman, *The World Is Flat: A Brief History of the Twenty-First Century*, Rev. Pbk. Ed. (New York: Picador, 2007).

7. This section draws from an excerpt from Tomi Ahonen's book, *Mobile as 7th of the Mass Media: Cellphone, Cameraphone, Iphone, Smartphone: futuretext 2008.* http://jasondaponte.files.wordpress.com/2009/05/tomiahonen-mobile7thmassmedia-excerpt1.pdf. (retrieved 3/19/10).

8. Robert Grassberger, personal communication with Michael Kroth, 3/19/10.

9. Sources for this section are the 2009 Telemedicine and Advanced Technology Research Center, 2009 TATRC Annual Report, also the TATRC Web site, http://www.tatrc.org/?p=home; also Sharon Kay, "Light Speed: Remote Surgery," *Innovation Online*, http://www.pbs.org/wnet/innovation/episode7_essay1.html (retrieved 3/20/10); and American Telemedicine Association, "Telemedicine Defined," http://www.americantelemed.org/i4a/pages/index.cfm?pageid=3333 (retrieved 3/20/10).

10. David Foster, personal interview with the authors, 2/1/10.

11. Brian Dolan, personal interview with David Clemons, 2/12/10.

12. Sources for this section include: *Time as a New Currency: Flexible and Mobile Work Strategies to Manage People and Products.* Knoll Workforce Research, Global Business Division. http://www.knoll.com/research/downloads/KnollTimeCurrency.pdf. Retrieved 8/30/10; Business in motion Managing the mobile workforce: A report from the Economist Intelligence Unit sponsored by Alcatel-Lucent. http://graphics.eiu.com/ebf/PDFs/Business_in_motion_April%202007_FINAL.pdf. Retrieved 8/30/10; A Study: Understanding and Managing the Mobile Workforce, July, 2007. http://newsroom.cisco.com/dlls/2007/eKits/MobileWorkforce_071807.pdf. Retrieved 8/30/10. Omniture Extends Web Analytics to Mobile, Jessica Tsai, July 22, 2008. http://www.destinationcrm.com/Articles/CRM-News/Daily-News/Omniture-Extends-Web-Analytics-to-Mobile-50025.aspx.

13. Measuring the Information Society, 2010: Executive Summary. International Tele-communications Union. http://www.itu.int/ITU-D/ict/publications/idi/2010/material/MIS_2010_Summary_E.pdf. Retrieved 8/30.10.

14. *Time as a New Currency: Flexible and Mobile Work Strategies to Manage People and Products.* Knoll Workforce Research, Global Business Division. http://www.knoll.com/research/downloads/KnollTimeCurrency.pdf. Retrieved 8/30/10.

15. For more information about schema, paradigms, and mental models, take a look at Marcy Perkins Driscoll, *Psychology of Learning for Instruction*, 3rd ed. (Boston: Pearson Allyn and Bacon, 2005); Peter M. Senge, *The Fifth Discipline Fieldbook: Strategies and Tools for Building a Learning Organization* (New York: Currency, Doubleday, 1994); Thomas S. Kuhn, *The Structure of Scientific Revolutions*, 3rd ed. (Chicago: University of Chicago Press, 1996).

16. Joel Arthur Barker, *Paradigms: The Business of Discovering the Future* (New York: HarperBusiness, 1993).

17. Joel Barker, personal interview with the authors, 2/17/10.

▶ CHAPTER 3

1. Bill Avey, personal interview with the authors, 1/4/10.

2. Telepresence T3, http://www.tandberg.com/totaltelepresence/pdf/Telepresence%20Brochure.pdf. p. 5 (retrieved 7/12/10).

3. Peter M. Senge and Society for Organizational Learning, *Presence: Exploring Profound Change in People, Organizations, and Society,* 1st Currency Ed. (New York: Doubleday, 2005), 5.

4. Karen Sobel Lojeski and Richard R. Reilly, *Uniting the Virtual Workforce: Transforming Leadership and Innovation in the Globally Integrated Enterprise,* Microsoft Executive Leadership Series (Hoboken, NJ: John Wiley & Sons, 2008).

5. For a discussion of transactional distance, see Michael Moore, "Theory of Transactional Distance." In Desmond Keegan, D., ed. *Theoretical Principles of Distance Education* (New York: Routledge, 1997), 20–35. For examples of how transactional distance can be applied, see Robyn Benson and Gayani Samarawickrema, "Addressing the Context of E-Learning: Using Transactional Distance Theory to Inform Design," *Distance Education* 30, no. 1 (2009): 5–21.

6. Cliff Kuang, "Holograms That You Can Touch and Feel," *Fast Company,* 8/5/09, http://www.fastcompany.com/blog/cliff-kuang/design-innovation/holograms-you-can-actually-touch (retrieved 2/28/10); and Cliff Kuang, "Samsung Unveils Gesture-Sensing Hologram, but It's Not World's First," *Fast Company,* 7/22/09,

http://www.fastcompany.com/blog/cliff-kuang/design-innovation/samsung-invents-worlds-first-gesture-sensing-hologram (retrieved 2/28/10). See also http://news.yahoo.com/s/ynews/20081104/pl_ynews/ynews_pl132.

7. Greg Kaiser, personal interview with the authors, 12/12/09.

8. Charlotte "Lani" Gunawardena, personal interview with the authors, 2/25/10. This section also draws from Charlotte Gunawardena, "Social Presence Theory and Implications for Interaction and Collaboration in Computer Conferences," *International Journal of Educational Telecommunications* 1, no. 2–3 (1995): 147–166. See also Charlotte Gunawardena and Frank Zittle, "Social Presence as a Predictor of Satisfaction within a Computer-Mediated Conferencing Environment," *The American Journal of Distance Education* 11, no. 3 (1997): 8–26; Charlotte Gunawardena, Fadwa Bouachrine, Ahmed Idrissi Alami, and Gayathri Jayatilleki, "Cultural Perspectives on Social Presence: A Study of Online Chatting in Morocco and Sri Lanka," In *American Educational Research Association 2006 Annual Meeting.* San Francisco, 2006; Tu Chih-Hsiung, "How Chinese Perceive Social Presence: An Examination of Interaction in Online Learning Environment," *Educational Media International* 38, no. 1 (2001): 45–60; Jennifer Richardson and Karen Swan, "Examining Social Presence in Online Courses in Relation to Students' Perceived Learning and Satisfaction," *Journal of Asynchronous Learning Networks* 7, no. 1 (2003): 68–88.

9. For a foundational discussion of social presence, see Charlotte Gunawardena, "Social Presence Theory and Implications for Interaction and Collaboration in Computer Conferences," *International Journal of Educational Telecommunications* 1, no. 2–3 (1995): 147–166.

10. Belle Linda Halpern and Kathy Lubar, *Leadership Presence: Dramatic Techniques to Reach Out, Motivate, and Inspire* (New York: Gotham Books, 2003). See also Steve Kayser, "What Exactly Is 'Leadership Presence'?" *Expert Access*, 9/7/09, http://expertaccess.cincom.com/2009/09/what-exactly-is-leadership-presence/, (retrieved 7-20-10); and Julie A. Fleming, "4 Steps to Growing Your Leadership Presence," *Ezine @rticles*, http://ezinearticles.com/?4-Steps-to-Growing-Your-Leadership-Presence&id=2343891 (retrieved 7/20/10).

11. Richard L. Hughes, Robert C. Ginnett, and Gordon J. Curphy, *Leadership: Enhancing the Lessons of Experience*, 6th ed. (Boston: McGraw-Hill Irwin, 2009).

12. James C. Collins, *Good to Great: Why Some Companies Make the Leap—and Others Don't*, 1st ed. (New York: HarperBusiness, 2001).

▶ CHAPTER 4

1. Peter DeNagy, personal interviews with the authors, 12/16/09 and 12/22/09.

2. Bob Grassberger, personal interview with Michael Kroth, 10/26/09.

3. M. Katherine Brown, Brenda Huettner, and Char James-Tanny, *Managing Virtual Teams: Getting the Most from Wikis, Blogs, and Other Collaborative Tools* (Plano, TX: Wordware Publishing, 2007), 22–23.

4. Jana M. Kemp, *Moving Out of the Box: Tools for Team Decision Making* (Westport, CT: Praeger, 2008), 133 and 138.

5. James M. Kouzes and Barry Z. Posner, *The Leadership Challenge,* 4th ed. (San Francisco: Jossey-Bass, 2007), 224.

6. Material from this section comes from a 1/19/10 personal interview with the authors and from Stephen M. R. Covey and Rebecca R. Merrill, *The Speed of Trust: The One Thing That Changes Everything* (New York: Free Press, 2008).

7. Don Cohen and Laurence Prusak, *In Good Company: How Social Capital Makes Organizations Work* (Boston: Harvard Business School Press, 2001), 29.

8. McKay Christensen, interview with the authors, 12/4/09.

9. Michael S. Kroth, *The Manager as Motivator* (Westport, CT: Praeger, 2006).

10. Nan S. Russell, *Hitting Your Stride: Your Work, Your Way,* 1st ed. (Sterling, VA: Capital Books, 2007), 170.

11. Roger C. Mayer, James H. Davis, and F. David Schoorman, "An Integrative Model of Organizational Trust," *Academy of Management Review* 20, no. 3 (1995): 709–734; and F. David Schoorman, Roger C. Mayer, and James H. Davis, "An Integrative Model of Organizational Trust: Past, Present, and Future," *Academy of Management Review* 32, no. 2 (2007): 344–354.

12. Jon R. Katzenbach and Douglas K. Smith, *The Wisdom of Teams: Creating the High-Performance Organization* (New York: HarperBusiness Essentials, 2003), 109.

13. Lisa Haneberg, *Focus Like a Laser Beam: 10 Ways to Do What Matters Most,* 1st ed. (San Francisco: Jossey-Bass, 2006), 30.

14. Greg Lowitz, personal interview with the authors, 12/11/09.

15. Lori Coruccini, personal interview with the authors, 1/29/10.

16. McKay Christensen, interview with the authors, 12/4/09.

17. Camille Venezia, interview with David Clemons, 2/22/10.

▶ CHAPTER 5

1. Sharon Allen, personal interview with the authors, 2/9/10.

2. John Berry, personal interview with the authors, 3/16/10.

3. References for this section include Alyssa Rosenberg, "Charged for Change," *Government Executive*, 2010, http://www.govexec.com/story_page_pf.cfm?articleid=44679&printerfriendlyvers=1 (retrieved 3/21/10); Joe Davidson, "Snowstorm's Possible Plus: Advancing Cause of Telework," 2/22/10, http://www.washingtonpost.com/wp-dyn/content/article/2010/02/10/AR2010021003715_pf.html (retrieved 3/21/10); Michael Hardy, "Government Re-Opens While Feds Talk Telework in Aftermath of Blizzard," *Washington Technology*, 2/22/10, http://fcw.com/Articles/2010/02/11/fed-telework-discussions.aspx (retrieved 3/21/10); "Federal Government Remains Closed After "Historic" Blizzard; More Snow Forecast," *VOANews.com*, 2010, http://www1.voanews.com/english/news/Federal-Government-Remains-Closed-After-Historic-Blizzard-More-Snow-Forecast-83804727.html (retrieved 3/21/10); http://en.wikipedia.org/wiki/Berry_Bastion (retrieved 3/22/10); http://www.federalnewsradio.com/?sid=1917223&nid=270 (retrieved 3/22/10); X. George Markfelder, "Telework: DON Keeps Working through Flu Season," NAVY.mil, 12/21/09, http://www.navy.mil/search/display.asp?story_id=50288(retrieved 1/16/10).

4. "Out of Sight, but Not Out of Touch: Federal Executives' Assessment of Agency Telework Policy: A Candid Survey of Federal Executives," *Government Business Council*, http://www.govexec.com/gbc/telework/.

5. Steve Lamont, personal interview with the authors, 10/13/09.

6. For more on ROWE, see Cali Ressler and Jody Thompson, *Why Work Sucks and How to Fix It: No Schedules, No Meetings, No Joke—the Simple Change That Can Make Your Job Terrific* (New York: Portfolio, 2008).

7. OPM's w/l Web site, http://www.opm.gov/Employment_and_Benefits/worklife/index.asp.

8. Peter DeNagy, personal interview with the authors, 12/16/09.

9. Barbara Wankoff, personal interview with the authors, 1/5/10. Guides provided via personal communication from KPMG.

10. Key points for this section come from Gundars Kaupins, Malcolm Coco, and John McIntosh, "Wireless Telecommuting for HR Managers," *SHRM White Paper*, 2007, http://www.shrm.org/research/articles/articles/pages/cms_020285.aspx (retrieved 11/30/09).

11. Visit the Telework Arizona Web site for more information about this very successful program: http://www.teleworkarizona.com/.

▶ CHAPTER 6

1. John Hale, interview with the authors, 1/19/10.

2. See Stephen Baker, "Management by the Numbers," *BusinessWeek*, September 8, 2008, 32–38, and Stephen Baker, *The Numerati* (Boston: Houghton Mifflin Co., 2008), for a fascinating, and scary, account of what organizations are developing to learn more about their workers.

3. Keystone and Island Pumping examples in this chapter provided by Mentor Engineering, www.mentoreng.com.

4. Mark Coffey, M., "Austin Energy Takes Laptops to the Field Efficiency," *Transmission and Distribution World*, October 2006, http://tdworld.com/distribution_management_systems/power_austin_energy_takes/.

5. "Cable&Wireless Selects and Implements ClickSoftware for Optimized Mobile Workforce Management," *PR Newswire*, http://www.prnewswire.com/news-releases/cablewireless-selects-and-implements-clicksoftware-for-optimized-mobile-workforce-management-81130182.html (downloaded 2/6/10).

6. Peter Manos, "Cutting Costs with Real-Time Mobile Data," *Public Utilities Fortnightly*, January 2006.

7. *Creating an Applications Infrastructure for 21st Century Water Distribution.* An Oracle Analysis, November 2009. Provided by Oracle to the authors.

8. Richard Mayer, personal interview with the authors, 2/25/10.

9. Personal communication from Cali Ressler and Jody Thompson, 2/26/10.

10. The content in this section is from Cali Ressler and Jody Thompson, *Why Work Sucks and How to Fix It: No Schedules, No Meetings, No Joke—The Simple Change That Can Make Your Job Terrific* (New York: Portfolio, 2008); and the *Results-Only Work Environment Business Case*, http://gorowe.com/wordpress/wp-content/uploads/2009/12/ROWE_Business_Case.pdf (downloaded 2/6/10).

11. The content in this section is from a 2/26/10 personal communication from Cali Ressler and Jody Thompson.

12. For an excellent summary of organizational citizenship behaviors, see Philip M. Podsakoff, Scott B. MacKenzie, Julie Beth Paine, and Daniel G. Bachrach, "Organizational Citizenship Behaviors: A Critical Review of the Theoretical and Empirical Literature and Suggestions for Future Research," *Journal of Management* 26, no. 3 (2000): 513.

▶ CHAPTER 7

1. Kathie Lingle, interview with the authors, 12/22/09. Information about the Alliance for Work-Life Progress can be found here: http://www.awlp.org/awlp/home/html/homepage.jsp.

2. Lori Coruccini, interview with the authors, 1/29/10.

3. Information for this section was taken from "Trucking Industry in the United States," *Wikipedia.org*, http://en.wikipedia.org/wiki/Trucking_industry_in_the_United_States (retrieved 2/2/10); Carl Stinson, "Introduction to the Trucking Industry," *Ezine @rticles*, http://ezinearticles.com/?Introduction-To-The-Trucking-Industry&id=470632 (retrieved 2/2/10); "Truck Driving Jobs: The History of Trucking," *JobMonkey.com*, http://www.jobmonkey.com/truckdriving/trucking-jobs.html (retrieved 2/2/10); "Making the Long Haul: A History of the Truck and Trucking Industry," *RandomHistory.com*, http://www.randomhistory.com/2008/07/14_truck.html (retrieved 2/2/10); "Missions and Values," *Con-way.com*, http://www.con-way.com/en/about_con_way/mission_and_values (retrieved 2/2/10).

4. Tyler Ellison, interview with the authors, 1/13/10.

5. Lyrics from Do-Re-Mi, *The Sound of Music*, Rodgers and Hammerstein, 1959.

6. Stephen R. Covey. *The Seven Habits of Highly Effective People: Restoring the Character Ethic* (New York: Simon and Schuster, 1989).

7. John Gentry, interview with the authors, 2/26/10.

▶ CHAPTER 8

1. Lori Coruccini, interview with the authors, 1/29/10.

2. James C. Collins. *Good to Great: Why Some Companies Make the Leap—and Others Don't* (New York: HarperBusiness, 2001).

3. Information from this section drawn from James Flanigan, "Working at Home Pays Off for Firms," *Los Angeles Times*, 5/9/04, http://articles.latimes.com/2004/may/09/business/fi-flan9 (retrieved 3/30/10).

4. John Gentry, personal interview with the authors, 2/26/10.

5. Lori Coruccini, interview with the authors, 1/29/10.

6. Doug Harward, interview with the authors, 12/4/09.

7. http://www.youtube.com/watch?v=FScddkTMlTc

8. Cisco Systems, Inc., "A Study: Understanding and Managing the Mobile Workforce," July 2007, http://newsroom.cisco.com/dlls/2007/eKits/MobileWorkforce_071807.pdf (retrieved 3/31/10).

9. Brent Lang, interview with the authors, 2/12/10.

10. Mike Cook, personal interview with the authors, 1/27/10.

11. Steve Franklin, personal interview with the authors, 2/1/10.

▶ CHAPTER 9

1. McKay Christensen, interview with the authors, 12/04/09.

2. For an excellent review of OCBs, go to Phillip M. Podsakoff, Scott B. MacKenzie, Julie Beth Paine, and Daniel G. Bachrach, "Organizational Citizenship Behaviors: A Critical Review of the Theoretical and Empirical Literature and Suggestions for Future Research," *Journal of Management*, 26, no. 3 (2000): 513–563.

3. Steve Lamont, interview with the authors, 10/13/09.

4. Michael S. Kroth, *The Manager as Motivator* (Westport, CT: Praeger, 2006).

5. Marsha Sinetar. *Do What You Love, the Money Will Follow: Discovering Your Right Livelihood* (New York: Dell Pub, 1989).

6. Patricia Kempthorne, interview with Michael Kroth, 12/2/09.

7. Stephen M. R. Covey and Rebecca R. Merrill, *The Speed of Trust: The One Thing That Changes Everything* (New York: Free Press, 2006).

8. Bill Avey, interview with the authors, 1/4/10.

9. Lori Coruccini, interview with the authors, 1/29/10.

10. For an in-depth explanation of managerial caring, see Michael S. Kroth, and Carolyn Keeler, "Caring as a Managerial Strategy," *Human Resource Development Review*, 8, no. 4 (2009): 506–531.

11. Mike Mansbach, personal interview with the authors, 12/18/09.

12. For a detailed and scholarly discussion of organizational commitment, see the work of John P. Meyer and Natalie Jean Meyer, for example, John P. Meyer and Natalie Jean Allen, *Commitment in the Workplace: Theory, Research, and Application* (Thousand Oaks, CA: Sage Publications, 1997).

13. Richard Morris, interview with the authors, 1/7/10.

14. There has been considerable work in the field of self-efficacy over the last several decades. Albert Bandura originally developed the concept and is the leading expert about it. For an in-depth discussion, see his book, Albert Bandura, *Self-Efficacy: The Exercise of Control* (New York: W.H. Freeman, 1997). For more information about expectancy theory see Victor Harold Vroom, *Work and Motivation* (Malabar, Fla.: R.E. Krieger Pub. Co., 1982) and Edward E. Lawler, *Motivation in Work Organizations*. 1st [Classic] ed., *The Jossey-Bass Management Series* (San Francisco: Jossey-Bass, 1994).

15. Edwin A. Locke and Gary P. Latham are leading scholars in this arena. See, for examples, Edwin A. Locke and Gary P. Latham, "Building a Practically Useful Theory of Goal Setting and Task Motivation," *American Psychologist*, 57, no. 9 (2002): 705; and Edwin A. Locke and Gary P. Latham, "What Should We Do

about Motivation Theory? Six Recommendations for the Twenty-first Century," *Academy of Management Review*, 29, no. 3 (2004): 388.

16. Cali Ressler and Jody Thompson, personal communication to the authors, 2/25/10.

17. For more about the relationship of goal setting, commitment, and volition see Corno, Lyn. 1993. The Best-Laid Plans: Modern Conceptions of Volition and Educational Research. *Educational Researcher* 22 (2):14-22;

18. For another good discussion of volition see Sumantra Ghoshal and Heike Bruch. 2003. Going Beyond Motivation to The Power of Volition, *MIT Sloan Management Review* 44 (3):51.

19. Found in Michael S. Kroth, *The Manager as Motivator* (Westport, CT: Praeger, 2006), p. 164. See also a Melaleuca case study, pp. 160—67 in the same book.

20. See *2009 Guide to Bold New Ideas for Making Work Work*, 2009, published by the Families and Work Institute, http://familiesandwork.org/site/research/reports/2009boldideas.pdf.

21. Patricia Kempthorne, interview with Michael Kroth, 12/2/09.

▶ **CHAPTER 10**

1. Jane C. Linder, "Continuous Renewal: Managing for the Upside." *U.S. Business Review*, http://www.usbusiness-review.com/content/view/485/ (retrieved 3/31/10).

2. Peter H. Lewis, "Keeping Up with the Phoneses," *The New York Times*, 9/24/96, http://www.nytimes.com/1996/09/24/science/keeping-up-with-the-phoneses.html?pagewanted=1 (retrieved 3/31/10).

3. Razib Ahmed, "Technology 1996: What We Had and Hadn't? A List of 50 Things," 8/2/06, http://techblogbiz.blogspot.com/2006/08/technology-1996-what-we-had-and-hadnt.html (retrieved 3/31/10).

4. M. Katherine Brown, Brenda Huettner, and Char James-Tanny, *Managing Virtual Teams: Getting the Most from Wikis, Blogs, and Other Collaborative Tools* (Plano, TX: Wordware Publishing, 2007).

5. Michael S. Kroth and McKay Christensen, *Career Development Basics* (Alexandria, VA: ASTD Press, 2009).

6. Michael Grahame Moore, "Editorial: First Thoughts on Metaskills," *American Journal of Distance Education* (2002), 16(1), p. 1–3.

7. Gary Hamel and C. K. Prahalad, *Competing for the Future* (Boston: Harvard Business School Press, 1994).

8   *WebProNews.com*, http://archive.webpronews.com/2002/0730.html.

9. For excellent discussions about learning organizations refer to Watkins, Karen E., and Victoria J. Marsick. 1993. *Sculpting the learning organization: lessons in the art and science of systemic change*. 1st ed, *The Jossey-Bass management series*. San Francisco, CA: Jossey-Bass, and Senge, Peter M. 1990. *The fifth discipline: the art and practice of the learning organization*. 1st ed. New York: Doubleday/Currency.

10. Steve Lamont, personal interview with the authors, 10/13/09.

11. Bala Chakravarthy and Peter Lorange, "Continuous Renewal, and How Best Buy Did It," *Strategy & Leadership*, 35, no. 6 (2007): 4–11 (retrieved 3/31/10 from ABI/INFORM Global, Document ID: 1369380701).

12. We thank Dr. Russ Joki for sharing the concept of consilience with us.

13. Brian Dolan, interview with David Clemons, 2/12/10.

14. For more on consilience, see "Consilience (Book)," *Wikipedia.org*, http://en.wikipedia.org/wiki/Consilience_(book); and "Consilience," *Wikipedia.org*, http://en.wikipedia.org/wiki/Consilience.

15. Steven Erickson, interview with the authors, 12/16/09.

 CHAPTER 11

1. Zev Barsky, interview with the authors, 12/14/10.

2. Information from this section was drawn from "World of Warcraft," *Wikipedia. org*, http://en.wikipedia.org/wiki/World_of_Warcraft; *Blizzard.com* (Blizzard Entertainment Web site), http://us.blizzard.com/en-us/games/wow; "Massively Multiplayer Online Role-Playing Game," *Wikipedia.org*, http://en.wikipedia.org/ wiki/Massively_multiplayer_online_role-playing_game (all retrieved 2/20/10).

3. *LEGO Universe Massively Multiplayer Online Game*, http://us.universe.lego.com/ en-us/NewsNetwork/Story.aspx?id=127607 (retrieved 2/20/10). See also http:// en.wikipedia.org/wiki/Lego.

4. Zev Barsky, interview with the authors, 12/14/10.

5. Brian Hoffmann, interview with the authors 1/15/10.

6. Peter M. Senge, *The Fifth Discipline Fieldbook: Strategies and Tools for Building a Learning Organization* (New York: Currency, Doubleday, 1994).

7. Peter M. Senge, and Society for Organizational Learning. *Presence: Human Purpose and the Field of the Future*, 1st ed. (Cambridge, MA: SoL, 2004), p. 34.

8. William A. Kahn, "Holding Environments at Work," *Journal of Applied Behavioral Science* 37, no. 3 (2001): 260.

9. This section drew upon these articles, which may be read for more depth of discussion about the virtual team development process: Stacie A. Furst, Martha Reeves, Benson Rosen, and Richard S. Blackburn, "Managing the Life Cycle of Virtual Teams," *Academy of Management Executive* 18, no. 2 (2004): 6–20; Guido Hertel, Susanne Geister, and Udo Konradt, "Managing Virtual Teams: A Review of Current Empirical Research," *Human Resource Management Review* 15, no. 1 (2005): 69–95; Chad Lin, Craig Standing, and Ying-Chieh Liu, "A Model to Develop Effective Virtual Teams," *Decision Support Systems* 45, no. 4 (2008): 1031–1045; Luis L. Martins, Lucy L. Gilson, and M. Travis Maynard, "Virtual Teams: What Do We Know and Where Do We Go from Here?" *Journal of Management* 30, no. 6 (2004): 805–835.

10. Bruce W. Tuckman, "Development Sequence in Small Groups," *Psychological Bulletin* 63 (1965): 384–399.

11. Interview with Shauna Wilson and the authors, 12/30/09. Also Shauna Wilson, *Successful Online Meetings*, Infoline: Tips, Tools, and Intelligence for Trainers: ASTD Press, 2009; Shauna Wilson, *InterneTeaming.Com: Tools to Create High Performance Remote Teams* (Portland, OR: Inkwater Press, 2005).

12. Interview with Kit Brown-Hoekstra and the authors, 1/20/10.

▶INDEX

A

Ability, 83
Actual presence, 69
Advancing employees, 191–192
Ahonen, Tomi, 31–33
Alfred P. Sloan Foundation awards, 201
Alignment issues, 14–15
Allen, Sharon, 26, 28–30, 93
API, 59–60
Apostolic work, 98
Apple, 7
Application protocol interface (API), 59–60
Arizona, 113–114
Assessment, 217
At-home mobile workers, 167–168
Atom, 231
AT&T, 114, 158
Austin Energy, 126
Autonomy or not autonomy?, 119–136
    employee satisfaction, 128–130
    false dichotomy, 154
    freemium, 122
    less autonomy, 126–130
    more autonomy, 130–136
    overview, 124
    ROWE, 131–136
    vignette (Trey), 135-136
Avey, Bill, ix, 51, 52, 54, 58, 68, 69, 190

B

Bad technology, 188
Baker, Stephen, 125
Barker, Joel, 21, 40, 41, 46, 47
Barsky, Zev, 221–225, 235
BDO Seidman, 201
Being present, 67
Being there (actual presence), 69
Benevolence, 83–84
Benko, Cathleen, 27
Berry, John, 94–103, 115
Berry's telework initiative, 98–101
Berry as missionary for telework, 98–99
    policy infrastructure, 99
    preparedness, 98
    resources and focus, 100
    riding the waves, 101
    trying things, 99–100
Best Buy, 7, 131, 214
Best practices, 17, 40
Biography. See Vignettes
Blended learning, 173, 181
Blind trust, 77

Blizzard (snowmageddon), 93–94
Broadband connections, 5, 64
Brown-Hoekstra, Kit, 73, 209, 234, 240–244
Building trust. *See* Trust or bust
Business review, 87–88

C
Cable&Wireless Worldwide, 127
Caesar, Julius, 198
Candor, 154
Capacitizing employees, 192
Capital One, 201
Capsule biography. *See* Vignettes
Career Development Basics (Kroth/Christensen), 211
Career opportunities, 26–31
Caring, 191–192
Cauldron, 229
CDN, 20
Cell phone, 32
Center of excellence, 15
Chakravarthy, Bala, 214
Challenging, meaningful work, 193–194
Changing rules of today's workforce, 41–45
Charismatic leaders, 68
Christensen, McKay, 80, 87–88, 183, 200, 211
Christiansen, Ole Kirk, 223
Cisco, 51, 53, 226
Cisco telepresence, 53
Citrix Online, 192
Clemons, David, 67, 163, 226
Clemons, John, 211, 212
ClickSoftware Technologies software, 127
CMS, 19
Colocated team container, 230
CoBank, 177–178
Cohen, Don, 79
Collaboration, 17, 215–216
Collaborative learning, 173
Collaborative whiteboards, 238
Collins, Jim, 68, 157

Command-and-control system, 73, 89–90
Communication, 80, 235, 243–244
Communication skills, 66
Competitive environment
economy, 102–103
employee, 103
global competitiveness, 104
technology, 104
Con-way Multimodal, 138–141
Conflict management, 90–91
Connecting with employees, 192
Connectivity, 46, 47, 48, 179
Consilience, 216
Consistency, 89
Content delivery network (CDN), 20
Content distribution network, 20
Content management system (CMS), 19
Context, 85
Cook, Mike, 170, 171
Core competencies, 211
Corridor mobile workers, 165–166
Corridor warriors, 26
Coruccini, Lori, 86, 137, 157, 160, 190
Cost/benefit analysis skills, 217
Cost savings, 102–103
Costs and benefits, 13–14
Covey, Stephen M. R., 74–78, 82, 86, 189
Covey, Stephen R., 74, 142
Credibility, 76
CRM, 18–19
Crossing the Rubicon, 198
CultureRx, 132
Customer relationship management (CRM), 18–19
Cutting expenses, 102–103

D
Daisy diagram, 237
Davis, James, 81, 83
Decision making, 73
Deloitte, 26
DeNagy, Peter L., 3, 71, 108, 109
Developing a mobile workforce strategy, 12–17

Developing your virtual team, 221–244
adjourning, 240
Barsky, Zev, 221, 223–225
Brown-Hoekstra, Kit, 240–244
collaborative work, 239
communication, 235, 243–244
confidence to trust your team, 240, 242
container, 229–231
equal access to technology, 242–243
focus, 229
forming, 233–234
freemium, 222
Hoffmann, Brian, 225–229
kickoff meeting, 234
learning together, 236
norming, 231–233
partnership, 228
people skills, 241
performing, 238–239
problem solving, 237–238
put it into gear, 228
relationships, 227–228
shared knowledge, 236
starting up, 242
storming, 236
strategic communications, 226–227
strategic thinking, 241–242
time zones, 243
transforming, 234–236
Dialogue, 55
"Distributed workforce," 11
Distributed workforce model, 37
Distrust, 77
Do What You Love, the Money Will Follow (Sinetar), 187
Dolan, Brian, 36, 216
Driving time, 179
Drucker, Peter, 226

E
E-presence, 58–60
Early adopters, 212
EDM, 19
Educational Services and Staff Development Association of Central Kansas (ESSDACK), 170

Eight principles model, 183–203
caring, 191–192
challenging, meaningful work, 193–194
Christensen's three steps, 200
foundational principles, 186, 189–192
freemium, 185
goals, 196–198
manager's role, 199–200
managing expectancies, 195–196
motivational arenas, 185
organizational commitment, 194–195
overview, 185–189
technology, 188–189
trust, 189
understanding your employees, 189–191
willpower, 198–199
Electronic document management (EDM), 19
Electronic management system (EMS), 19
Ellison, Tyler, 138–142
Employee responsibility, 44–45
Employee satisfaction, 111–112, 138–130
EMS, 19
Enabling others to act, 73
Endnotes, 244–255
Energy companies, 126
Enterprise analysis of "mobile readiness," 106–108
Enterprise resource planning (ERP) system, 18
Erickson, Steven, 218
ERP system, 18
ESSDACK, 170
Evaluation and reward, 153–154
Expectancy manager, 195
Expectations, 152
Expense cutting, 102–103
Expressiveness, 67
Extending trust, 76

F
Face-to-face meetings, 225
Facts and figures, 9–10, 38–39

Failing forward, 99
Federal government, 97, 101. *See also* Berry's telework initiative
Feedback
  difficulty of observing behavior, 88
  eight principles model, 199–200
  from employees, 172
  high-priority communication, as, 17
  performance management, 140
  support, and, 153
  virtual team, 239
Fifth Discipline Fieldbook, The (Senge), 229
Flexible policies, 40
Flexible work arrangements, 40
Flexible workplace, 202
Focus, 229
Focus Like a Laser Beam (Haneberg), 82
Foster, Dave, 36
Foster, Justin, 65
Franklin, Steve, 177–178
Freemiums
  autonomy, 122
  hiring and preparing, 164
  keeping up, 217
  leadership, 105
  mobility, 4
  motivation, 185
  paradigm, 22
  performance, 151
  presence, 61
  trust, 78
  virtual team, 222
Friedman, Thomas, 31

G
General Electric, 101
General Services Administration (GSA), 94
Generation Y (Gen Y), 171
Gentry, John, 146–151, 159, 169
Geographic distance, 54
Goals, 143, 196–198
Going global, 39–40
Good to Great (Collins), 68
GoToMeeting, 192, 218
Grassberger, Bob, 33, 34, 71–72

Green initiatives, 101
Group discussion, 91
GROW, 238
GSA, 94
Gunawardena, Charlotte (Lani), 61–64

H
Habits, 199
Hale, John, 119–124, 152
Halo system, 52–53
Halpern, Belle Linda, 67
Haneberg, Lisa, 82
Harward, Doug, 162–163
Healthwise, Inc., 36
Hewlett-Packard, 51–53, 158, 225–229
Hiring and training, 145–147, 157–181
  at-home mobile workers, 167–168
  baseline technology, 172–177
  blended/collaborative learning, 173
  building blocks of mobile training, 178
  corridor mobile workers, 165–166
  example (public schools), 170–171
  freemium, 164
  Gen Y trainees, 171–172
  managers, 180
  mobile road warriors, 168–169
  organizational culture, 174
  questions to ask, 158–159
  steps in hiring process, 160–161
  strategic content plan, 172–173
  supporting infrastructure, 179
  technology, 161–164, 172–177
Hitler, Adolf, 68
Hitting Your Stride (Russell), 81
Hoffmann, Brian, 225–229, 234, 235
Holding environment, 229
Hologram, 57, 58
Home-based mobile worker, 167–168
Hospital, 23–25
HP Printer Museum, 225
http://gorowe.com, 132
Hudson's Bay Company, 54
Huettner, Brenda, 73
Hull, Jane, 114
Human API, 60, 145
Human nature, 190

I

iGeneration, 171
Immersive telepresence, 53
In Good Company: How Social Capital Makes Organizations Work (Cohen/ Prusak), 79
Individuality, 190
Innovation, 214
Integrate mobile practices into existing systems, 16, 18–20
Integrity, 84
Inter-institutional cultural issues, 72
InterneTeaming.com: Tools to Create High Performance Remote Teams (Wilson), 236, 238
Interpersonal connections, 88–89
Inviting employees, 191
iPad, 7
Irreversible commitment, 198
ISB Global, 59
Island Aggregates, 128

J

James-Tanny, Char, 73
JetBlue, 158
Job description, 160
Job design, 144–145
Joki, Russ, 254
Jones, Jim, 68

K

Kahn, William, 229
Kaiser, Greg, 59–60, 163
Katzenbach, Jon, 81
Kay, Sharon, 34
Keeler, Carolyn, 191
Keeping up with the phoneses, 207–219
   assessment, 217
   collaboration, 215–216
   consilience, 216
   example (UBS Financial), 218
   freemium, 217
   learning organization, 211–213
   metaskills, 211–217
   renewal, 214–215
   sticking it out, 219
Kemp, Jana, 73

Kempthorne, Patricia, 189, 202
Keystone Excavating, 126
Kouzes, James, 73
KPMG, 111-113, 119-124
Kroth, Michael, 81, 185, 191, 211
Kuhn, Thomas, 40

L

LaBrie, Jodi, 26-28
Lack of trust, 79
Lamont, Steve, 99, 184, 213, 215–216
Lang, Brent, 23–26, 165
Leadership, 69–70
Leadership Challenge, The (Kouzes/ Posner), 73
Leadership presence, 67–69
Leadership Presence (Halpern/Lubar), 67
Learner autonomy, 55
Learning management system (LMS), 19–20, 173
Learning organization, 211–213
LearnKey, 211–212
LEGO, 222–224
Linder, Jane, 207
Lingle, Kathie, 137
LMS, 19–20, 173
Lojeski, Karen, 54
Lorange, Peter, 214
Loss of trust, 86
Lousy technology, 188
Lowitz, Greg, 84, 146
Lubar, Kathy, 67

M

Manager as Motivator, The (Kroth), 81, 185
Manager overcontrol, 89–90
Managing expectancies, 195–196
Managing Virtual Teams (Brown-Hoekstra et al.), 210, 240
Mansbach, Mike, 192–193
Mashup network, 215
Mass Career Customization (Benko/ Weisberg), 27
Mass career customization (MCC), 26, 27, 28

Mass product customization (MPC), 27

Massively multiplayer online role-playing game, 222

Mayer, Rick, 128, 129

Mayer, Roger, 81, 83

MCC, 26, 27

Meaningful work, 193–194

Mediocrity, 199

Meetings, 141

Melaleuca, 80, 200

Mental models, 40

Mentor Engineering, 126

Merrill, Rebecca, 189

Metadata skills, 215

Metaskills. *See* Keeping up with the phoneses

Micromanaging, 44, 89

Millenials, 171

MMORPG, 222

MobiHealthNews, 36

Mobile channel, 32

Mobile performance management process, 137–155
  evaluation and reward, 153–154
  expectations, 152
  goals, 143
  hiring, 145–146
  job design, 144–145
  orientation, 146
  overview, 141
  start at the beginning, 142–143
  support, 153
  training, 147
  what needs to be done, 143
  work tools, 145

Mobile performance management technology, 120, 128

Mobile road warriors, 168–169

Mobile strategy, 6

Mobile trust-building strategies, 87–91

Mobile work strategies, 40

"Mobile workers," 11

Mobile workforce
  at-home mobile workers, 167–168
  corridor mobile workers, 165–166
  e-presence, 58–60
  leadership presence, 67–69
  mobile road warriors, 168–169
  personal presence, 64–65
  social presence, 61–64
  statistics, 9–10, 38–39
  terminology, 11
  working definition, 48

Mobile workforce management technology, 127

Mobile Workforce Registry, 4

MobilHealthNews, 216

Mobility
  all-encompassing nature, 31–33
  individual, and, 12
  manager, and, 12
  ubiquitous, 7–8
  what is it, 8–9

Moore, Michael, 55

Morris, Richard, 195

Motivational arenas, 185

Motivational tools. *See* Eight principles model

MPC, 27

Multimodal services, 140

My online virtual me, 64–67

N

Neeleman, David, 158

New Business of Paradigms, The (Barker), 41

New rules, 41–45

Notes (endnotes), 244–255

Numerati, The (Baker), 125

O

Obama, Barack, 93, 96

Objectives, 143

OCBs, 133, 184

Office of Personnel Management (OPM). *See* Berry's telework initiative

Old *vs.* new rules, 41–45

OPM. *See* Berry's telework initiative

Organizational citizenship behaviors (OCBs), 133, 184

Organizational commitment, 194–195

Organizational goals, 143

Organizational standards, 152
Orientation, 146
"Out of Sight, but Not Out of Touch:
    Federal Executives' Assessment of
    Agency Telework Policy," 99
Overcontrolling, 89–90

P
Paperwork, 126–128
Paradigm, 21. *See also* Workforce
    paradigm
Paradigm shift, 104–105
Past experiences, 85
Patent and Trademark Office, 94
People skills, 241
Perfectionism, 91
Performance, 119
Performance cycle, 141
Performance evaluation, 87–88, 153
Performance expectation creep, 134
Performance management, 142, 154,
    239
Performance management process. *See*
    Mobile performance management
    process
Personal branding, 65
Personal lives, 69
Personal presence, 64–65
Pilot projects, 15
Pilot test, 99–100, 213
Platform, 108–110, 113
Policies, 16
Polycom, 53
Poor technology, 188
Posner, Barry, 73
Potomac Electric Company, 127
Propensity, 85, 86
Predix Inc., 86
PRES, 67
Presence, 51–70
    actual, 69
    current situation, 57–69
    distance, 54–56
    e-presence, 58–60
    freemium, 61
    future advances, 56–57
    leadership, 67–69

overview, 53, 58
personal, 64–65
social, 61–64
stage, 67
Presence (Senge et al.), 54
Principle sharing/principle following,
    84
Problem solving, 237–238
Prusak, Laurence, 79

Q
Questions to ask, 106–108, 158–159

R
Reaching out, 67
Real-life examples. *See* Vignettes
Recursive model of manager-employee
    caring, 191
Redesigning a job, 144
Reilly, Richard, 54
Relationship building, 235
Relationships, 45, 79, 227–228
"Remote Surgery" (Kay), 34
Renewal, 214–215
Ressler, Cali, 131–134, 146, 197
Results-only work environment
    (ROWE), 100, 131–135, 197, 239
Reward, 153
Rewards systems, 202
RipCode, 84, 146
Risk taking, 81–82
Robotic combat casualty extraction and
    evacuation system, 36
Roles and expectations, 16
Roman Empire, 55
ROWE, 100, 131–135, 197, 239
Rumor mill, 91
Russell, Nan, 81

S
Samsung Mobile, 108
Satava, Richard, 34
Schema, 40
Security, 16, 113
Self-efficacy, 195
Self-knowing, 67–68
Self-renewing, 214

Senge, Peter, 40, 54, 69, 229
Setting expectations, 123, 152
7th of the Mass Media (Ahonen),
    31
Shared thinking space, 225
Shoorman, David, 81, 83
Simplicity, 16
Sinetar, Marsha, 187
Sloan, Alfred, 226
Small successes, 90
Smart trust, 77–78
Smith, Douglas, 81
Snowmageddon, 93–94
Social capital, 72, 79
Social presence, 61–64
Sound of Music, The, 142
*Speed of Trust: The One Thing That
    Changes Everything, The* (Covey/
    Merrill), 74, 189
St. Luke's Episcopal Health System,
    201
Stage presence, 67
Staples, 7
Star Wars, 57
State government (Arizona), 113–
    114
Statistics and industry trends, 9–10,
    38–39
Sticking it out, 219
Storming, 236
Strategic communications, 226–227
Strategic feedback, 199
Strategic fit, 12–13
Strategic leadership, 93–115. *See also*
    Competitive environment; Tele-
    work
Strategic mobile workforce platform,
    110
Strategic platform, 210. *See also* Plat-
    form
Strategic thinking, 241–242
Strategies, 15–17
Structure, 55
Success stories. *See* Vignettes
Support, 153
Sustainable competitive advantage,
    98

T
Target, 7
TATRC, 35, 36
Team. *See* Developing your virtual
    team
Tech troubles, 188
Technology, 121, 179, 188–189
"Tele-workforce," 11
Teleconsultation, 35
Telemedicine, 35
Telemedicine and Advanced Technol-
    ogy Research Center (TATRC),
    35, 36
Telepresence, 51. *See also* Presence
Telepresence T3, 53
Telerobotics, 36
Telesurgery, 36
Telework
    Arizona, 113–114
    government initiative, as, 94–95
    KPMG, 112
    OPM. *See* Berry's telework initiative
    savings, 102–103
    snowmageddon, 93–94
    sustainable competitive advantage, 98
    worker autonomy, 124
Telework Arizona Web site, 250
Telework Talk Blog, 99
Thompson, Jody, 131–134, 146, 197
360-degree feedback process, 140
"Time," 40
Time zones, 243
Tracking progress, 200
Traditional (Tuckman) team develop-
    ment process, 232
Training, 147
Transactional distance, 55
Transatlantic surgery, 34–36
Transformational leaders, 68
Trial and error, 213
Trucking industry, 137–139
Trust, 17, 68. *See also* Trust or bust
Trust-building principles, 80–86
Trust dividend, 75
Trust or bust, 71–92
    ability, 83
    benevolence, 83–84

blind trust/distrust, 77
communication, 80
conflict management, 90–91
consistency, 89
context, 85
Covey, Stephen, 74–78
credibility, 76
decision making, 73
extending trust, 76
freemium, 78
group discussion, 91
importance of trust, 73–74
integrity, 84
interpersonal connections, 88–89
lack of trust, 79
loss of trust, 86
mobile trust-building strategies, 87–91
outcomes, 85–86
overcontrolling, 89–90
performance evaluation, 87–88
propensity, 85, 86
principle sharing/principle following, 84
relationships, 79
risk taking, 81–82
small successes, 90
smart trust, 77–78
social capital, 79
trust-building principles, 80–86
trustworthiness, 82–84
Trust tax, 75
Trustworthiness, 82–84
Tuckman, Bruce, 231, 232, 236
Twiga Foundation, 202
2009 Guide to Bold New Ideas for Making Work Work, 202

U
UBS Business University, 218
UBS Financial Services, 218
Undercover Boss, 180
Understanding your employees, 189–191
Uniting the Virtual Workforce (Lojeski/Reilly), 54

Universality of knowledge, 46
U.S. Patent and Trademark Office, 94

V
Values, 152, 161
Venezia, Camille, 89
Verges, 47
Video conferencing, 224
Virtual API, 59–60
Virtual business review meeting, 88
Virtual distance, 55
Virtual Instruments, 146, 147–148
Virtual team. *See* Developing your virtual team
Virtual team container, 229–231
Virtual team development process, 231–240
"Virtual workforce," 11
Virtual you, 64–67, 70
Vocera Communications, 23
Volition, 199

W
Wal-Mart, 101
Wankoff, Barbara, 111–112
Weisbaum, Jack, 201
Weisberg, Anne, 27
Welch, Jack, 226
When Work Works, 202
Why Work Sucks and How to Fix It (Ressler/Thompson), 131
Willpower, 198–199
Wilson, Shauna, 236–238
Windshield time, 178
Wisdom of Teams, The (Katzenbach/Smith), 81
"Work," 41–42
Work-life balance, 49–50, 100, 159
Work tools, 145
Worker autonomy. *See* Autonomy or not autonomy?
Worker satisfaction, 128–130
Workforce paradigm, 21–50
    all-encompassing nature of mobility, 31–33
    benefits, 46
    career opportunities, 26–31

Workforce paradigm *(Continued)*:
  costs, 47
  everyone is on bandwagon, 37–40
  freemium, 22
  how work gets done, 23–25
  new rules, 41–45
  work and worker in different loca-
    tions, 33–37

Working cross-culturally, 69
Workplace flexibility, 202
World of Warcraft (WoW), 221, 222
Written policies, 15
www.telework.gov, 99

Z
Zittle, Frank, 62

ABOUT THE AUTHORS

David Clemons CEO of Achieve Labs Inc., has provided leadership and innovation to the digital publishing industries, specifically the enterprise online learning space, since 1990. Today, David is speaking nationally and internationally within the mobile industry as a mobile strategy expert, an executive of LearnKey, Inc., and founder of Achieve Labs Inc., (LearnCast.com and PushMobileMedia.com) focusing on the delivery of digital content to the mobile workforce and providing the enterprise with strategies and educational delivery platforms. David lives in Eagle, Idaho as a true mobile worker and employs a large "mobiForce" including international partners and content specialists.

Michael Kroth, Ph.D., is an assistant professor at the University of Idaho in Adult/Organizational Learning and Leadership and a recipient of the university's Hoffman Award for Excellence in Teaching. He has written three books, *Transforming Work: The Five Keys to Achieving Trust, Commitment, and Passion in the Workplace* (2001), Perseus Publishing, coauthored with Patricia Boverie, about passionate work; *The Manager as Motivator* (2006), Praeger Publishing, which provides practical tools leaders can use to develop highly motivating work environments; and, *Career Development Basics*, coauthored with McKay Christensen, and published by ASTD press. He is a member of the National Speakers Association.